THE NAKED TRUTH

THE NAKED TRUTH

Behind Every Woman is a Story

40 PERSONAL GOD- INSPIRED STORIES FOR WOMEN

DAILY/WEEKLY REFLECTION JOURNAL

By

KIM WALTMIRE

MILL CITY PRESS, INC.

Mill City Press, Inc.
2301 Lucien Way #415
Maitland, FL 32751
407·339·4217
www.millcitypress.net

Unless otherwise indicated, Scripture quotations taken from the Holy Bible, New Living Translation (NLT). Copyright ©1996, 2004, 2007 by Tyndale House Foundation. Used by permission of Tyndale House Publishers, Inc.

Scripture quotations taken from the Amplified Bible (AMP). Copyright © 1954, 1958, 1962, 1964, 1965, 1987 by The Lockman Foundation. Used by permission. All rights reserved.

Scripture quotations taken from the New King James Version (NKJV). Copyright © 1982 by Thomas Nelson, Inc. Used by permission. All rights reserved.

Scripture quotations taken from the King James Version (KJV)—*public domain.*
Printed in the United States of America.

ISBN-13: 9781545606964

A special thanks to my family
for hearing my heart, encouraging me over the years, and keeping me in prayer.
May you always live to give one life lesson at a time. You have spoken into my life,
more than you know, and I am truly blessed and grateful.

This book was finally published due to prayers answered over many years.
We didn't have the money to self-publish due to various circumstances you will
learn more about in this book. Over the course of several years, I have prayed to
the Lord about these stories, whether they should be published, and when, or how
we could afford this investment. After several years of tears, patience, and prayers,
I found this envelope on my door on 1/23/17; less than 24 hours after I gave the
book back to the Lord in prayer and His perfect timing. My heart burst with joy and
amazement that I would receive such an extravagant and anonymous gift.

"Now to him who is able to do immeasurably more than all we ask or imagine,
according to his power that is at work within us." Ephesians 3:20

God knew my heart's desire and in His timing, He revealed himself in a miraculous
way and I am so grateful. What a confirmation when I read my name and the
note at the bottom of the money order checks: Book Publishing. This had to be
confirmation from God to show up at my door in an envelope with my name on it.
He knows me by name; and He knows you by name too!

"What God can and will do through your book will bless many.
Be that blessing!" Anonymous

Dear Lord,
Thank you for loving me and thinking enough of me to use an anonymous giver
(you know by name) to bless me and the publication of this book.
May these stories bless many women and bring them closer to you.
I pray I can be that blessing.
Amen!

"With man this is impossible, but with God all things are possible."
Matthew 19:26 (NIV)

CONTENTS

Acknowledgements

First and foremost, I thank God for the strength He has given me when I was weak, the guidance He has given me when I felt alone, for the forgiveness He has given me when I felt unforgivable, and for the love He has given me when His arms were opened wide on the cross that precious day he died with me on His mind.

I love you Lord.

The Lord gave me an amazing husband who has encouraged me to get this book done. It was my husband who reminded me that I can achieve my dreams and writing this book was one of them. I am amazed by all the walks and excursions we could retreat and reflect on while he was committed to completing his Masters of Divinity. He still took time away from his studies and job when I was crying and needed someone to talk with. He is my best friend.

I love you Hank.

My daughter, Jacquelyn, is one of the sweetest and kindest young ladies any parent could ever hope for in life. When I began writing this book, God used my daughter to comfort me in moments of need. She was the one who gave me the hugs when I needed them most or rubbed my back reassuring me that everything would be okay. She listened to me express my innerthoughts and without her I would never have written my personal stories.

I love you Jacquelyn.

A special thank you is given to my friends and family who prayed and encouraged me along this journey. I thank them all for their support and belief in me, and for all the times I shared my heart and stories along the way. Thank you for listening.

I love you friends and family.

Finally, I want to thank all of you who are reading this book. Thank you for your support and I pray that these stories inspire you to tell yours one day.

God Bless all of you.

Leaving a Legacy

Dear Friend,

I t wasn't long ago when I realized the importance of leaving a legacy for my daughter. Twenty-three years ago, I began a journal of my daughter's life experiences. When she turned sixteen, I gave her all the journals and was thrilled to know that she can read them at any time and quickly be brought back to various memories and learn about them from her mother's perspective. Then I thought how important it would be for me to write about my life lessons, highlighting major events in seasonal order. These personal stories would include my family; more importantly, become a legacy for Jacquelyn to know her mother more intimately. Jacquelyn is my greatest legacy and I want her to know the 'real me.'

Are you ready to reveal the naked truth? Are you ready to learn through your life lessons and share your story before someone else does? These were questions I pondered for quite awhile. I have read various books, listened to many sermons, and spoke to friends and strangers throughout my life and I have come to the same conclusion; we all have a story. Unfortunately, many of us are uncomfortable with sharing our story due to our personal pain, hidden secrets, or uncertainty; for fear that others won't believe us, gossip about us, or not even care. If you are like me, perhaps it has crossed your mind that you don't have a story worth sharing. Everybody we meet or see in a life-time has their own unique story and we will never truly know it unless we take the time to ask, listen carefully, and encourage one another to share it. So, what's holding you back from sharing your story for others to know who you really are?

Who am I, you might ask? I was given away at birth, adopted out of admiration, feared failure, aimed to please people, acquired acceptance from others, perfectly imperfect, and had a low self-esteem. I lived internally insecure and eternally concerned. I always second guessed myself, feared change and taking risks. I was afraid of making mistakes, never felt intelligent, concerned about making friends, obsessed with physical fitness, and often felt lonely in a room full of people. I was an over-achiever, overcame cervical cancer, and experienced loss from death to relationships along the way. I am now a loving mother, very creative, more outgoing, enjoy public speaking and blessed to be a teacher. I love children, have an amazing daughter and I am happily married to the most wonderful, godly husband. I'm inspired by creativity, finding inspiration in community service and enjoy inspiring women. More importantly, I am a Christian woman, transformed by God, seeking His power in my purpose, holding onto His hope and plan for my life, and desiring to make a difference one day at a time.

Okay... These are just a few phrases to sum-up "who I am", before and after I accepted the Lord in my heart, but I guess you must read the rest of this book to learn the details. How we choose to live through our life lessons makes all the difference. I want my daughter and other women to know about some of the joys and hardships I experienced and how I lived through them. I want my daughter to remember how I overcame adversity, and found my purpose through faith, hope, and love only God can give. I decided to reveal the naked truth and write my personal stories in the attempt to leave a legacy and I pray that you would desire to be more transparent and honest with yourself and share your story someday too.

Are you going to keep your story hidden, or will you leave a lasting impression on people's lives and live beyond yourself? When I asked myself this question, I knew how I wanted to be remembered. If my life were asked of me today, I'd like to know that I lived the most meaningful life I could; well beyond myself. I'd like to know that my teaching, creativity and community projects made a difference in the lives of my students. I want to be remembered for being a sensitive and caring daughter to my adoptive parents. I pray my birth parents remember that there are no hard feelings about my adoption and I love them for choosing life and not abortion. I hope my friends were touched, encouraged, and supported along our journey together. I want my husband to remember me as a loving and caring wife, as well as how proud I was of him for following his heart into the ministry and how excited I have been working alongside him for the Lord. I want my husband to remember how honored I was to be our daughter's mother and to be remembered for loving her with all my heart. I'd like to know that our daughter, Jacquelyn, will have my life stories so she can know the real me and pass this legacy onto her children some day. I'd like her to know that if my life were asked of me today; she is my greatest legacy. I pray God would be pleased with me and say, "Kim, you did well with what I gave you." I pray that if at least one of my stories could touch someone's heart or inspire another to give their heart to the Lord, the Author of our lives, then my life was well worth it all.

I want to honor God with my whole life. I learned through my life lessons that I will please God when I am completely devoted to living a life for Him and willing to tell others about my transformation. My personal stories will reveal the results when I centered my thoughts and life on Him, as well as the consequences when I didn't live a life for the Lord or rely on Him. These stories you are about to read are not meant to impress you, but to influence you. They are my personal stories and it took many hours and years of healing and digging deep into my heart to write with such transparency. There were many months I felt as if I was walking the loneliest desert walk of my life. Sometimes not a friend was in sight, but it wasn't until I walked through these lonely times that I realized I had no place to look but up and not necessarily lean on those around me. I learned that if I could just give all my fears, concerns, pain and bitterness to the Lord, He would see me through all my circumstances. Some lessons were easy to remember and others were painful and draining, I just wanted to quit. I cried through some of my writing and laughed through others. I smiled and frowned on so many occasions as I decided to emotionally and spiritually connect with the truth. I decided to share the details and be as transparent as possible and after writing with such integrity, I feel as though a huge burden has been lifted. Each story became another chapter of my life told and put to rest. "God's truth will set you free," right? Well I did just that. As the pages of this book unfold, you will read the naked truth. You will read about the life-transforming news that Jesus loves, saves, forgives, cleanses and eliminates all the "junk" we have collected over the years.

> *"God loves you and me just the way we are, but He loves us too much to let us stay there."*
> *Kerry Shook*

Maybe there will be a story that will influence you. Just maybe one of these stories will persuade you to make a change, press on, and even encourage you to write your own life story so others will know the "real you." Wherever you may be in your life's journey, I invite you to turn the pages and experience the reality that we have been given a limited amount of time to influence others and truly make a difference. When we place God in the center of our lives and choose to live to influence others for Him, His story can be told through your life lessons and His legacy can be passed on from generation to generation.

> *"Say what you want to say when you have the feeling and the chance. My deepest regrets are the things I did not do, the opportunities missed and the things unsaid."*
> *Jim Keller*

Lovingly,

Kim Waltmire

How to Use This Book

My Inspiration

Often, I would read devotionals and feel the pressure of having to keep up with my reading based on the daily structure of the book. Life would get in the way and the next thing I knew, I wasn't on schedule and fell days behind in my devotional readings. As much as I desired to keep up with my devotional commitment and journaling, when I did fall behind, I felt like I failed again. I am not saying that everyone feels this way, but when I decided to write this book, I asked several women how they felt when this same scenario happened in their lives and they agreed; it truly frustrated them that they couldn't keep up, especially if it was a daily, year-long devotional.

Another commonality was the pressure of journaling. Fifty percent of the women I spoke with wanted to journal and reflect on their reading and fifty percent would rather read the story and move on. Recently, I found myself being inspired by devotionals that focused on events within a month's time. This allowed me to feel like the end was in sight, but the study guide emphasized a commitment to completion within the 30 days. Again, with busy schedules and other obstacles, I have failed at this attempt on occasions and felt frustrated all over again.

Given my personal experiences, one day my husband arrived with a small book tucked under his arm. "Kim, I bought this book from a new author. I talked with him at his booth after the seminar and decided to support his endeavor and invest into his ministry," he eagerly remarked. I read this book in a few days and what inspired me was one chapter after another that detailed how the author came to know the Lord based on his life experiences, in chronological order. It fascinated me to read his personal stories with such transparency. I wanted to reflect on a few chapters, but unfortunately there was no room on the pages for journaling. Immediately I thought how wonderful it could be to journal my own personal stories for my daughter and structure the book so that it could be used in multiple ways. Coupled with my current experiences reading devotionals and my need to leave a legacy for my daughter, I decided to write my own personal life lessons and give women the option to journal and reflect on a *weekly* or *daily* basis, and perhaps use the book as a women's bible study, depending on their preference.

Ways to Use this Book

The following chronological stories are separated into chapters.

* You can leisurely read the stories, perhaps several in a sitting, without following a calendar or journaling.
* Try reading one chapter and journaling your reflections daily.
* Read one story, journal your feelings, and focus on the life lesson for a week at a time.
* Read one story, journal your feelings and share at a women's bible study weekly.
* Utilize your journaling to inspire writing your own personal story.

Enjoy your experience
with or without a friend during this time
and remember,
YOU
truly matter,
one life lesson at a time.

Identity Reversibly Changed

I was five years old when the neighborhood kids told me my parents were not my parents. You can only imagine how confused I felt. Kids are mean sometimes, aren't they? Puzzled by their insensitive and persistent comments, I ran home to tell my mom immediately and her response was concerning. "We need to talk about this Kim. Your father and I are your parents and we love you like any parents would love their child. But, what the kids were trying to tell you is that we are not your birth parents. You didn't come from my tummy. You came from another woman's tummy and she is your birth mother, or as the kids would say, she is your real mother. You were adopted and your father and I are considered your adoptive parents. Your real mother and father were young and unable to take care of you, so we decided to take you home with us and care for you as our own child and eventually we could adopt you and now, we have become a real family. Out of all the babies we saw, you were the one we chose. We chose you Kim because you were special". *During these impressionable years, my identity crisis was birthed.*

I appreciated my parents telling me the truth so early in my life, as I am convinced it took them by surprise the way I found out. Nonetheless, my self- esteem and identity became challenged as the years progressed. I spent 24 years struggling with my identity. In my earlier years, I questioned who I was and why I was adopted. How can my birth parents give me away? Can my adoptive parents truly love me? They aren't my real parents. What if they change their minds and don't want me anymore? I reflected on these thoughts day after day; circumstance after circumstance. I was beginning to think it would be better if I just didn't exist. *During these impressionable years, my fear of rejection was birthed.*

Throughout my childhood, I found myself very envious of my younger adoptive brother. I felt as if he got away with more things, didn't do as many chores, and received a lot of attention. I even remember thinking it was possible my parents loved him more than me. I also remember a time when I thought our family was the strange family because my brother and I were adopted. Surely every other family had to be great because they had their real parents. It amazes me today just how easy it was for me to think I was worthless and a bother, even possibly a waste of time. *During these impressionable years, my insecurity was birthed.*

I became consumed with fear and quite nervous as I grew older. I was resistant to change; I became more introverted and retreated to my room a lot. Sadly, I feared failure. I wanted to please my parents, but mostly my father. I thought if I could make him happy, he would be glad he adopted me. I found myself aiming to please my father and I did everything I could to gain his approval. Despondently, I didn't always feel I had his approval, nor heard the words "I love you." I unfortunately remember moments when my father made me feel that women were second class citizens. I watched my father look at other women and persistently comment about their appearances and body types as if that is why women were placed on earth. I was convinced there was no altering my identity at this stage of the game. *During these impressionable years my lack of self-worth was birthed.*

I began working out at the school gym, started biking and jogging. I joined the baseball team and even played Varsity Softball in High School. I would jog up the front yard hill with the push mower just so I would feel like I "worked out." It was imperative that I was thin, beautiful, and looked like the women on the cover of those magazines; especially the ones my father bought. I remember the movies he rented and the shows we watched and the magazines he read. My father made it very clear that this is what a real woman was all about. *During these impressionable years, my resentment was birthed.*

I achieved more awards and honors than most people my age. I was inclined to do my best and be the best at whatever I put my mind to doing. I wanted my father to think I was special and that women are also intelligent. I had a longing to be accepted and recognized for being smart. *During these impressionable years, my lack of intelligence was birthed.*

All throughout high school and my college days, I continually struggled with where I came from. Who do I look like? Why was I rejected? Soon, I found a lot of my focus was on being successful. If I excel at everything, then my successes would outlast my failures and failure was never an option. *During these impressionable years, a fear of failure was birthed.*

As I lived out my college days, my appearance was the most important because I knew that's what people noticed first. My father continued to make comments about my appearance which shattered my self-esteem. Some of his comments hurt so deeply over time and his actions were very telling. Sadly, the one I tried to please failed me. *During these impressionable years, my identity crisis was revealed.*

By the time I graduated college, I was a fractured and broken young woman. I continually feared rejection and failure and I naturally used my adoption to justify my emotions. My adoption became my excuse in life. *During these impressionable years, blaming others was birthed.*

As I ended my college career, I was stricken with pre-cervical cancer and two venereal diseases with no medical history except a history of one bad relational experience after another. I was immediately hospitalized with no insurance, surgery pending and a reality check. I was all alone and very scared. As far as I was concerned, my identity was irreversibly changed and that would be the end for me. I decided I would await my consequences as I lay there in a very sterile, cold hospital room all alone. I had no one to hold my hand and reassure me that I would be okay. The walls felt as if they were closing in on me. I became more and more isolated in my thoughts of despair. My boy-friend arrived with concern on his face. He apologized for my situation and proceeded to tell me that he had two diseases and wanted me to know it was his fault. I was devastated. I knew my parents liked him, but it was my previous boy friend my father didn't like. I knew I didn't have the heart to tell them it was the guy they liked who had the diseases, for fear of what my father may do or say. I decided to lie and eventually told them it was my previous boy-friend at fault. I knew immediately in my heart that I failed myself and I most certainly failed my father. My parents arrived and I felt my mother's concern right away. My father was immediately disgusted with me. He was extremely unsupportive, called me a whore and said he wished he never adopted me. As time passed, friends were disappearing, boyfriends dared not commit to me, and I felt utterly alone. *During these impressionable years, I felt totally ostracized and abandoned.*

My life as I knew it, hit rock bottom and there was no place to look but up. Why do we fall? I guess we fall so we can learn to pick ourselves back up. At that very moment, I had to get up, swallow my pride, and go home with my parents for the summer to recuperate and heal. I had to pay my consequences, physically and emotionally. *During these impressionable years, I felt humiliated and unforgivable.*

It took me two more years before I realized my true-identity. Perhaps I never would have realized the answer had I not experienced these trials and tribulations. When I fell I always looked up to see who was there to hold my hand and guide me. Sadly, I never saw anyone. It took time for me to realize my eyes were on those around me or my own circumstances, and they were never on the One who was there all along.

> *God knocked on my heart and whispered, "Kim, your identity is in me. Your identity is reversibly changed through me. Just open your heart and let me in. I will change you for eternity."*

It was an instant revelation. I was looking up towards God and never realized it. I remembered all the times I felt rejected, insecure, worthless, resentful, unintelligent, fearful, ostracized, abandoned, humiliated and unforgivable. Throughout these emotions and tragic times in my life, the One I should have been reaching towards was there reaching out His hands ready to pull me towards Him all along. It was the Lord and I never truly saw Him.

> *Revelation 3:20*
> *"Behold, I stand at the door and knock. If anyone hears My voice and opens the door, I will come in to him and dine with him, and he with me." NKJV*

I decided I didn't want to be indifferent to God. His offer is of lasting satisfaction and we must constantly keep the door of our hearts open if we want to hear the knocking of our heavenly Father. Letting Him in our heart is our only hope for lasting fulfillment.

I remember being told early on in my Christian walk that once I asked Jesus into my heart and believed in Him as my Lord and Savior, I was adopted into the Kingdom of Heaven. What? Is that possible? God, the Creator of the Universe loves me that much that He would adopt *me* into the Kingdom of Heaven so I can live with Him forever? I was told He is preparing a place for me to be with Him for eternity. God created me in His image. I now have someone who I can identify with for the first time in my life. My identity crisis had come to an end. *My identity has been reversibly changed* because of what Jesus did for me on the cross. I have unmerited favor and unconditional love from the heart of the Father. He accepts me just as I am. I don't have to measure up to someone's standard of performance any more. Praise God!

> *Romans 8:14-17*
> *"For as many as are led by the Spirit of God, these are sons of God; For you did not receive the spirit of bondage again to fear, but you received the Spirit of adoption by whom we cry out, "Abba, Father." The Spirit Himself bears witness with our spirit that we are children of God, and if children, then heirs- heirs of God and joint heirs with Christ, if indeed we suffer with Him, that we may also be glorified together." NKJV*

I learned that I can have a new relationship with God. Likewise, when you and I become a Christian, we gain all the privileges and responsibilities of a child in God's family. We are led by His Spirit and even though there will be days you and I will feel like we don't belong, God's Holy Spirit will remind us who we are in Him. When we understand our identity is in Christ, we are changed. Our full identity, as his children, exists and now we must choose it. My identity wasn't as an adoptee here on earth. On the contrary, my identity is reversible and I am an adoptee into the Kingdom of Heaven. As soon as I came to this realization, I felt a huge weight lift from me. Yes, I feel insecure, resentful and worthless at times, but when those moments pour in like a flood, I turn to my Daddy in Heaven who wants to lighten my burden. He wants to remind me that I belong to Him and his family. The hope of my eternal identity has been realized. *During these impressionable years, my identity was reversibly changed.*

Remember that there is a God, your heavenly Father, who has covered your past; your sins and ungodly emotions. He wants to give you a new identity in Him. His arms are open wide and He wants to embrace you in the folds of His love. Find that secret, quiet place and listen for His knock on the door of your heart. Let Him into your life. Let Him fill your soul and identify with you and you will never wonder who you are or who you belong to again.

Who will you identify with? Is your identity in and of yourself or is your identity in Christ alone? Tell Him about it and tell others.

Establish a Spiritual **B.A.S.E.**
<u>B</u>elieve- I believe that Jesus Christ died on the cross for me
<u>A</u>ccept- I need to accept God's forgiveness for my sin
<u>S</u>witch- I will switch to God's plan for my life
<u>E</u>xpress- I express my desire for Christ to be the Director of my life

"Dear God, I believe You sent Your son Jesus to die for me and my sins so I could be forgiven. I'm sorry for my sins and I want to live the rest of my life the way You want me to. Please put Your Spirit in my life and lead me all my days. Amen!"

Week 1/ Day 1: Identity Reversibly Changed

Explain about a time you experienced an identity crisis:

_____

_____

_____

Write briefly about a time you felt rejected or insecure:

_____

_____

_____

Do you feel this way now? _____ What changed?

_____

_____

_____

How has your self-worth been affected over the years? Explain:

_____

_____

_____

_____

Have you ever been afraid to fail at something? How did you overcome your fear?

_____

_____

_____

_____

Who do you indentify with during these difficult times? _____ If you haven't chosen God, what is holding you back?

_____

_____

_____

Is your identity in and of yourself, or is your identity in Christ alone? Explain your reasons

_____

_____

_____

Choose the Lord today if you haven't already. Pray with all your heart and follow the ABC's:

Accept the Lord as your Savior; **B**elieve in Jesus as the Son of God who died for you and your sins; and **C**onfess your sins

_____

_____

_____

If you were to choose one word to describe how you feel now, what would it be? Why?

_____

_____

_____

What life lesson have you learned through this story?

_____

_____

_____

_____

A Father's Love

My adoptive father was a key person in my childhood who taught me what character is all about. He chose to use "tough love" most of the time, but unfortunately, I struggled with perfectionism, rejection and fear of failure and this made it difficult for me to feel or accept my *father's love* when I needed to most.

For instance, one phrase my father used frequently was, "Your word is as good as you. Mean what you say and say what you mean." To illustrate this point, my father told me one day that if my grades went down I would have to quit the varsity softball team. Of course, I agreed. I was a varsity player and was involved in many extracurricular activities. I knew how hard I had to work to participate in every event and I was confident my grades would be fine. The next thing I knew, my grades arrived home before I did and one of my final grades fell from a B to a B-. My father came to the ball field to tell me I could no longer stay on the team. I was devastated. He said, "Kim, what did I tell you? My word is as good as me. And you agreed if your grades go down, you are off the team. If you can't hold true to your word now, what will you do when things really get tough?" I heard this message loud and clear and as bold as my father was at times, I always remembered the importance of thinking before I agree and to choose my words wisely. I will remember a lot of things, such as being a leader and not a follower, honesty is the best policy, never giving up, always working hard, doing my best, sitting in the front row and showing that what I am listening to is important, and that first impressions truly matter. I didn't like the intensity of some of these life situations, but they taught me lessons I will never forget.

During another season of my life, my brother found me at an off-site college apartment that my boy-friend was renting. My father was livid I was dating this guy and spending time there, so he sent my brother to take my car that was insured by my parents, to teach me a lesson; "If you don't follow my rules, you lose. I never should have adopted you". Regrettably, he left me alone with no transportation, which inevitably caused me to rely on my boy-friend even more. In all actuality, I spent nights there so I could get transportation which made me more vulnerable to my boy-friend's abuse and control, as well as my father's incessant need to reel me in on every decision I was making. He followed up my lesson stating that there was no way I would be able to get my own car and challenged me on what I would do without his help. I knew at that moment I had to prove him wrong because I was so scared I may have to walk everywhere. What if it wasn't safe? How would I get to my jobs? The fear was unsettling. I met with a banker about my circumstances and my desperate need to borrow $1.000.00 to purchase a used car. After one appointment, she mentioned that she was so impressed with me and with how I chose to go about solving my problem that she lent the money to me in good standing. I purchased my first car for $900.00 and paid off my loan within the year. I didn't like the intensity of these life situations, but they taught me life lessons I will never forget.

I am not claiming to know what you have *been* through or what you are *going* through, but I can distinguish this; knowing you are loved, despite your circumstances and consequences, is what will undoubtedly get you through your challenging life lessons. Rules and regulations ultimately equated to the fear of failure and rejection throughout my childhood. If I made a mistake I felt like a failure and feared being rejected; sadly, due to how my earthly father decided to handle these situations. Sometimes the expectations of me were too high and appeared unachievable. Often my father made me feel I wasn't good enough for his standards. But intently, I decided I would work hard to gain his approval because feeling loved and accepted was my main priority and I believed that perfection and winning awards would ultimately gain my father's approval and love. These experiences caused me to become a high achiever and instead, I relied on my earthly father's arms to embrace me and sadly, I met those expectations with rejection. It wasn't until I found the Lord years beyond that I realized the 'increase' in my life was because of God and I owed my gratitude to Him only. I finally grew to understand that my love and acceptance should be focused on God, my Heavenly Father, who loved me enough that He sent his only son to die for me on a cross with His arms opened wide. It was His arms I needed to rely on to embrace me through my circumstances, but, unfortunately, I never learned early on that God's love was sufficient. My earthly father didn't display God's love that way at all, but eventually I grew to know a Heavenly Father who loves me and claims me as His own.

Stormie Omartian was once quoted saying, "Parental love is often how children actually open themselves to God's love and come to understand it early in life." Earthly fathers will fail us. Some will be abusive, nonexistent, or even passive, but God our Father and His discipline is perfect and purposeful. Am I saying that life's lessons and discipline aren't worth living through? Not at all, but I am suggesting two things. First, remember life serves you tough love sometimes and secondly, there is a God who loves and accepts us unconditionally through all our situations. He loves us like a father should. Will there be consequences with our life lessons? Yes. Do we or will we always agree with how His love is shown through our life lessons? No, but…

> Hebrews 12:10-11
> *"For our earthly fathers disciplined us for a few years, doing the best they knew how. But God's discipline is always good for us, so that we might share in His holiness. V.11… No discipline is enjoyable while it is happening- it's painful! But afterward there will be a peaceful harvest of right living for those who are trained in this way." NLT*

God is our loving, heavenly Daddy and His example in and for our lives is more than we can ever imagine. Whether we had a wonderful or challenging relationship with our earthly father, we need to learn from Him through our life lessons and live and leave the love of God to our family, friends and strangers.

That does not negate our mother's influence in our children and those around us, but daughters, ask God what you can do to receive God's unconditional love and acceptance so when life's lessons knock at your door, you can answer it with His confidence, in His love, and with His acceptance. A *Father's Love* is to be cherished. Will you rely on your earthly father's love and acceptance or embrace a Heavenly Father who will see you through your circumstances?

"I may not be perfect, but Jesus thinks I'm to die for." Author unknown

Week 2/ Day 2: A Father's Love

What kind of relationship have you had with your earthly father? Explain.

_____

_____

_____

_____

Define a *father's love*:

_____

_____

_____

_____

How has your relationship with your father affected your other relationships? Why or why not?

_____

_____

_____

_____

How have your choices benefitted you and those you are involved with?

_____

_____

_____

_____

Have you asked God into your heart and relationships? _____If something is holding you back, what is it? If you have asked God into your relationship(s), describe your experience(s).

_____

_____

_____

_____

Ask the Lord what unique perspectives you can bring to your relationships to make them healthier. List your responses. (i.e. listening, open communication, sharing responsibility, acknowledging mistakes)

_____

_____

_____

_____

If you need to search for reconciliation, ask the Lord for guidance. What steps are you willing to take?

_____

_____

_____

_____

What life lesson have you learned through this story?

_____

_____

_____

_____

_____

Agree to Disagree

Typically speaking, men carry a 'tool box' and women carry a 'Kleenex box'; Men want to 'fix it' and women want to 'emotionalize it'; Men can 'forget it' and women 'hold on to it'. Sound familiar? Have you noticed how different men and women are when it comes to relationships, the way we talk, the way we listen, or the way we argue? If there is one thing that challenges us all it would be receiving forgiveness or extending it. Another challenge for me has been saying 'sorry' and agreeing to disagree. No matter what relationship we are involved with; co-worker, friend, spouse, boy friend, family or fiancé, we are all different and we bring to that connection various emotions and experiences. One of the questions we need to ask ourselves though; are these relationships working?

> James 3:17
> *"But the wisdom from above is first of all pure. It is also peace-loving, gentle at all times and willing to yield to others. It is full of mercy and good deeds. It shows no favoritism and is always sincere". NLT*

I grew up with a controlling father at times. My father was 'boss' and whatever he said was the final answer. My father knew I was a visual learner and he didn't hesitate to press his thumb down on the kitchen table, twisting it back and forth as a reminder I was under his thumb; under his control. You could say I understood that visual loud and clear. I was intimidated until I grew into my teenage years and decided I had feelings and a voice and I was going to use them. I noticed my mother never said very much over all those years. I assumed she thought 'father knows best.' But I thought otherwise and one day, during an argument, I decided to shove the kitchen chair across our small kitchen and dared my father to hit me, I was so angry. My heart was filled with sin when I shoved the chair that day. I didn't have a relationship with the Lord at that time and all I wanted to do is get back at my father and show him that I would not be controlled any more just because I was a girl. I even took it a step further and yelled at him and told my father I didn't like how he treated my mom at times and it needed to stop. I abruptly left the kitchen because I was done with it. I could feel the heat of my father's anger as I left the house despite his warning not to leave. A lesson learned here was simple for me; I just disagreed and that was it! There was no room for agreement and certainly no room for apologies. My pent-up emotion spilled over into anger that day and I dealt with it the only way I saw fit. I left the house and that was the end for me.

My college days were no easier, especially without having the Lord in my daily walk. Every guy I dated had similar traits to my father and for some reason I gravitated towards the familiar; being controlled. My father had an addiction to pornography and you guessed it, I would soon find out that a boyfriend of mine was the same. I was surrounded by pornographic posters, magazines and the playboy channel. Not only did he compare me to 'other girls', he would pinch my skin and tell me if I was too fat or beautiful enough on any given day. I was told to get to the gym for another workout and to change my outfit because I wasn't to embarrass him as 'his trophy'.

Subsequently, he would get angry with me and I never knew when his temper would flare. You see, he did steroids as well. I knew he was taking them, but I was afraid to leave him because he told me nobody would like me anyway. Trust me, we had conversations, but I always agreed rather than disagreed to avoid the conflict as much as I could. I retreated when the emotions flared. It was my only means of survival. He was a handsome body builder who weighed 250 pounds and I wasn't about to argue with him, especially after he threatened me time and time again.

One day we were enjoying a ride in his sports car when suddenly he slammed his breaks at an intersection, got extremely angry, and threatened me to get out and drive. I had no idea why he got so angry; nor did I know how to drive a stick-shift. I got inside the driver's seat and instantly his abusive language filled the car as I continued to grind the gears. When we arrived at his apartment, he exited the car and bent down reaching for something under his seat. I got out of the car and in a split second a wrench was thrown at me. Miraculously, I ducked just in time as the metal wrench landed several feet behind me while the words "I'm going to kill you," echoed across the vacant parking lot. I never felt so scared and controlled in my life. Immediately, he took me by the arm and into his apartment. I thought, just maybe I could muster up enough strength to talk to him and calm him down. Maybe if I give in and tell him he is right and I am wrong and let him know he is in control; that would help. The next thing I knew he dragged me into the bathroom and told me he needed to be injected with his steroids. At that moment, I realized his mood swing was due to this powerful drug. He slapped his thigh, signaling the area of injection and instantly, I am handed a syringe and threatened that if I don't inject him he would turn it on me. Obviously, there was no time for a nice conversation and I wasn't about to succumb to his request and let fear consume this conflict. I dropped the syringe, turned, and headed for the door. Suddenly, I slowly felt the air being squeezed from my body while my elbows were bruising and my arms were painfully being pulled from my shoulder sockets. I was bracing myself between the narrow doorway as he lifted me with all his might and tugged me back through. I couldn't endure the painful pressure and my arms fell weakly to my sides. He fell back and we both landed on the floor. I ran out the door again and he grabbed me, took me by the back of the hair with one hand and with the other hand intently lifted the cover to his snake tank and tried to stick my head in the tank. Panic stricken, I yelled, "You win." At that very moment I was convinced that running or facing this conflict head- on wasn't worth it. I never did inject my boyfriend that day or ever for that matter, but unfortunately the story doesn't end there.

My father didn't like this guy and I didn't care what my father had to say about it at the time. I guess you could say I agreed to disagree. The next thing I knew, he and my brother learn of my destination off campus and confiscate my car. "If you are going to live like a whore then it won't be with this car. Now, let's see you get out of this one. Sometimes I wish I never adopted you." I was left in the middle of the city with no transportation or a means of escape, but I would never tell my father about that. My father's words pierced my heart that day. Words can do that you know.

> *Ephesians 4:29*
> *"Let everything you say be good and helpful, so that your words will be an encouragement to those who hear them." NLT*

Years later I met my husband Hank. He learned immediately that I was fragile and my feelings were hurt easily. We both entered our marriage with hurts and pains and sadly, without the Lord in our lives. Our relationship was tenuous at times. Hank was a 'fix it' man and I was 'emotional'. He carried the tool box and I always carried the Kleenex box. He would raise his voice and I would raise mine louder. He would get me angry and I threatened to leave him because I didn't need a guy to define or control me. Our conversations were not seasoned with peace and Godly guidance and sometimes we used harmful words and not helpful words.

Thankfully, Hank was not physical or violent, but had a loving heart. I was always the one to drag the past into the present and that made Hank furious. Without Godly wisdom, I found myself accountable to nobody other than controlling the situation, especially with men. I refused to be controlled by a man or be made to feel inferior because I was a woman. My only goal in our conversations or conflicts was the '*resolution*' and not '*reconciliation*'.

Over a year into our marriage an eight-year-old girl witnessed to me in my classroom and told me Jesus loved me. A few months later Hank and I gave our hearts to the Lord and vowed to follow Christ as our eternal savior and accept Him into our daily lives and marriage. Are things perfect now? No! We are perfectly imperfect. We are an imperfect couple with unique perspectives; perspectives that God truly designed us uniquely with to bring to our relationship. Sure, we still have hurts and pains, baggage and claims, but here's the difference; the One who is made perfect in and through our conversations and conflicts is God. He is our audience of one. He is the one we want to please. It is God who taught us to agree to disagree. It is God who taught us patience and how to listen to each other. It is God that reminds us that we are to achieve His will for our lives while loving others in all our relationships, no matter how hard it is.

Hank and I have grown closer day by day, month by month and year by year. Our relationship is a work in progress and we are committed to our relationship until eternity. We are learning to grow through our mistakes and take accountability when necessary. We ask God for forgiveness and ask each other as well. Hank and I have set boundaries for our conversations. We sit down frequently and discuss ways to help us have a healthy conversation. I need eye contact and sometimes I must write things down to help me organize my thoughts. Hank doesn't want me to bring up the past, but rather be a part of finding a solution. I told him to leave the tool box in the closet because I don't always want to be fixed, just listened to. We also agree on the best locations to talk and how to make it work. If we are talking or arguing, we won't answer the phone or we just take the phone off the hook. Sometimes we just go for a walk or out to dinner, especially if it is a private discussion. I learned to let Hank know whether the timing is right and seek a better time to talk. We realized that phone conversations are kept for emergencies and quick messages, and not to resolve issues or begin conflicts. I know not to target Hank just as he walks through the door, but rather wait a half hour until he is settled or gives me the cue. I also learned that if I need a touch or facial expression, to think in advance about the best time and location to talk. And often we get excited and have unrealistic expectations of our loved ones or friends and we end up disappointed when they don't respond the way we would like them to.

Spiritually speaking, God created us differently, but we live our lives unconcernedly. There was a time when Jesus got angry and He expressed His emotions in the temple as He turned over the tables... Did Jesus sin during that experience? No! Sometimes anger and frustration will find itself in our conversations and it's our indifferences that consume our conflicts. God created us uniquely and He desires for us to bring our unique perspectives to each conversation or conflict. The only way for this to happen is to allow God to be in the center of it all.

Ever since our daughter Jacquelyn brought home a bracelet with WWJD- What Would Jesus Do? embedded around it, I have begun to break down every situation, conflict or conversation I have had and ask myself this question...What would Jesus do? What a difference it makes when we put God in the center of our choices. I can guarantee when you allow God to control your thoughts, only then will your speech, response, and heart be encouraged. Only then will

you begin to see through your conversations and conflicts with hope and a purposeful direction. Only then will it be easier to 'agree to disagree'.

What a difference the Lord can make in your relationships when He is in the center of your life. Sure, men and women are different, but we are perfectly and uniquely made for His purpose. Some parts of my college days and childhood may not have exemplified the healthiest relationships, but when forgiveness abounds and when we can agree to disagree, it softens our conversations and conflicts. More importantly, it pleases the Lord. I thank God that I can forgive my father and previous boyfriends. I thank God, He forgives me. If God can forgive me, how much more do I need to forgive others? Now, let me ask you again; are your relationships working?

Whether you hold onto the Kleenex box or he grabs the tool box, remember, a healthy relationship begins with you accepting the Lord into your heart. It is as simple as accepting God as your Lord and eternal Savior; admitting you are imperfect and asking God for His forgiveness. When you seek after a healthy relationship with your Daddy in Heaven, your life and relationships will never be the same. If your relationships are not working, it's time to address them now.

What kind of relationships will you choose to have? Will you ask God into your heart and into your relationships? Will you ask Him about the unique perspectives you can bring to your conversations? If you have a conflict, can you agree to disagree and search for reconciliation? What will you do to continually show God's love? Remember, God wants to reconcile you unto Himself. Perhaps this is the relationship you need to focus on first. He is waiting; now it's your turn to respond.

Week 3/ Day 3: Agree to Disagree

Have you ever agreed to disagree? What happened?

_____

_____

_____

Are your relationships working? Why or why not?

_____

_____

_____

What needs to change in your relationships to make them more fulfilling?

_____

_____

_____

Do you need to reconcile with anybody? _____ If yes, explain what for and why haven't you?

_____

_____

_____

What is the worst thing that can happen if you don't reconcile with this person?

_____

_____

_____

_____

What is the best thing that can happen if you reconcile with this person?

_____

_____

_____

_____

_____

Is God in the center of your relationships? Why or why not? Explain:

_____

_____

_____

_____

_____

God wants to reconcile you unto Himself. What can you do to make God the center of your relationships?

_____

_____

_____

_____

_____

What life lesson have you learned through this story?

_____

_____

_____

_____

The Source of My Significance

M y whole childhood and young adult life I lived in fear. I remember clear as day; I worried about being lonely and not having enough friends. I worried about others not seeing the importance of my life, not being intelligent or beautiful and thin enough, or the basement flooding during rainstorms and "fine things" my family couldn't afford. My fears as a child translated to concerns... I longed to hear the words "I love you" more often and have more hugs too. I wanted my family to say they were proud of me because pleasing them was imperative. If my birth parents could give me away, there must be something wrong with me; then it was only a matter of time before my adoptive parents would do the same thing, right?

All throughout my childhood and into my early adult life, I defined my existence through, fear and failure. It was an obvious pattern that I allowed to uniquely weave itself through my daily existence. If I failed to fear then I was content for awhile, but as soon as fear failed me I immediately was convinced my life wasn't worth anything. I believed I was just a big mistake. I began living my life based on my emotional existence and eventually I felt my hopes and dreams were meaningless; I hadn't a purpose, and perhaps the world would be a better place without me. The source of my significance was in question.

Although I attended church every week and prayed to God every day, I wouldn't say that I understood the relationship I had with Him. I prayed for things and talked a lot with the Lord, but I had no understanding of heaven and hell. I would hear my adoptive father's words ring continually in my mind; "There is no hell. Hell is here on earth." I distinctly remember worrying about death and how it would happen to me. What would it be like when I am gone? Will I feel anything? Where would I go? Will anyone miss me when I am gone? Is there really a heaven? Why am I here on earth? What is my purpose? All I desired was peace and joy, but instead, fears and worries consumed me and I lived my younger years with uncertainties and reservations until one precious day God had a child's prayer for *me;* a prayer she prayed with her Sunday School Teacher that led me to the Lord; a decision that changed my life for eternity.

In 1989 my husband and I began our marriage with a lot of baggage and no godly relationship or direction. I found myself needing validation and often considering the mirror only to see rejection and not God's reflection. I considered my mirror and saw flaws and imperfections. Therefore, I found myself continuing a life-style of obsessive physical fitness, setting high standards for myself and seeking approval from my father and those around me. I tried everything to prove to the world that I was worth loving.

Hank, on the other hand, tried seeking approval from corporate executives believing he needed to prove to the business world that he was 'somebody'. His eyes were fixated on the things of this world and moving up the corporate ladder, only to find out his ladder was up against the wrong building. Tension and mistrust mounted between us as we sought approval and acceptance from the world around us and unfortunately, we grew further and further apart as a couple.

A year and a half into our marriage, in May of 1991, my husband Hank was in Kansas City on business training for 3 weeks. We had never been separated this long. Unfortunately, he did not keep in touch with me on a regular basis and instantly I found myself beginning to mistrust his intentions; a characteristic of mine that never really did me any good. I was convinced Hank must have found someone more attractive and our marriage, perhaps, wouldn't be worth saving.

You could say that an unforgiving spirit of contention and frustration mounted between us. It didn't matter what question I asked him when we finally spoke on the phone; I was already convinced I wouldn't believe him and he was convinced I wouldn't listen anyway.

We both began our careers at the same time. I was already teaching and found myself spending 12 hour days at school preparing lessons and activities. I was a bit consumed and at the time I didn't mind. In addition to working so many hours, I was working out at the gym 2 hours a day, as well as starving myself in hopes to lose weight and look better for fear my husband would not think I was attractive enough when he got home. I began to lose weight, which made me happy, but sadly, I ignored the warning signs as my body gave way. I was dizzy, nauseous and very weak. Teaching became more difficult as I found myself quickly holding onto bookshelves, walls or anything more stable than me, in hopes I would not faint and alarm anybody. Then one day in my 2nd grade classroom, an 8-year-old girl named Natalia interrupted my unwavering thoughts saying," Don't worry Mrs. Waltmire. Jesus loves you." I was shocked! I couldn't believe a young girl would say something like this to me. What did she just say? Jesus loves me? "Thank you, Natalia, you can sit down now". Jesus loves me? I thought to myself. Why would Jesus love me?

Days and weeks passed. Hank and I were reunited after three long weeks, going about our normal routine of course. We talked about our time apart as fear and mistrust still gripped me, but I accepted these feelings because it was my comfort zone. It's all I knew; worry, worry, worry. But there was one thing we didn't hesitate to talk about and that was Natalia's comment. Week after week, I told Hank about Natalia and her family and the encouraging notes they would send me. Their kindness and love for me and my husband throughout the school year was immeasurable. But one question remained; what did Natalia have that we didn't?

This burning question remained with me for many weeks. As my husband and I began to get to know Natalia's family, we witnessed a peace and joy that pierced our hearts. There was such a calm and confident direction they had in their lives and over time they began to share the Lord's love with us meekly and gently. Throughout that summer, we could watch this precious family live a life with purpose and significance. We continued to talk about our lives and found the commonalities and concerns Hank and I had along the way. Thereafter, we were invited to their church. Hank and I heard the word of God preached simply and powerfully. As time progressed, we began to have answers to our concerns, while Natalia's family continued to share God's truth whenever we asked.

As our relationship grew, Hank and I decided to accept Jesus Christ as our Lord and Savior in our hearts one evening in their living room. What a blessing it was to do this with my 8-year-old student praying alongside me. I remember Natalia thanking God for answering the prayer she had been praying that her 2nd grade teacher would give her heart to the Lord. Tears streamed down my face as we prayed that Jesus would forgive us of our sins and cleanse us of all our wrong doings. We thanked the Lord for dying on the cross for our sins and agreed to follow Him, the Son of God, for the rest of our lives. Immediately, I was set free. My burdens were lifted. I felt free of stress, cleansed and filled with the peace and joy I longed for my whole life. Suddenly, I realized that I am adopted into the Kingdom of heaven and I am a child of God. My identity is in Him and not my earthly family. The bitterness I carried about being adopted began to melt away. I soon realized that God loved me enough to adopt ME into His family if I choose; really? My life has a purpose! He is the source of my significance and the world will be a better place when God is in the center of it. And to this day, I am so taken back by the overwhelming love and acceptance that my Lord has for me, despite my fears and failures, mistakes and imperfections. My sins are nailed to the cross and He bore all my pain and sorrow. I get to have a "do over"! That day I met my Creator who forgave me of all my sins and I am forever transformed, praise God! How precious my life has been since giving my heart to the Lord with my husband that same summer day in 1991.

> *Romans 12:1-2*
> *...Give your bodies to God because of all He has done for you. Let them be a living and holy sacrifice-the kind He will find acceptable... Don't copy the behavior and customs of this world, but let God transform you into a new person by changing the way you think." NLT*

My life is more fulfilled now. I realize more than ever that happiness can come under any circumstance when I put my complete trust in God. Nick Vujicic was once quoted saying, "God's love is so real that He created you to prove it." These words have always stuck with me. You know, He loves you too. He created me and I know I will be in heaven one day and I don't have to worry another moment. I don't worry about death anymore. I have comfort in knowing I will be with my Lord when that time comes and nothing can turn me away from the love of God and what He did for me. He has a plan for my life and I know He has a plan for you too.

> *Jeremiah 29:11*
> *"For I know the plans I have for you," says the Lord. "They are for good not disaster, to give you a future and a hope." NLT*

What's holding you back? Are you putting your life on hold, dwelling on your past hurts and pains? Perhaps you are waiting until your life is in order or until you are perfect and presentable before you talk to the Lord. Maybe you are blaming God for your circumstances rather than asking Him to see you through them. I could have given up many times, but I decided to keep on striving for a better life and I found it. God answered a child's prayer and used her to tell me in the middle of my classroom how much He loves ME. He met me right where I was, but loved me enough not to leave me there and He will do the same for you. Will you let Him into your heart? What are you waiting for?

> *Isaiah 11:6*
> *..."and a little child will lead them." NLT*

It's having hope and faith in One who is bigger than all your situations that will see you through the next day. Life without hope is meaningless and life without hope is faithless. I lived this way for years and it doesn't work. I promise you though; the good that awaits you when you surrender your heart to the Lord, surpasses all understanding. His arms are open wide and He is calling your name to come and cast all your cares, fears, worries, ugliness, insecurities, pain and tragedies at the foot of the cross. He will give you peace, joy, and assurance that will take you into eternity if you would just believe in Him and the plans He has for you. You are not a mistake; you are a miracle, so live like one! What are you waiting for? Give it all to Him right now. He placed you in your mother's womb. He created you and suffered on the cross for you out of love, so let Him embrace you today and give you rest. Come to Him like a child. I did... A child led me right to the cross... right to His feet and I bowed my heart and I cried like a child. It was the best decision I ever made and it will be yours too. Let Him be the source of your significance. Don't wait any longer... He's calling you; will you answer?

Week 4/ Day 4: The Source of My Significance

What word or words define your significance? Why? (Example: Try using words before you knew the Lord and after; see how you have changed) Explain:

_____

_____

_____

_____

What do you think your purpose in life is? How do you know this?

Do you believe God's love is so real that He created you to prove it? _____ If so, give examples. If not, tell why you don't believe this.

_____

_____

_____

_____

Give examples of what's holding you back from fully committing to the Lord or if you have committed your life to the Lord? How has it affected your life?

_____

_____

_____

_____

Describe your "God moment" when you accepted Him into your life, and if you haven't already, make today the day you can say "This is my God moment!"

_____

_____

_____

Will you let Him into your heart? What are you waiting for?

You can pray this prayer of forgiveness and ask Jesus into your heart right now:

> *Dear Jesus,*
> *Please forgive me of my sins. I want to live my life for you. I believe you are the Son of God and the source of my significance. I accept you as my Savior and thank you for dying on the cross in my place when I am the one who is unde-serving. Help me to turn from my worldly ways and be more like you. Lord please help me to live the rest of my days desiring your will and purpose for my life. Thank you for hearing my prayer. In your name I pray this; Amen!*

What life lesson have you learned through this story?

_____

_____

_____

_____

_____

_____

_____

_____

_____

_____

_____

_____

_____

_____

_____

_____

_____

Listening and Responding

Second grade should be fun and exciting, but it wasn't always that way for Frankie. His mother had multiple personalities and this young boy was always worried and wearied every time he entered the classroom. I never knew what personality I would be speaking to when his mother arrived and I could only imagine how difficult it must have been for Frankie.

One cold January day Frankie walked to his seat with his head held low and with no joy in his heart. His smile was gone and he despondently answered my questions all morning. Something was clearly wrong. I approached Frankie and gave him a hug. "What's wrong Frankie? Why are you so sad?" "When my sister and I got off the bus yesterday, we were locked out of the house. Mommy was crawling on the floor like a two-year-old. She couldn't unlock the door so we stayed in the shed until dad got home. You don't understand Mrs. Waltmire. You don't understand what it is like to have to take care of your mom. I am only 8 years old and I'm tired." I gave Frankie a big hug and prayed secretly in my heart that God would protect him and give him peace.

A few days later, Frankie told me that his family was moving to a nearby town, just a few blocks away from the new casino. I was so concerned, considering his fears and challenges with a mother who was diagnosed with schizophrenia. On my way to school one day, I prayed the Lord would give me a sign that Frankie would be okay. Hours later, I taught a lesson about Martin Luther King. I asked the children to *listen* to the story about his life and *respond* in their writing journals. Amazingly, our class conversation and written responses were powerful. Half of my inclusive class had special needs children and I was deeply touched by some of their individual expressions and interpretations. "Thank you, Lord," I thought to myself. Immediately following our discussion, the children began responding in their journals. Soon after, I asked my students if they felt something. Many responded that they felt a breeze, but the windows were all shut and it was the middle of winter. Suddenly, Frankie approached me saying," Yes Mrs. Waltmire; what do you want?" "I didn't call you Frankie," I responded as he walked back to his seat. A few moments later Frankie approached me again. "Yes Mrs. Waltmire, what do you want?" "Frankie, I didn't call you." Frankie walked slowly back to his seat a bit puzzled and instantly I knew... The Lord reminded me of the story of Samuel in the Bible.

> *1 Samuel 3:4-10*
> *"And he answered, "Here I am!" So, he ran to Eli and said, "Here I am, for you called me." And he said, "I did not call; lie down again." And he went and lay down. Then the Lord called yet again, "Samuel!" So, Samuel arose and went to Eli, and said, "Here I am, for you called me." He answered. "I did not call, my son; lie down again." (Now Samuel did not know the Lord, nor was the word of the Lord yet revealed to him.) And the Lord called Samuel again the third time. So he arose and went to Eli, and said, Here I am, for you did call me." Then Eli perceived that the Lord had called the boy. Therefore, Eli said to Samuel, "Go, lie down; and it shall be, if He calls you, that you must say, "Speak Lord, for Your servant hears." So, Samuel went and lay down in his place. Now the Lord came and stood and called as at other times, "Samuel! Samuel!" And Samuel answered, "Speak, for Your servant hears." NKJV*

"Lord", I prayed... "You heard my heart's cry this morning when I asked for a sign that Frankie would be okay. You know how concerned I am that his mother has multiple personalities and one of those personalities is quite sensual. Lord, you know that he and his family are moving right next to the Casino. What will happen to Frankie? What will their life-style be like? Lord, is this a sign from you?"

In Samuel's day, God's word became rare during the three centuries of rule by judges. The Lord called the young boy Samuel while lying down and Samuel listened to the voice and responded, "Here I am", to Eli, but it was not Eli who called him by name. It was not Eli's voice at all. After three calls, Eli realizes that Samuel was called by the voice of the Lord and he needed to respond to the Lord's call. Samuel returned to his room and heard the voice of the Lord and responded...

"Speak Lord, for Your servant hears." v. 10

As I am standing a few tables away from Frankie in my quiet classroom, I see him look back over his shoulder as if he saw someone. A smile spread across my face in great anticipation of a miracle that was happening right before my eyes. I felt my eyes swell with delicate tears and heat surge through my body as if I had a temperature. My heart began to pound as Frankie rose from his tiny seat and approached me for the third time. I knew it was the Lord speaking to him... "Mrs. Waltmire?" he said softly. "Yes, Frankie. What's happening?" "I think I am supposed to tell you something. I think I am supposed to tell you everything is going to be okay."

I tightly hugged Frankie as tears streamed down my face. I bent down to my knees and looked him directly in the eyes. "Frankie, how did you know?" I asked. He sincerely smiled and replied," I felt a touch on my shoulder and looked back and an angel told me to tell you that everything will be okay; so, I did." Frankie listened and responded that cold January day and God listened and responded to me too.

Listening and responding is vital to our relationship with the Lord. Some people may have experienced an audible voice, felt a tug on their heart, heard a friend's encouraging thoughts, or listened to God speak visibly to them through His Word. Frankie heard a voice that clearly wasn't mine that day and he actively listened and responded. I am so blessed God revealed himself to me in such an exceptional way. If we want to hear His message, we must be ready to listen and respond too. God chose to work through an 8-year-old to remind me that my prayers are heard and I thank God with all my heart that he chose Frankie to tell me the good news.

Frankie moved a few weeks after he told me everything would be okay and to this day I believe that God has him in the palm of His hands. That year I learned that 'with God all things are possible.' So be prepared; God will work in any place, at any time, and through anyone He chooses. It's His voice, our choice. He heard my heart's cry and He will hear yours too. Now what will you do? Will you listen and respond?

Week 5/ Day 5: Listening and Responding

Think of a time when God answered your prayer. Write about it:

_____

_____

_____

_____

Think of a time you felt you had a sign from God. What happened and how did it make you feel?

_____

_____

_____

_____

Think of a time you heard from the Lord and you responded? Explain:

_____

_____

_____

_____

What life lesson have you learned through this story?

_____

_____

_____

_____

_____

_____

Footprints in the Sand

Many years ago, I experienced much persecution during a budget crisis in our Town District. Many teachers were to be laid off my second year of teaching and I happened to be one of the educators. Moreover, one evening I felt lead to appear at the Board of Education meeting and speak on the teacher's behalf. Now mind you, not only did I live fifty minutes away from this school district, I had no idea that speaking on behalf of the teachers was politically *incorrect*. At this point, I have already driven home and felt such heaviness in my heart. I really felt the Holy Spirit tugging at my heart and encouraging me to go all the way back to school and put my name on the list of public speakers to gently voice my concerns. Instantly, I was scared. I never thought that this would be 'politically incorrect'. All I thought about were the words to say. How could my words make a difference? Their minds are probably made up and I am not a veteran teacher, whose job is worth saving. Thereafter, softly I felt God whisper…

> *"With me, all things are possible Kim. Now go and I will give you the words to say, just as I did Moses."*

Immediately, I called my husband and told him what happened. He supported me and when Hank got home, we took a long drive back to the Board of Education meeting and followed my God-inspired heart. When my husband and I arrived at the meeting, the room was filled. I squeezed my way to a table and signed my name to be one of the speakers that evening. We sat where there was room and it happened to be two chairs left in the very front row. As we sat down and waited for the meeting to begin. I glanced around me with heavy anticipation and suddenly heard, "Mrs. Waltmire; Hi Mrs. Waltmire." It was one of my second-grade students. I smiled and waved in response. Noticeably, there was a lot of attention towards me, as I was one of the teachers being laid off. The meeting began and surprisingly, a few of my student's parents stood up and moved toward the front of the room. They faced the crowd and read a petition to save my job along with the other teachers as well. The parents felt there had to be another alternative. My mouth must have dropped open wide when they mentioned there were a few boys who wanted to share their hearts as well. Slowly, one of my students approached the front of the room, as his mother read his speech. The other boy was his older brother confidently standing beside him. The letters were so touching and the crowd's prolonged clapping was the nicest reward. What amazed me more was the tenderness and purity of their heart-felt letters. They not only told the throng of people that they valued Mrs. Waltmire, but honorably mentioned the *other teachers* as well. 'For such a time as this', I thought to myself; I felt I was in the right place at the right time. It was precious and I was so proud of the boys for standing firm in their beliefs. Similarly, I could speak and God undoubtedly gave me the words to say. I focused every comment on the importance of *all* the teachers keeping their jobs, as well as highlighted the value that each of them would have with the children they were called to teach. The audience applauded and I sat down in quiet assurance.

The next morning, a newspaper article was printed, titled <u>Two Boys Try to Save Teacher's Job.</u> I was shocked! Unfortunately, the article was slanted toward the boys speaking on *my* behalf and the other teachers were *not* mentioned at all. When I arrived at school, I was shunned by most of my colleagues. A few days later, the local TV station called to interview me, my second-grade student, and his mother. The TV personality mentioned she was touched to the point of tears when she read the article and wanted to publically tell the story to get others to understand what would cause a young boy to be so passionate and speak on behalf of his own teacher. Although the article was misinterpreted and slanted towards me and not saving the other teachers, the Superintendent approved the interview and with permission, we accepted.

I'll never forget how my student mentioned that I taught him public speaking, how to use his voice, and the importance of standing up for what he believed in. That is what prompted him to write a letter. He wanted everybody to love all his teachers like he did. The interview proceeded and his mother was asked about her alternative to passing the budget. She replied, "*Maybe the district could freeze the teacher's salaries and save their jobs.*" I was not asked a word about the alternative during that interview and immediately, I realized this would not go over well with my colleagues. I would be guilty by association and sure enough, when I arrived back at school the next day, my life as a teacher was not as I knew it. I had no friends and became extremely isolated. I had a visitor a few times after school hours making threatening comments to me about my audacity speaking at a board meeting and to never open my mouth again. One teacher also told others I must have paid the boy's parents and the reporter to have the article written. I lost friends and acquaintances that year. When the budget crisis came to an end, the district followed the mother's advice and all thirteen jobs were saved. Nothing was ever said again, but the pain remained in my heart for years to come.

This was one of the hardest and loneliest times of my life. I remember moments when I wondered if God was there. I wondered if He heard my heart's cry. My drive back and forth to school was so time-consuming and tiring. It took everything in me to continue praying to the Lord for strength and the courage to go back to an unfriendly place. I would walk through the hallways and some teachers would stop walking their class and wait for me to pass them by and then proceeded when I wasn't near them. Other teachers would mock me with comments and those who were silent never let me know their feelings either way. What hurt even more was when a student of mine mentioned that the teachers act like they are mad at me. I remember hearing my name over the intercom and for a moment, I was ashamed of my name because of either the tone in which it was used or how I was allowing others to make me feel. I had to get a handle on these emotions right away and I knew, without the Lord and His strength in my weakness, I would not be strong enough to conquer my fears and frustrations.

A few mornings later, I thought I had it all figured out. I would leave real early and get to school before all the other teachers. This way, I could escape and hide in the confines of my classroom before I had to endure the harsh and uncaring looks from others.

> "*Lord, please carry me through this day. I am scared and tired of the isolation and hard looks from others. I feel all alone and there is no way I can walk any further without you carrying me. Please help me! Please carry me though this.*"

I pulled into the school parking lot and there happened to be one other vehicle. I assumed it was a custodian at 6:30 in the morning. I wiped away my tears after my prayer and slowly approached the side double door entrance in hopes that God would carry me through the day. I walked through the doors and there on the other side was a fifth-grade teacher waiting with a paper bag tightly gripped in his hand. "Good morning Kim, I've been waiting for you." In amazement, I asked him why he was there so early. He replied, "I believe God told me last night to give this to you this morning. I took this off my wall. Kim, remember you're not alone. Open the bag." He handed me the paper bag and I opened it with such anticipation. There inside this paper bag was a plaque titled: *Footprints in the Sand*. My heart sank deep into my chest as I began to cry. "Thank you so much," I whispered. The poem ended...

> *"My precious child, I love you and I would never leave you. During your times of trial and suffering, when you see only one set of footprints, it was then that I carried you."*

For all those times, I wondered or questioned whether God heard me or was even there, that day I learned one of the greatest lessons: We are never alone. He may give you just the words to read or just the words to hear. God told us that He will never leave us. He told us we would never be forsaken by Him. That morning my Lord used a teacher's obedience and faith to speak to my heart and answer my prayer. It was God who was carrying me all along.

> *Lord, thank you for loving me enough to answer my prayers and speak to my heart. It was then that I was reminded that we may be...*

> *11 Corinthians 4: 8-9*
> *"Pressed on every side by troubles, but we are not crushed and broken. We are hunted down, but God never abandons us. We get knocked down, but we get up again and keep going." NIV*

As hard as it will be at times in your life, you *will* persevere if you rely on the Lord. His promises are true. He hears your heart's cry and knows your pain and suffering. He was persecuted, beat-down and carried the cross for you and me. Now He wants to carry us through everything if we would just ask. Trust in His footprints... Will you lean on your understanding or His when you are suffering? Are you going to lie down and give up or will you commit your pains and tribulations to the One who will never abandon you? Ask Him and be assured... It's not too late!

Week 6/ Day 6: Footprints in the Sand

Recall a time you felt persecuted. What happened and how did you handle it?

_____

_____

How did the Lord make a difference in your decision to handle this situation?

_____

_____

Has God ever used you or another to speak into your life? Explain:

_____

_____

Have you ever questioned if God hears your heart's cry? Why or why not? Then, whose understanding do you lean on when times are difficult? Explain:

_____

_____

_____

Will you turn to the Lord for strength and lay down your pains and circumstances to the One who will never abandon you? Why?

_____

_____

_____

What life lesson have you learned through this story?

_____

_____

_____

Risky Reliance

We were so excited when we heard the news...You're pregnant! Many questions flooded our minds. My husband and I thought about whether our baby would be a girl or a boy; what or who would our baby look like, will our baby be healthy and would our present location be the best place to raise a family. After these thoughts settled in our minds, one remained... it would be wonderful to move out of the city life and into the country life. It didn't take long for us to ask the Lord for guidance.

"Lord, please help us find a home in the country, closer to where I teach. Lord, you know our hearts and desires. If it be your will Lord, please guide us and help Hank and I make the right decision. Thank you, Jesus."

After my prayer, I rose from my knees to the phone ringing. It was a parent of a former student of mine. She said, "Kim, you won't believe this, but I just had a dream about you last night. I dreamt that you were looking for a new home. Are you?" I couldn't believe it! I responded with a "yes" and thanked God immediately in my spirit. You see, this woman was a realtor in the country town I was presently teaching. How perfect was this, right? Well you guessed it. We scheduled an appointment right away.

Looking for a new home can be quite exhausting and exhilarating. By the end of a very long day, we stumbled upon what we thought to be the ideal home. Unfortunately, the listing price was out of our price range and seemed impossible to attain. We knew instantly we needed to wait. Hank and I continued to rely on the Lord's guidance, trusting God for his direction along the way.

We felt confident that;

> Matthew 19:36
> *"With man this is impossible, but with God all things are possible." NIV*

We knew in His timing that everything would work out just fine, so what could possibly go wrong?

Although we had a realtor, one day we decided to go about it on our own. We decided to look at some other homes in the area. One particular home caught our attention right away. It was remotely nestled up against the quiet woods with sky lights and big windows and a patio. It looked remarkable. We proceeded to get more information and noticed the listing price was more than the first home we adored. Somehow the desire for a gorgeous home out-weighed the price. Although the paperwork would exhibit we qualified, the banker wouldn't know we tithe to the church as well. We knew the price was an indication to walk away and be patient. We knew that we were focused on our "wants" and not our "needs". And we knew we had to work too hard to take this risk and yet we pulled over along this winding dirt road and prayed again.

"Lord, give us a sign. Let us know if you want us to buy this home or not".

Immediately, our prayer was interrupted by a car erratically driving by us. When the dust settled, the license plate appeared... 666. Now mind you, we were on a private, long dirt road with no one to be seen. There may have been 3 houses in this secluded area. Where did this car come from? Shockingly, Hank and I stared at each other. One would think this was a sign from the Lord.

> *"Lord, we know you are not a God of fear. Lord, please give us a sign. Speak to us and let your will be done."*

We drove away in silence. I knew this wasn't right and Hank kept insisting we could afford the home and we can't live in fear. Suffice to say, our drive home was long and extremely hushed. Weeks passed and we discussed our concerns with one another. I told my husband that it was too risky to go ahead with this home. It was a risky reliance leaning on our own justification. God has answered our prayers all along, so why are we not listening now?

Moreover, as the weeks passed, my husband tells me the Lord spoke clearly to him at work. He was on a sales call when a car sped by him on his way to meet a client. It sounded all too familiar... As Hank was pulling into a parking lot, the car intended to pull beside him. The woman abruptly left the vehicle and Hank noticed the license plate...666. It was the same car we saw awhile back on the winding dirt road. My husband decided to follow her into the same building he was visiting and noticed the door she entered was bolt locked and chain linked. Nothing appeared right about her location and demeanor. Hank returned to his car and glanced in the back of her vehicle and saw several promotional materials about the anti-christ. Through further inquiries, we found out that this woman's residence was on the same street we were looking to purchase our new home.

> *Psalm 118:8*
> *"It is better to trust in the Lord than to put confidence in people."* NLT

"Lord, please forgive us for putting more trust in the desires of what we see, rather than in the confidence of Your guidance. Why is it Lord that we are more inclined to put our trust and confidence in our own understanding, a plane ride or a car ride to get to our destinations? Help us Lord, to take residence with you. How futile is it to trust anything or anybody more than you God?"

Another week or two passed when we received a phone call from our realtor. We were told that there were unique circumstances presenting a promising purchase. The price was lowered for the first home we adored earlier. Hank was also a veteran and first time home buyers could purchase a home with a VA loan with no money down. We waited patiently until God's timing was revealed. There was no risky reliance when we diligently leaned upon the Lord. God worked it out in His glory and in October 1993 we were honored with the opportunity to acquire our first home in the town that I teach. A few weeks later our daughter Jacquelyn Marie was born healthy and beautiful.

This story never ceases to amaze me. My husband and I were walking with the Lord, praying daily and seeking His guidance. How is it that we can think we are about the things of God and miss His voice? It astonishes me to think that we are easily won over by our own understanding and justification.

Proverbs 3:5-6
"Trust in the Lord with all your heart; do not depend on your own understanding.
Seek His will in all you do, and He will show you which path to take." NLT

Sometimes when we are confronted with important decisions, we can't seem to trust anyone, not even the Lord. We need to remember that God knows what is best for us. Whether He answers our requests in our timing or the way we want him to, really doesn't matter. What matters is that we must trust Him with everything, which includes all our thoughts, intentions and choices. It's God's voice, but our choice.

My husband and I brought our prayers before the Lord, but we needed to be reminded of the importance of following His leading, hearing and recognizing His voice and using the Bible as our guide. There are risks in life, but remember when we rely on ourselves and justify what we think and feel, it is a risky reliance not worth taking. Will you rely on God's leading? Trust in Him to make your paths straight. You will be glad you did.

Week 7/ Day 7: Risky Reliance

Explain a time you went about things your own way and why it didn't work.

_____

_____

_____

_____

Tell about a time you were 'warned' about danger or potential problems and you didn't listen.

_____

_____

_____

_____

Share how you will rely on God's leading in all circumstances. How can this benefit you and others?

_____

_____

_____

_____

What life lesson have you learned through this story?

_____

_____

_____

_____

The Birth of a Princess

April 16, 1993 was one of those days I will never forget. It was the day my pregnancy was confirmed. My due date was January 1, 1994... A New Year's baby! I loved being pregnant. My first two trimesters were wonderful. I had the summer to relax, write in my journal, go for walks, and continue my involvement in church activities while talking with friends about pregnancy and my anticipation of motherhood. Unfortunately, though, my adoptive mother couldn't share the details of pregnancy with me because she was unable to have children. Therefore, I spent a lot of time talking with friends or other family members that loved to share their experiences and advice and I contributed what I learned to my mother so we could share it all together.

We decided we would wait until the baby was born before we chose a name. The two names we had in mind were Jacquelyn Marie or Joshua Ryan. We planned on a baby registry, began the plans for a baby's room and my husband and I felt everything was falling into place. The names were all set; we had jobs, and friends and family supporting us along the way from leaving our condominium to buying a new home. God's timing was perfect...

Well, on the eve of November 15th, surprise! My water broke while I was in bed. "Hank, my water just broke. I can't believe it. It's so soon," I apprehensively stated. "It's okay Kim. God's timing is perfect," Hank replied. The contractions continued and I was rushed to the hospital. The doctor on call stated that the baby was breeched, and being six weeks early and the possibility of an emergency c-section, they felt I would be better served at another facility an hour away. My husband called to inform the family and off we went in the most uncomfortable ambulance ride; bump after bump. By the way, did I mention I didn't have adequate lesson plans for a substitute teacher for the next day? In between contractions, I gave Hank the school number to secure my request for a substitute. Additionally, I asked the emergency medical technician to hand my husband paper and a pen so he could write down my lessons so the teacher could have the most successful experience with my students. Between panting, perspiring, and prescribing lessons, it was an hour I would never forget.

Fortunately, when we arrived, the finest doctors were available to assess the possibility of an early arrival, with hopes of little or no complications. They quickly wheeled me into the birthing room and after a very thorough evaluation, conclusively they stated their concerns. The doctors were concerned about our baby being breeched, the possibility of being born six weeks early with underdeveloped lungs, as well as the prospect of my contracting an infection. They felt to alleviate infection and leave time for my baby's lungs to develop, I should be placed on steroids so the contractions would stop and remain on bed-rest; this way my baby can have more time to develop.

Soon thereafter, Hank and I were joined by family and close friends. We informed them of what needed to take place then Hank and I prayed that God's will be done. I felt the baby kicking and it appeared as if I would give birth at any moment. Steroids or not, I believed my baby was going to be born sooner than later.

I was wheeled into a new single suite. It perfectly suited our needs. Bed-rest seemed inevitable until a few hours later and the contractions increased instantaneously. Hank buzzed the nurse on call and I was immediately rushed to another room. A nurse asked me to lift my back up off the bed and placed a pillow up underneath me, arching my back. I was quite uncomfortable for a time. Meanwhile, my privacy was interrupted as several interns entered the room discussing my medical condition; from a baby being breeched, to a possible c-section, a premature birth, and the dreaded sexually transmitted disease that I contracted years before. The interns were asked to observe me and tell the attending doctor what their assessment would be; should we try to turn the baby and allow for natural childbirth or should we perform a c-section? They all started to converse as if I wasn't even there and then they decided to check and see if I was having an out-break. "Awkward", I thought to myself. Can it get any more humiliating? Anyway, this observation would determine whether the baby should enter the birth canal or not. A few argued not to take the chance of passing the disease onto my baby and then the decision was made. I was going to have a c-section. "Hello," I thought to myself. Does anybody care that I am right here? I couldn't believe what I was hearing, not to mention how embarrassed I was; but at this point, I guess it didn't matter. I just wanted to give birth and move on. Instantly, I felt my heart palpitate and this overwhelming sense of fear gripped me.

> *"Lord, forgive me again for the mistakes I made before I was married. I gave myself to someone who knew they had a disease and didn't tell me and my child doesn't deserve it. It appears that if I have a c-section, then I won't have to worry about the possibility of passing it onto my baby. Thank you for protecting us and keeping us healthy. Help me to cast all my worries upon you and let your will be done. I trust my care into your hands Lord. I pray for the doctors and the nurses, that they would make the right decisions and put our needs first. I pray for the opportunity to be the best parents we can be; just please protect my baby Lord. Thank you, Jesus!"*

The evaluation was complete and I was quickly wheeled to the birthing room. To my surprise, I was greeted by another intern who would be giving me a spinal for their first time. I was moved to the gurney and asked to lean forward. "No, no, not there," a voice bellowed. "You could paralyze her. Be careful and go slowly." My heart sank and I nearly fainted. "Okay Kim, sit up and lay back carefully." The nurse introduced me to the anesthesiologist to prepare me for the c-section. She poked me to determine whether the numbing has taken effect and to assess my breathing as well. The doctors were prepared to begin surgery and Hank was there to hold my hand. The incision was made and I felt pain, so the technician gave me more medication and I couldn't remember many details after that.

Suddenly, on November 17, 1993 at 2:06 pm, I heard a baby's cry and Hank responding, "There she is... She is beautiful Kim." "I knew her lungs would be fine. She's crying." I said with confidence. Instantly, I turned my head to see Jacquelyn, but I only caught a quick glimpse and she was whisked away. Tears of joy streamed down my face and exhaustion spread across my body. The longest part of the surgery was putting me back together and in what little humor I had at that moment, I reminded the doctors to do a little liposuction while they were at it and we all laughed. Throughout the rest of the procedure, Hank said I was quite funny and kept the doctors smiling.

After giving birth to Jacquelyn, hours later I remember waking up in what appeared to be a side closet area. It was strange and scary. The dim lights of monitors reflected off the narrow window pane. I could see people rushing by the partially opened blinds, up and down the hallway. It took awhile to rub my eyes and regain clarity and suddenly panic struck. Where am I? Where is my baby? Where is my husband? "Hello?" I yelled. I felt numb and extremely tired, but the anxiousness wouldn't leave me. "How can I get someone's attention? How will anybody ever hear me? What if they forget I'm here?" Darkness seemed to captivate my thoughts until a stream of light trickled through my doorway and a familiar nurse entered with a comforting smile on her face. "Hi Kim, you're awake." How do you feel?" she asked. "I felt lonely and scared until you arrived. How is Jacquelyn? Can I see her?" "Let's get you unhooked and take you back to the room. Jacquelyn is in an incubator. She is 5.6 pounds and 19 inches long. She is a great size for a premature baby." "That's wonderful! I can't wait to see her. When can I see her?" The nurse smiled and proceeded to push me down the corridor to my suite. The room was filled with flowers and cards. I slipped uncomfortably into my bed and the nurse reassured me that I could see Jacquelyn when I demonstrate I can walk on my own. In the meantime, my husband finally arrived and shared with me that a princess was born. We talked at length, but the medicine hadn't worn off and I felt a tad bit loopy waiting to see my daughter for six hours. Later that evening, the nurse arrived with a Styrofoam cup with a slit on the bottom. I curiously looked at her when, to my surprise, she pulled out a Polaroid picture of Jacquelyn and placed it in the slit as a picture stand. I grabbed the picture and cried. I couldn't believe this was my daughter, let alone, the only way I could see her.

Sadly, everybody could see my daughter except for me and I was her mother. I was so concerned that I wouldn't bond with Jacquelyn because we were separated for so many hours. A steady stream of tears ran down my face. I began to feel sorry for myself, as well as reminded that this must be a familiar feeling my birth mother had when I was born. Did she hold me or even see me before I was handed off to the adoption agency? What was my birth like? My heart was broken and filled with joy all at the same time. I missed my daughter immensely and I was envious that my husband and family could see Jacquelyn and not me. I remember struggling with my emotions when suddenly the nurse arrived with Jacquelyn in an incubator. She was a princess. Her tiny body lay there asleep, innocent and precious right before my eyes. I couldn't believe the tiny tubes and monitors she was attached to and of course I started to cry again. I was only able to spend 15 minutes with her and it was the fastest 15 minutes of my life.

I had complications with the C-section and unfortunately, I was hospitalized for a week. Jacquelyn was born the same time as three sets of triplets. The Neonatal Unit was extremely busy and we had to leave Jacquelyn in the hospital for 25 days for observation and time to grow. It was the hardest thing for me to do. I couldn't imagine giving birth and not bringing my baby home. We transitioned an hour and a half, back and forth each day until it was time for our daughter to be discharged. In the weeks to come, we prayed with and for other families who were having difficulties in hopes we could bring a little comfort to their situations. We all shared smiles, tears, words of encouragement and experiences through the weeks ahead and twenty-five days later we were the first family out of the group that were told we could bring Jacquelyn home because she had no problems with breathing and finally gained enough weight. When that day arrived, we were as happy as could be.

Weeks later I asked my husband why I had to spend so much time away from Jacquelyn hours after she was born. That very moment, he sat me down and revealed the truth of what happened. I prefaced his response with my thoughts about how odd it was to be kept from her for so long. Hank reassured me that he didn't keep this information from me to hurt me, but to protect me because he knew how sensitive I was. He told me that Jacquelyn stopped breathing at least three times and needed to be resuscitated and knew I wouldn't handle the news very well. I hugged Hank and reassured him he made the best decision after all. I was so grateful God spared me from the unnecessary details until the time was right. "See Kim, His timing is perfect. He provided for Jacquelyn's every need. Every moment was laid out just as He planned."

Psalms 139:13-16
v.13"You made all the delicate, inner parts of my body and knit me together in my mother's womb. v.14 Thank you for making me so wonderfully complex! Your workmanship is marvelous-how well I know it. v.15 You watched me as I was being formed in utter seclusion, as I was woven together in the dark of the womb. v.16 You saw me before I was born. Every day of my life was recorded in Your book. Every moment was laid out before a single day had passed." NLT

The remarkable birth of a princess had taken place. No, she didn't arrive by chariot. She was exposed bottom first, vulnerable and dependent on those around her. Jacquelyn's most delicate inner parts were knit together in my womb, formed by God, her King, in utter seclusion. Woven together, He saw her before she was even born. No, I didn't have a crown to place on her head. Her King wore the thorny crown in her place so the humble could be crowned with remarkable significance. Her glory and honor as a princess of the King derive from her creation in the image of God. Instead, we placed a tiny knit cap on her head. We wrapped our bundle up and proudly took her home to the castle that awaited her; I as her mother and God as her King.

Overwhelming emotions flooded my soul. I was honored to be her mother, to be chosen for such a responsibility, excited to teach her all that the Lord has hidden in my heart. Moreover, a healing began that only time will reveal in its' completion. Through God's comforting guidance, He allowed me to conceive a baby that was a part of ME! For years, I longed to know who I looked like, my nationality, what characteristics I inherited and finally, the time has come and it didn't matter anymore.

When I gave my heart to the Lord I was so touched to learn that He is my Heavenly Father who wants to adopt me into the family of God. My identity is in Him and He makes me complete. A huge burden was lifted that day and through the birth of a princess, He has shown me once again that I am a princess too; 'fearfully and wonderfully made;' Amen!

Isaiah 49:15-16
v.15 "Never can a mother forget her child. Can she feel no love for the child she has borne? But even if that were possible, I would not forget you. v.16 See, I have written your name on the palms of My hands..." NLT

Our Lord was born of a virgin, wrapped in swaddling and laid in a manager. It wasn't the way we think a King should be born, but it was perfect. And your life is significant and has a purpose too. Maybe you weren't born in the perfect place or for the perfect reason in your eyes, but the Lord thinks differently. You are infinitely loved and cared for by the King of Kings and the Lord of Lords. Like a mother who never forgets her child, He will never forget you. You are a beautiful gem, uniquely and perfectly engraved in the palm of His hands. Just remember there is a God... there is a King that is calling you Princess. He has a crown of glory He wants to place on your head if you would surrender your heart and accept His gift of life eternally with His family. It's time to accept your royalty... He is robed in Majesty and awaits your answer. He is calling you just as you are; so, forget the ball gown, the glass slippers, your chariot and jewels. Forget the makeup, coach purse and styled hair. Come to Him like a baby, bare, vulnerable, and dependent upon Him and I promise you, His regal life-line will change your life forever. You are His princess.

Week 8/ Day 8: The Birth of a Princess

Tell about a time you were faced with a difficult situation and the Lord helped you to focus on the needs of others and take your eyes off yourself. How did it make you feel?

_____

_____

_____

_____

How do you know you are infinitely loved by God? Explain.

_____

_____

_____

_____

Share how your life was like before you knew you were a princess of the King and how you feel now.

_____

_____

_____

_____

What life lesson have you learned through this story?

_____

_____

_____

_____

Wanting the Wheel

"Control is not in doing things your way, but yielding to God's way".

On December 6, 1996, my husband reminded me that he had the day off to help a friend finish our basement and that meant Hank would keep Jacquelyn home with him as well. I was always thrilled, of course, when at least one of us could be home with Jacquelyn. God provided us Auntie Joy to be with our daughter during our work hours in her early childhood years. Sometimes I had to drive twenty-five minutes out of town first thing in the morning to drop her off and drive another twenty-five minutes just to get back to my classroom on time. At the end of the day, I would do the same thing, no matter what the weather; back and forth on the highway. Nonetheless, we were so grateful that God gave us a beautiful Christian woman to help our daughter in those times of need.

We were usually figuring out who was bringing Jacquelyn home and coordinating afternoon meetings, while respecting Auntie Joy's hours with our daughter. But this morning was different. Hank was staying home with our Jacquelyn on a last-minute decision and I was off to school; a choice that undoubtedly changed our lives.

As the day progressed, I remember the children running through the classroom with their noses pressed up against the cold window- pane peering out at the first snowfall. We couldn't believe our eyes. Winter was officially upon us. We were only in school for an hour before it started and it didn't let up at all. A few hours into the morning, we had accumulated several inches of snow followed by an announcement from our principal saying, "We are moving to an emergency half day schedule. Please see that the children know where they are going." Immediately, my class was filled with cheers and laughter. I, on the other hand, was frantic because I was responsible for their departure and correct destinations.

I remember saying goodbye to the last student who slowly turned the corner out of my class-room door and that was my cue to get my bags and head home for the day. I rushed through the hallways and out into the slippery parking lot. My car was blanketed with inches of snow. I opened the trunk and found my scraper and cleaned the windows, along with my colleague who couldn't find hers. Instantly, I was concerned about the roads, especially with the first snowfall of the year. The winds began to increase. The ride would be challenging, but I have driven in worse weather before. "I can do this", I thought to myself.

I managed to get down the street and onto the back roads where we lived. I am only six minutes from the school, so I was hopeful I would be home soon to be with my family and bunker down for the rest of the day. I approached my winding, slippery, snow -covered street with confidence, knowing every twist and turn because I have driven this road for years. Unexpectedly though, I turn a corner and everything drastically changed.

I tried turning the steering wheel and it automatically turned back. How could this be possible? I turned it again and the wheel automatically turned back. I felt as if I was on an iced track without control. Regrettably, it looked as if I was either going to head for the only tree on the upper right-hand side of a hill along the edge of the street or I would pass the tree and go hundreds of feet down a front yard hill and into a house. In a split-second I grabbed the wheel again, but I was not in control. I prayed to God, let go of the wheel, and let the car do what it was going to do and hit the tree head on. The pain instantaneously spread through my legs as the front end of my car crumpled back into my dash board, cutting me off at the shins. The air bags alarmed me with a punch to my face that left it so numb; I thought I was bruised for sure. The impact of the car pushed the driver's door right open, hurting my left hand badly. As I began to open my eyes, thanking Jesus that I really was alive, I started to tremble from head to toe. Even the passenger's door was pushed open. How could this be? I know these roads. I am a good driver. I wasn't going that fast. What do I do Lord? Do I stay in the car? Do I drag myself out? I don't even have boots to wear... Can I walk? Do I try to walk home? What if nobody sees me for a long time?

"Lord, I tried grabbing the wheel!"

But I wasn't in control. Isn't life like that sometimes? We think we know all the answers... and it dawned on me. "Kim, you aren't in control; I am", said the Lord in my heart that day. I wanted the wheel, I grabbed the wheel, and it wasn't for me to control.

God was in control.

With tear filled eyes, I sat there and prayed a prayer of forgiveness and protection. I was fully convinced this accident wasn't my fault. I knew the road, I thought. I'm a good driver; I was only going about 30 mph. The police will see that it was the weather and not my fault. It looked like someone else did the same thing before me. I was on an iced track because of an accident before me. That's why I got in the accident.

It was the Lord that protected me that day and my pride that almost ended my life. As I sat there trying to regroup and reason with myself, I was reminded of how Jacquelyn was suppose to be in the car with me. My car was totaled at 30mph. I kept thanking God it was me and not my daughter in this accident. I looked at myself in the rear-view mirror and thought for sure I would look like a raccoon. My face was perfect. There was no bruising at all. I held my hand and the lump was the size of a small grape. I placed my other hand on the bump and prayed for a healing and the bump appeared to stop swelling and started to miraculously disappear. Tears streamed down my face uncontrollably.

> *"Lord, please forgive me for not allowing you to be in control of my life at times. My devotions have been sporadic; I have been rushing to meet expectations; trying to be perfect in every situation. I couldn't wait to get home and even prayed to you while I was on these back roads. I feel like I have failed you. Lord, I was very confident with my driving and thought I knew the road because I travelled it many times. I am so humbled by your love for me and the second chance you just gave me and with my family. Please forgive me for my pride and thank you for your protection and healing me in my pain. Help me to stop taking the wheel and let you guide me and direct my journey. Please help me find a way back home safely today. Thank you, Jesus!"*

I carefully stepped out of the car and I turn to see the first vehicle heading slowly towards me. The head-lights of the car glistened off the fresh, snow-covered road. The car began to slow down and to my joyful relief, it was Hank! I cried out in tears with such gratitude, I thought my heart would burst. Hank saw my car from a distance and told me of the panic he had when he realized it was my car stranded along the barren road. Immediately he prayed that I was alive and okay. Praise God He answered yes to Hank's prayer too. Hank mentioned he and our friend needed to get supplies for the basement and was grateful they made that decision last minute. I smiled and knew that God's hand was in our midst that day, every step of the way.

Life is like that you know... We want to grab a hold of the wheel and sometimes we drive the car right off the road. I remember clearly during this season when life was nothing but busy and busier. I remember telling the Lord that I will settle down when 'this' and 'that' are done. I remember the restlessness without the rest. When life comes at us from all directions, we tend to take the wheel and drive ourselves. It's not until we are bitterly humbled, when we decide to let go of the wheel.

I learned a lot about the importance of placing myself under God and His control that day. We humble ourselves, He lifts us up, and sometimes life's lessons humble us too. Sometimes we grab the wheel and the outcome is humbling. Sometimes we don't grab the wheel and the outcome is humbling. Other moments we let God grab the wheel and the outcome remains humbling, but if we let God take the wheel in all our circumstances and h*umble ourselves*, we will begin to see the path He has chosen for us.

There was a time when Jesus and His friends were gathered together sharing an intimate meal with one another. A deep sorrow overflowed the atmosphere while Jesus revealed that they would all betray Him; even Peter. Peter had many weaknesses that would make him stumble just like you and me, so Jesus added that He prayed for Peter. Imagine that...

> *Luke 22:33-34*
> *"Peter said, "Lord, I am ready to go to prison with You, and even to die with You." But Jesus said, "Peter, let Me tell you something. Before the rooster crows tomorrow morning, you will deny three times you ever knew me." NLT*

Later that day guards arrested Jesus, mocked and began beating Him. Peter had denied ever knowing Jesus three times before the rooster crowed the next morning. When Peter was reminded of His Savior's humbling words, he left the courtyard weeping bitterly.

How often do you and I let our pride take the wheel? I was sure I knew those roads and I thought I was driving slowly enough to avoid an accident, but the results were telling. When the officer came upon the scene he said," Miss, do you know the speed limit on this road?" Humbly, I admitted that I thought it was 30mph. "The speed limit is 25mph and yes, there was a minor accident earlier today in this same location, but it had nothing to do with your accident. We must fine you for driving hazardously at 30mph in this inclement weather." And then it struck me...I had to take personal responsibility for my accident. The warning signs were there, but I neglected them. Jesus warned the disciples and they neglected the signs too.

God never promised us we would avoid trials and tribulations; but He promises to see us through them; just like he did the day He was orchestrating my circumstances all along. So why would I take the wheel now? Interestingly though, it was when I let go of the wheel that the car headed right into the only tree along the edge of the road. If I literally grabbed the wheel and fought the tension, I most likely would have missed the tree and headed down the hill and into a house. I can't imagine what damage would have been done or pains and trauma I would have endured. I couldn't help but thank Jesus for His protection that day. I was clearly rushed, but God provided for me in those conditions with a lesson learned; *let go of the wheel.*

I remember the fear I felt, thinking about getting behind the wheel again. Perhaps that is the best place to be. No matter what our circumstances, God's power is perfected in our weaknesses when we surrender to Him. Every time I feel the pain in my shins, shave my legs or feel the indentation and see the scars left behind, I am reminded that although God hasn't taken away my physical pain, His power works through me in my weakest moments.

> *2 Corinthians 12:8-10*
> *"Three different times I begged the Lord to take it away. Each time He said, "My grace is all you need. My power works best in weakness." So now I am glad to boast about my weaknesses, so that the power of Christ can work through me. That's why I take pleasure in my weaknesses... For when I am weak, I am strong." NLT*

The accident I described was humbling and life changing. Like any overwhelming experience, we learn the importance of staying on track, but it is His track that will take us where we need to go. God doesn't promise the track will be easy or we won't stumble along the way, but He loves you and me enough to pick us up and move us forward for His purpose if we would just let Him.

I am continually reminded to let go of the wheel and let God direct my life's journey. I may slip and forget at times, but I praise the Lord that I have a God who wants a relationship with me because He loves me. I praise the Lord because I have a God who loves me enough to help move me and guide me onward, despite my failures.

Think about where you want God to take hold of the wheel. Is it in your marriage, job, family, relationships, finances, projects or dreams? Recognize that area of importance and release your grip. Give your circumstances to God and let His power and control lead you through your weaknesses. Keep your eyes on Him and trust the One who died for you with His arms opened wide. Give it all to God and watch what the Lord will do. He wants to take the wheel; will you let Him?

Week 9/ Day 9: Wanting the Wheel

Think of a time you were absolutely in control and it didn't work. Tell about it.

_____

_____

_____

Think of a time you were over-confident and the situation back-fired.

_____

_____

_____

Write about a time you had to ask for forgiveness for controlling or being over-confident in a situation.

_____

_____

_____

Think about a time you allowed God to take your wheel. How was this experience and outcome different from your previous decisions?

_____

_____

_____

What life lesson have you learned through this story?

_____

_____

_____

Sin Stains

I couldn't sleep in any longer, so I quietly got up without waking my husband and I brewed my favorite coffee. All I could think about was my cup of coffee and how the warm cup feels in my hands. Momentarily, the aroma spreads across the room and when it's time to add my hazelnut cream, I somehow always fill it to the brim and stir it with anticipation of my first sip. It's like starting my day with a decadent dessert.

This particular morning, I sipped my coffee along the edges of my cup and walked towards my favorite spot on the couch. Suddenly, my hand slipped and the coffee spilled all over the rug. I knew the carpet would eventually absorb the coffee and possibly leave a stain, so I set the coffee cup down and immediately began cleaning the remnants with a paper towel; of course, it was the only thing I could quickly get my hands on. For a moment, it appeared to have not left a stain and a smile spread across my face. Unfortunately, the next thing I knew, a stain suddenly appeared. Without hesitation, I got a wet rag and rubbed deeply to remove what I thought was left of the coffee stain, but soon thereafter, I could still detect a stained remnant. Obviously, my efforts were not enough, but it dawned on me what would work; the stain remover. Why didn't I think of that in the first place? That spray is so powerful; it would certainly remove the stain with no problem. Can you believe the remover was in front of me the entire time; What was I thinking? A couple of sprays and rubs later, the stain disappeared. If I only relied on the stain remover, I wouldn't have worked so hard and certainly would have enjoyed warmer coffee.

I poured another cup more carefully this time and sat down to reflect on what just happened. If only I had not filled my cup to the brim. If only I walked slower and more cautiously. If only I remembered the stain remover my first attempt. Who knew I would be starting my day taking matters into my own hands, without relying on the very thing that would have made all the difference in the world. Have you ever started your day taking matters into your hands?

As I sat there, God brought to memory the many times I have filled my life to the brim with too many things. He reminded me of the times I didn't rely on Him to remove the stains in my own life when He was there all along. When my life is filled to the brim I must walk just as cautiously, worried that I am going to make a mistake; concerned I will spill over into other areas of my life. It's an exhausting way to live, but it's a choice. I often bite off more than I can chew and somehow, I believe that I can balance all these areas; without the stain remover. That Saturday morning was no exception. Sure, I saw the warning signs and I sipped back the coffee settling around the rim of my cup, but it still spilled over and made a mess.

Isn't life like that sometimes? I can remember many warning signs that would have helped prevent quite a few sins in my days, if I had just paid attention. There were many sins I repented for when I realized that God would forgive me and cleanse me. Whether I sat or knelt on my knees, I felt the Holy Spirit gently tug on my heart and extract that which tainted my past. I remember asking God to remove the remnants so I could continue my walk with a clean heart. I realized early on in my Christian walk that He was and is my stain remover. We just need to rely on the One who can remove the stains from our lives.

Isaiah 1:18
"Though your sins are like scarlet, they shall be white as snow; though they are
red like crimson, they shall be like wool." NKJV

When we study the word 'scarlet' or 'crimson', we learn of its deep color. It is a deep red permanent dye. Its rich stain is practically impossible to remove from any clothing. When we are reminded of our sin stained lives, we may think of our sins as equally permanent, but God promises to remove our sin's stains. Sure, most of our articles are stain resistant, but nothing is guaranteed. What we need to know is that we can't be without the Lord's protection. Can you imagine going through life permanently soiled for all to see? Thank God, we don't have to. Moreover, I learned to keep His word hidden in my heart. I realized the importance of being prepared and I began to recognize the value of praying and the significance of asking the Lord to guide me and bring a balance to my life. If I determine to change my ways and follow Him, Christ forgives me and removes my most stubborn stains; and He will for you too.

That unforgettable Saturday morning undoubtedly added to my life lessons. It was obvious that all my efforts to remove the coffee stains were not good enough. My self-determination didn't succeed. We think we can remove the stains from our lives, and in some cases, it appears we have. Seriously though, we need to grab a hold of the stain remover immediately and admit we can't get the job done alone, nor properly. We need His help. No matter how hard we try or how good we think we are at it, the remnants will still be there. Just lift the rug and look underneath.

Lord, fill us to overflowing with your living water. Only you can satisfy our souls
and remove all our stains. Forgive us of our sin stained lives and help us to be
more stain resistant. Lord, help us to obey you and rely on you to quench our
thirst and admit that you are the only One to remove our tainted pasts. Thank
you with all our hearts Jesus.
Amen!

What will you do to remove your sin stained remnants? Will you rely on your own efforts or will you rely on the God that's not limited by your stains? God is your stain remover, so now it's time to let Him do His job.

Week 10/ Day 10: Sin Stains

Think of a time you could *not* remove a stain. What did you do to try and remove it? How did it make you feel?

_____

_____

_____

_____

Relate this stain to your sin-stained life. Give an example of your sin and what happens when God is not the One you call on to remove it.

_____

_____

_____

_____

What steps can you take to rely on God to remove your sin's stains?

_____

_____

_____

_____

What life lesson have you learned through this story?

_____

_____

_____

_____

_____

Quick to Listen and Slow to Speak

I slowly moved my way towards the front row as the guest speakers prepared for their presentation. I happened to know about the direction these facilitators were taking, as we just spoke about this topic for my master's class the week prior. I stood up and approached both speakers and introduced myself with a brief handshake, welcoming them to our school district and quietly sat back down in the front row, all by myself. The room began to fill with laughter and discussions as I organized my notes and thoughts. The voices become louder as they surrounded me in the second row, still leaving me and my thoughts to myself. As always, nobody ever likes to sit in the front row, I thought to myself, at least until this one time...one colleague eased her way to the front and sat right next to me.

The easel was placed behind an empty table right in front of us as a mother and father received their directions before they sat down. I slowly glanced towards the woman as a faint, but cautious smile spread across her gentle face. I was impressed with the facilitators, as I knew why the parents were there and I couldn't help but to return her smile with one of my encouraging ones, in hopes to put her more at ease. Momentarily, one of the facilitators turned the chart paper over to reveal the title of the presentation: Home-School Collaboration and instantly I knew that this staff was in for an impressive surprise.

The purpose of the workshop was to provide teachers with the tools and strategies for conferencing, but seeing the process through the parent's point of view. It was a powerful experience, as the session confidently reminded me of the natural way I speak to my families throughout the school year. It excited me so much that when the facilitators asked questions and needed examples, I eagerly raised my hand to share a teacher's perspective when there was no response from the audience. Although they didn't call on me every time; the times they did, I noticed the facilitator would write my responses on the chart. I didn't think much of it at the time, as others would respond and have theirs highlighted up on the chart as well.

We broke into three sessions; the first being a discussion about the 'how-to's' and the 'expectations of dialogue' between parents, teachers and administrators. The second session would be two different mock conferences between separate teachers and the parents. The third session would be to analyze what worked and what needed improvement to have a more successful parent-teacher conference.

During the break after the first session, I approached the facilitators and volunteer parents, thanking them for their suggestions and encouraging them that this workshop is just what we all needed to hear. All my colleagues moved about the room while caught up in conversations, had a few snacks, and sat down for the next session.

The session began with a call to have a mock conference with the two parents. The facilitators 'set the expectations' and one hand raised to take the challenge. The Teacher of the Year sat in her chair and with assurance, conducted the mock conference from the back of the room. When she completed the mock session, the audience applauded and the facilitators thanked her for her courage. Thereafter, another invitation was given. My heart began to pound slightly, as it always does when I feel the Holy Spirit prompting me. I was so excited to share the techniques I use during conferences, as 'communication and putting others at ease' is one of my gifted areas. Nobody responded and I was sure I knew why... The teacher who spoke was deemed as a master teacher and by participating in the next mock conference would undoubtedly look like a challenge to her expertise, but deep down inside, I knew I would have done the conference differently. I slowly waited for the facilitators to make another invitation for a willing teacher to participate. The waiting seemed like forever and then it happened. It was as if my hand was raised uncontrollably. You could hear a perpetual gasp when the facilitators welcomed me as the second courageous colleague. My friend to the right of me placed her supportive hand on my leg and smiled half-heartedly. Was she thinking what I was thinking? Who in their right mind would dare to participate after the Teacher of the Year, but this isn't a competition. I'm not competing; I'm showing another way to have a conference. What am I doing Lord?

I arose from my seat and asked the parents if I could sit beside them and they smiled and replied a 'yes' with certainty. I sat beside the two of them and proceeded with the conference and to my surprise, at the final moments; the mother began to cry. The facilitators gave a clap and it sporadically began to spread across the room. Unfortunately, I could hear the whispers over the few claps and then I knew it... the rest of the workshop was going to test me to my limit.

The mother and father shared their hearts and revealed that the way I made them feel valued was enough to make them cry. They loved that I sat next to them and not across the table and appreciated how I touched the mother's hand. As the parents expressed their gratitude, the facilitators followed it up by listing on the chart all the strategies that I used. Noticeably, the last session ended with their words of support, stating that every teacher should conduct conferences just like I did. My heart sank as those words echoed across an anxious room... I sat there 'quick to listen and slow to speak' as the deafening silence fell upon all my colleagues; it was so uncomfortable. If I get through the after-math of this session, it will undoubtedly be a miracle.

The presentation came to an end and the parents thanked me for my comforting conference skills and the facilitators told me that I was clearly an exception to the rule. I picked my things up off the front row seat and made my quick departure towards the back of the room, smiling at anyone who would look at me on the way out the door. Before I made it half -way down the deserted hallway, I could hear the rumbling; "I saw her shaking hands with them before the presentation. It was fixed. She must have been paid or she paid them to look so good. Who does she think she is?" And I kept walking, never saying a word.

The next day was a lonely day. Many colleagues gave me the cold shoulder and it broke my heart. I knew I didn't do anything wrong, but that wasn't the consensus. I sat down at my desk wishing I could quit when apparently one of my students was having a questionable moment as well. He sadly approached me telling me that he could not sleep the past few nights. He mentioned he was hearing voices and the voices or monsters were scaring him around 3:00 am every morning. "Mrs. Waltmire, I want the voices to go away. Can you help the voices go away?"

> *"Lord, I have my own trials right now; what can I possibly do for this boy? I feel like I am going to cry right in front of him. Lord, help me to get my eyes off myself and be 'quick to listen and slow to speak."*

I asked Brent what he watches or reads before he goes to bed and he mentioned that he reads scary stories sometimes. Then I asked him if he would like to get some ideas from his classmates that might help him sleep through the night better and he loved the idea. At morning meeting with the class, I chose one of my girls to be the recorder and I called upon all the classmates that had an idea to share with Brent. As the children contributed to the conversation, I was amazed by how easy it was to take my eyes off myself and help bless another. My students were so happy to share, especially Alyssa who mentioned that she reads scripture from the Bible and has a glass of milk every night before she goes to bed. When the list of ideas was complete, I wrote a note to Brent's mother about his request for a list of things to choose from to help him sleep and proceeded with the rest of the day.

That evening, I prayed that Brent would be able to sleep through the night and I asked God to help me through my situation as well. I fell fast asleep until I awoke around 2:50 am.

> *"What Lord? Oh Lord, please help Brent to sleep through the night. Father, protect him from the voices he has been hearing and let him hear your voice and bless him this night Lord. Thank you, Jesus... Amen!"*

...And back to sleep I went. Morning arrived just like every other morning and my students arrived just like they do every day, except for Brent. He came barreling through the door and nearly knocked me over at my table. "Hello Brent! Why are you so happy today?" I asked. With a huge smile spread across his face, Brent told me that he slept through the night without hearing scary voices. "Mrs. Waltmire, I woke up at 3:00 am again, but this time I didn't hear scary voices and I fell right to sleep". "That's wonderful Brent. Did you do anything different this time?" I showed my list to my mom and Grandpa and we chose to read the Bible and drink some milk before I went to bed. Here, we read in the Book of James and I want to give you this scripture.

> *James 1:19*
> *"Understand this, my dear brothers and sisters: You must all be quick to listen, slow to speak, and slow to get angry." NLT*

> *Lord, I can't believe Brent gave me this scripture. I have been quoting this for the past few days. Thank you for answering my prayers and taking care of Brent. What a testimony to your Word being heard and coming to life. Brent heard your Word and listened to Your voice, which overshadowed the dark last night. Thank you, Jesus."*

No sooner did I hug Brent and share my heart with the Holy Spirit that morning, a substitute teacher came through my door and told me that she was taking over my class while I go to the office to meet with the Principal. I was stunned and unprepared for this announcement, so I thought. I inquisitively walked to the office to await my conversation. The Principal told me that there were many rumors about my 'conduct' at the recent home-school collaboration presentation and my mock conference offended a lot of colleagues. Then, it all made sense to me; 'be quick to listen and slow to speak.'

> *"Lord, you were preparing me all along for such a time as this. You knew I would be confronted by the Principal and I had to be 'quick to listen, slow to speak and slow to anger". Father, you were stirring in my heart all along and you used a child to confirm that your voice was the one I was hearing. What a miracle Lord... Thank you Jesus!"*

In my flesh, I wanted to yell at the principal and give her my resignation. It amazed me how ridiculous these accusations were. She even had the nerve to mention that there were rumors that I knew the facilitators and the presentation was fixed to make the Teacher of the Year look bad. Through it all I remained quiet... I was "quick to listen, slow to speak and slow to anger." As the Holy Spirit gave me peace, I reassured the Principal that the rumors were just rumors and that I didn't intend to hurt anyone's feelings. I reassured her that I did nothing wrong and I was sorry to waste her time. She thought I should apologize to the Teacher of the Year and I diverted her from this inappropriate request, bowed out of the accusatory conversation gracefully and headed back to class.

Was my pride and integrity bruised that day? Was I offended? You bet, however, I wasn't about to show my anger. I wanted to honor the miracle God performed in my life. He chose to use my circumstances and speak through a seven-year-old. How could I get angry? My desire is to never intentionally communicate that 'my' ideas are much more important than others. I take great pride in adding value to other people and showing them that I care about their viewpoints. The Principal clearly took sides and it was an injustice, but getting angry wasn't the answer. I'm not sure I won the argument with the Principal that day, but I do know that I walked away representing my Lord.

There will undoubtedly be times in your life when injustice creeps around the corner and catches you when you least expect it. You will be offended and there will be times when your integrity and pride will be challenged and hurt as well. But remember not to let your selfish anger get in the way of God's truth. Be "quick to listen, slow to speak and slow to anger" and indisputably you will speak with more clarity; Just see what happens. These are qualities needed in trials and trust me, you will have them. Will you let God perform a miracle in your life? Turn your trials into trust. It will make all the difference in the world.

Week 11/ Day 11: Quick to Listen Slow to Speak

Can you remember a time you were accused of something that wasn't true? Tell about this moment.

_____

_____

_____

_____

Getting angry isn't always the answer. Share about a time you showed your anger, rather than held it in. How did this make you or others feel?

_____

_____

_____

_____

Speaking too quickly and not listening carefully can place you and others in uncomfortable circumstances. Think of a time you decided to listen carefully and spoke with clarity. What was is like for you to turn your trial into trust?

_____

_____

_____

_____

What life lesson did you learn through this story?

_____

_____

_____

_____

Sensibly Speaking

S ociety doesn't hold much stock in 'words' today. Words don't have much value and unless it is in writing, some say you are bound to the words; and even then, it is questionable.

Matthew 12:36-37
"But I say to you that for every idle word men may speak, they will give account of it in the Day of Judgment. For by your words you will be justified, and by your words, you will be condemned." NKJV

Jesus reminds us all that what we say reveals what is in our hearts. Have you ever thought of what kind of words come from your lips? I can't believe some of the things I have said. Think about the many times you and I have said, I'm sorry, I didn't mean to say that." The very words we utter are an indication of what is happening in our hearts. The question is... what really lies in our hearts? Why do we speak the way we do? Perhaps it is a heart problem or maybe we were taught that way. And if we clean up our speech, will we heal our heart issues as well? The problem we have today is that we don't value 'words' at all. We have forgotten how our words can affect so many people. It's not until we allow the Holy Spirit to fill us with a brand-new attitude, that we will be changed and others will be blessed. It's not until we change our motives, that our speech will be respectable all the way to the source.

I remember a time when I arrived at the school parking lot with my daughter and a driver sped quickly by, slammed on their breaks, just missing us. Rather than looking out the side window to acknowledge our neighbor driving sporadically, I stalled to get our bags and waited for him to leave. We exited the car when suddenly a colleague approached me with a few insensitive words to describe the gentleman driver. Not thinking, I responded with a few comments myself, recounting him as our neighbor who is loud, uses profanity and drives fast all the time. Jacquelyn interrupted our conversation and told me she would meet me in my classroom. When I joined Jacquelyn, she was quite sad. "Why are you so sad Jacquelyn?" I asked. "Mommy, what you said in the parking lot was like gossip and you told me we should not do that." My heart began to pound. "You're right. I never should have said those things. I gave too much information and I was wrong. Please forgive me Jacquelyn." "I do mommy." "I'll be right back. I need to apologize to Mrs. P." I added. "Okay mommy; do it." I apologized to the teacher for what I said and she saw absolutely nothing wrong. I told her I needed to do this because of the wrong example I was setting for my daughter. "Oh, just tell her that we're friends and friends share stuff like that," she responded.

Our words really do matter...

Think about marriage vows. Men and women are getting married every day, repeating after one another, "Until death do us part." Months or years later, often their marriages fail and the words they once shared don't have the same meaning any more. It can be as simple as the rules of a game. The rules are stated right off the top and many children are caught changing the rules to benefit themselves. We either laugh or look away because 'kids will be kids,' right? What about that job promotion your boss promised you and the employee next door just had their name tag added to the new office? You never saw that was coming, now did you?

We will encounter many people with various opinions, comments and unfulfilled promises and these types of people will inevitably hurt us. Unfortunately, responding and reacting to these individuals will be our most difficult challenge. Remember, whatever has been spoken, cannot be taken back.

1. Telling the truth-

> *Ephesians 4:25*
> *"Therefore, putting away lying, "Let each one of you speak truth with his neighbor, for we are members of one another." NKJV*

Anger, lies and deceit can hurt others and we must always choose our words wisely. Even when we are angry, we must remember to handle our anger properly; sensibly speaking. Angry words can hurt and destroy relationships. It can cause us to become bitter and ache from within. The lying and deceit can cause us to bring about division just by mentioning the wrong words. We live in a world where lying is natural and expected. I see it all the time in my classroom. I am constantly reminded by other adults that 'kids are kids.' Well, that's what I call a heart problem. We can't condone this way of speaking because it will only continue. When our children continue to lie, they are not trusted and then they wonder why it is so hard to have friends. And so, the cycle continues until it is broken. There is nothing more unattractive than a girl who speaks falsely. Remember, if you are a mother, you are setting an example for your children. If you are a daughter, you are setting an example and honoring your parents as well. How do you see yourself in this area? Would God be pleased?

2. Keeping your word-

If you and I will say we will do this or that, then we must keep our promises. Children are observing this every day. I should know as a teacher. Every day someone asks me to let them do something and I always respond, "I hear what you are saying and I will do my best to let that happen." I never make a promise I can't keep. If we do not respect children enough to respond this way, it will naturally carry over to other areas of our lives and adults are not that forgiving.

3. Speaking slowly-

We must always think before we speak. Our words can build up or tear down. We must speak sensibly and not be ashamed of anything that one might hear us say. Have you ever heard another tell a joke or make fun of someone, but thought they were being funny? Imagine how the other person might feel. Regretfully, the results could be detrimental.

> *Titus 2:8*
> *"Be sound in speech that cannot be condemned, that one who is an opponent may be ashamed, having nothing evil to say of you." NKJV*

One more thing to remember is that our actions give our words a greater impact. If we can follow up our sound speech with acts of kindness, it will help. If we are impulsive or unreasonable with our words, we are more likely to start arguments and less likely to convince others with our comforting words.

4. Speaking with grace-

No, not your Grandmother Grace... We must always preserve our speech and not allow it to be degrading.

> *Colossians 4:6*
> *"Let your speech always be with grace, seasoned with salt, that you may know how you ought to answer each other." NKJV*

We must be gracious in what we say. If we are not courteous, we will lose our effect on others. We must respect others enough to listen to them and in turn, hopefully, they will respect us when we speak. If we can speak with a lasting 'tasty' impression, leaving others to want to hear more, we are seasoned with salt and they will surely want to come back and hear more.

5. Being noble in speech-

> *Proverbs 8:6-7*
> *"Listen, for I will speak of excellent things, and from the opening of my lips will come right things, for my mouth will speak truth; Wickedness is an abomination to my lips." NKJV*

We need to be careful with the words we choose to use. The other day I was in the grocery store and a very tired and angry mother referred to her daughter as stupid. A few moments later, the Grandmother approached the two of them and said both were stupid for blocking the isle. Mother, like Grandmother... We must break the cycle!

6. Speaking about God without fear-

It takes courage to live fearlessly. We must speak fearlessly and faithfully of Him when we are in difficult situations and when things are going well. When we speak confidently about God, we will also be an encouragement to others around us.

> *Philippians 1:14*
> *"And most of the brethren in the Lord, having become confident by my chains, are much bolder to speak the word without fear." NKJV*

7. Being a good example-

What is good Christian speech without being a wonderful example? Think about how many girls are watching you and aspiring to be more like you. Whether you are a mother or a daughter, you never know who is watching, so why not be the best example you can be?

> *1 Timothy 4:12*
> *"Let no one despise your youth, but be an example to the believers in word, in conduct, in love, inspirit, in faith, and in purity." NKJV*

Regardless of our age, we must be careful to earn respect from others and put value to our choice of speech and God will use us. We must live so others may see Christ in us. And we must speak so others may hear that Christ lives in us too.

8. Gossiping-

At times, we may be surrounded by those who gossip or criticize us. Verbal cruelty is horrible and can hurt any one of us deeply. It's at these times we must be careful to not respond hatefully, but rather, talk with the Lord to get us through. I have had a hard time with criticism. It has been difficult when I have been wronged and I want to talk about it with someone who has experienced the same thing or even witnessed it. I have had to ask God countless times to forgive me and help me not to say too much and move on. I need Him to help me to forgive others before I say something I will regret.

Another way I have worked through this challenge is to step away from the situation for a period and begin the healing process. I even pulled away from people so I could have space and reflect. I have asked myself if I might have been a part of the situation and then had to pray to the Lord for guidance. I have also tried to practice a response. For instance, "I know it has been difficult and I don't agree with them, but I have given it to the Lord and it is time to move on. If you have any concerns, perhaps you should bring it up to that person." These are a few ways I have tried to work on gossip. Believe me, it isn't easy sometimes.

> *2 Thessalonians 3:11-12*
> *"For we hear that there are some who walk among you in a disorderly manner, not working at all, but are busybodies. Now those who are such we command and exhort through the Lord Jesus Christ that they work in quietness and eat their own bread." NKJV*

Rumors are tantalizing and make us all feel like we have the 'inside scoop.' Remember, words encourage or discourage; tear down or build up. When we gossip, we are likely damaging another's reputation. Sadly, others may choose to believe what we say and regrettably, we can't take those words back. Gossip creates a gap between you and the one you are slandering, as well as you and your healthy walk with the Lord. Choose your words wisely and speak when it's necessary. Only then will you be heard and taken seriously.

What will you do to display Christian speech? Is this an area that you need to work on? Ask the Lord to give you the words this time and see if it makes a difference in your walk with Him and others. Without a doubt, your circle of Godly influence will increase in numbers.

Week 12/ Day 12: Sensibly Speaking

Do you value your words? What does this mean to you?

_____

_____

_____

Write what each of the following areas mean as they relate to you.

Telling the truth-

_____

_____

_____

Keeping your word-

_____

_____

_____

Speaking slowly-

_____

_____

_____

Speaking with grace-

_____

_____

_____

Having noble speech-

_____

_____

_____

Speaking about God with no fear-

_____

_____

_____

Being a good example-

_____

_____

_____

Words can encourage and discourage; tear down or build up. What area do you need to still work on? What will you do to change this behavior?

_____

_____

_____

What life lesson did you learn through this story?

_____

_____

_____

_____

_____

Choice Not Chance

In 1999, I was invited to Washington, DC as a recipient of a National Teacher of the Year Award. It was that weekend I visited the Smithsonian Institute and was captivated by the most colorful array of quilts. I asked a sweet woman to tell me about the display. She proceeded to tell me that the exhibit was to honor and highlight an era in our history that many of us know nothing about. "It brings us back to a stitch in time", she gently remarked. The woman elaborated about various African American slave women who stitched messages in their quilts as a form of communication and direction for the slaves to escape into the Promised Land. She continued, "These women worked tirelessly to weave a path of freedom into their labored quilts. The signs were there and the plantation and slave owners loved the quilts as well, but missed all the signs. Many slaves otherwise, noticed the signs and sought to understand them and eventually followed the path to freedom; a choice that changed their lives forever. You see, life is a matter of choice, not chance."

For a moment, my mind began thinking of how many times I have seen the 'signs' and chose to ignore them? I began thinking of how my husband would explore the roads and miss the road signs, rather than use a map. "If we get lost we can use the GPS. With advanced technology and a personal GPS installed in our car, we don't need to look at all the signs, right?" he said with a smirk. We may giggle, but it is a terrible reality. How many times have you and I burned a meal because we chose not to read the directions or were distracted along the way? Has your body ever revealed those signs of fatigue and unhealthy concerns, but you decided to ignore them as well. How is it that so many of us can have all the resources and signs, yet chose not to address them?

"By the way Kim, look at the stitching and symbols on these hand-made quilts," her words passionately echoed. This woman's passion and genuineness drew me deeper into our conversation and throughout my tour I knew God inspired me with a vision to teach my second-grade children, in a predominantly white community, the value of diversity. I wanted to create a voice to be heard through our own quilt and poetic interpretations, but how could I move beyond the district's standard public school curriculum and teach about historical events that impacted African Americans?

We concluded our conversation as this kind woman told me of a children's book <u>Sweet Clara and the Freedom Quilt</u>. We walked intently over to a wooden bookshelf as she gently took the book off the shelf and held it lovingly against her chest. "You will learn that life is about choice and not chance", she softly spoke. "I encourage you to read this story to your children and I promise you there will be many lessons learned." I smiled with assurance and agreed to read the story. We hugged one another, somehow feeling more than just strangers. "God bless you," I said, "and thank you for keeping this history alive." As I left the exhibit, a promising smile spread across my face with anticipation of my return to the classroom. I knew in my heart that my children would be inspired and soon after my return to the classroom, the "Voice of Freedom" program began to unfold.

I knew instantly I wanted to share African American quilting and history with my children. I always read the story of Ruby Bridges and taught lessons about Martin Luther King. I even read stories about Rosa Parks and many other African Americans that have made a difference in our world, but this year would be different. I wanted my students to learn that life is about choice, not chance.

Immediately, I met with our school librarian and a local quilter to help me adorn our classroom with artifacts and stories. A Latino woman, a parent of one of my students, decided to get involved with my program as well. She spoke to many African American leaders throughout various communities and immediately my children were introduced to incredible speakers and resources. This mother and I spoke frequently about her hurts and concerns about diversity. She shared her story with me, telling me that she never had the opportunity to learn about other cultures due to a lack of history lessons around Latinos and African Americans; an integral part of our society. Her transparent feelings consumed my thoughts and made this program even more meaningful.

I read <u>Sweet Clara and the Freedom Quilt</u>, along with other African American stories to my children and each child responded with their poetic interpretations. They created a quilted handprint, a written legacy they could leave the world, similarly to the legacies Harriet Tubman or Ruby Bridges left behind, but moreover, these children began to view the world differently: "Freedom is being able to think for yourself and make your own choices," said Taylor. "Diversity is having equal rights," said David. One mom writes, "Michelle educated me about Ruby Bridges one night before her prayers. She whispered to me that Ruby Bridges prayed for those who hurt her. It was clear to me that Michelle had learned to empathize with others and that she could look with awe at the strength of one little girl; one not so different from her."

All of the children's work was compiled into a poetry book and is now traveling with the Amistad captain and crew. We included pictures of our trip to the Amistad, as well as donated our 3' by 5' legacy quilt to travel nationally with the historic ship. This program has left an enduring impression on my students that will undoubtedly last a life-time. Our poetry has become a written message to inspire others to learn more about African American history and the importance of learning lessons of the past, moreover, forming solutions for "our" future. This program has also shaped me as a teacher and as a person. Our experiences allowed several generations to come together as one; embracing diversity, causing us to question, challenge ourselves, and dare to dream for a brighter tomorrow. I am honored to be a teacher and blessed to be a part of so many children's lives.

Maybe you have a story not so different from this one. As a Christian public school teacher, I have learned that my teaching and inspirational vision is a gift from God and it's not by *chance*. I knew the chance I was taking by focusing on the spiritual elements woven through African American History and I made the *choice* to teach my second graders the value of diversity and learning lessons of the past, without a district approved curriculum in place. I had the choice to leave my comfort zone, pave the way for new historical topics to be shared at my school, as well as listen to others with more experience and bring to fruition life lessons that will undoubtedly change anyone's heart and I don't regret my choices at all. But what if I looked at my circumstances as if they happened by chance only? Where would I be? Where would Harriet Tubman, Ruby Bridges, or Rosa Parks be? If their choices had no conviction, would their stories be the same?

Every year I teach my students about historical African American figures. I choose to discuss diversity, adversity, slavery and persecution. I never mention God, but His Holy Spirit guides my conversations every year and my students are always blessed. More importantly, they are often transformed. Every year my children benefit from learning the importance of standing in the gap, even if it's not comfortable. When my students learn about these historical figures and the impact they have had in this world before they were born, they want to carry on their legacy. Now these are life lessons worth choosing to teach. I believe with all my heart that it wasn't by "chance" I met this sweet woman at the Smithsonian Institute. My steps were ordered that day by a God who knew all along the path I would take to create the

"Voice of Freedom" program. I made the choice to follow His prompting, no matter how scary it was without a school curriculum in place. Now, over the years, more and more teachers are learning about African American History in my district and can read our poetry book with their students as well. It certainly was the right choice after all!

Harriet Tubman freed over 300 slaves, risking her life on countless return missions, escorting them into the Promise Land. Every year, one of my students would ask," What if Harriet decided not to free the slaves?" My students learned over time that Harriet's story would not be the same if she made a different choice. And that was just the point. She had the chance to free the slaves and she did, despite the death threats and fear along the way. Inevitably, one of my students would always say that they wanted to be brave like Harriet too. Meaningful moments like these brought us closer throughout the years. Our discussions were rich and authentic. I walked a very fine line making the choice to teach African American history without an approved curriculum, just as my students making the choice to leave their comfort zone and face their educational fears head on. Soon after, many of my students decided to make better choices and work harder to become the best reader, writer or speaker. They were so inspired by these stories and I am so glad I chose to share them.

> *Exodus 13:17-18*
> *v.17"When Pharaoh finally let the people go, God did not lead them along the main road that runs through Philistine territory, even though that was the shortest route to the Promised land. God said, "If people are faced with a battle, they might change their minds and return to Egypt. V.18 So God lead them in a round-about way through the wilderness toward the Red Sea. Thus, the Israelites left Egypt like an army ready for battle." NLT*

God didn't guide the Israelites along a direct path from Egypt to the Promised Land; instead, He took them the longer route to avoid fighting with the Philistines. Like Harriet, there were times she blazed a new trail to avoid danger even though it would have made her journey longer. We need to remember if God doesn't lead us along the shortest path to our goal; we mustn't complain or resist. Every year my students learn that although Harriet Tubman experienced pain and suffering along the way, she had the choice to complain or believe in a miracle that would see her through her treacherous journey. Harriet knew that God was her guide and she chose to follow Him willingly and trusted He would lead her safely around the unseen obstacles, just as He did for the Israelites and just as He will do for you and me. God knows and can see the end of our journey. He knows the safest route, so will you choose to follow in His path?

As for my students, although I don't mention God, they inevitably take to heart the life lessons taught through African American history and in some small way, try to become braver themselves during 180 school days; all because I made the right choice.

Do you live your life based on chance or do you let the choices you make today be the choices you can live with tomorrow? Jesus lived to give and that was a choice. He chose to die for you and me so we can live. He gives us life eternally; if we would just choose to believe and follow Him. Will you step out of your comfort zone and choose Him today? Will you choose to rely on God to direct your path, to stand in the gap, or leave His legacy for others to follow? Harriet Tubman did and she reached the Promised Land. Now it's your turn. You need to remember that life has many twists and turns; we just need to know when to bend a little. It's not by chance you are reading this today so what choice will you make? He is waiting...

Week 13 / Day 13: Choice Not Chance

How many times have you seen the signs and chose to ignore them? Tell about one of these moments.

_____

_____

_____

Have you or someone you know, ever made a choice you realized you couldn't live with? How did it make you or this person feel? Tell about this time.

_____

_____

_____

Have you chosen to follow Jesus as your Lord? You can't take the chance not to. He is waiting, so what choice will you make? If you chose the Lord, you have made the best choice of your life. Praise God!

What life lesson have you learned through this story?

_____

_____

_____

_____

_____

_____

_____

_____

_____

The Edge of Expectation

I remember waking up with no expectations at all. It was a cold, sunny March day and my daughter and I were playing and creating for hours, as we always did. We were using her art easel in the kitchen most of the time and to my enlightenment I realized my daughter was a budding artist. What parent wouldn't, right? I was so proud of her rendition of 'mommy' drawn with chalk. I had a disproportioned head in accordance to the rest of my rather slender body. I also had a smile that spread across my entire face. It lifted my spirit to know that Jacquelyn saw mommy in such a joyful way. It amazes me how much we can learn through children's art. Of course, parents always think the best of their children. March 6, 1999 was one of those special days; a day I will always treasure in the depths of my heart, but interestingly, it had nothing to do with the art. But rather, it had everything to do with a little girl's heart and a lesson she taught me that I will take with me all the days of my life.

The morning continued and we were totally engrossed with one activity after another. We stopped for lunch and soon it was time for a bible story before naptime. We rocked gracefully back and forth reading the story of Ruth. "Read it again mommy," Jacquelyn requested. We read it one more time and decided to take a nap together. I awoke before my daughter and instantaneously I noticed the peace on her face as she continued sleeping. At that very moment, I began to think about the precious gift children are from the Lord. I felt as if I fell in love with Jacquelyn all over again. Then I wondered how God must feel about His children when He looks at us.

Moments later, I quietly got up and sure enough, Jacquelyn awoke with my disruptive moves. She rubbed her eyes, I gave her a big hug, and off the bed she jumped. Jacquelyn was strangely attracted to the edge of the window sill overlooking the side yard. It was still bright and sunny as the heat from the sun warmed up the window pane. Jacquelyn pressed her tiny cheek up against the warm glass and a smile spread across her face. She began to talk about how the warm window pane felt against her cheeks. "It feels so good mommy." I watched her in amazement as she repositioned her body, gently tilting her face upward and resting her hands against the heated glass as if she saw something. Her eyes widened as I stood there still, so not to break the silence. Jacquelyn started talking as her eyes peered lovingly toward the clouds.

"You are Jesus," Jacquelyn softly and confidently replied. "Yes Jesus," she spoke again. "Mommy, sheep are people, right?" "Yes Jacquelyn, why do you ask?" "We have to feed the people," She answered. I asked Jacquelyn who she was talking to. "Jesus was on that cloud. I saw Him. He was talking to me. He asked me if I knew who He was and I told Him he was Jesus. Then he asked me if I love him and I said yes. Jesus said to feed his sheep." I intently fell to my knees and hugged Jacquelyn tightly as tears streamed softly down my face.

I gently released my grip from around Jacquelyn and curiously looked out the window trying to see Jesus, but I couldn't see Him at all. Isn't that typical of adults? How many miraculous moments have we missed out on when we are expecting our sight to drive our faith. I believed my daughter that day. My six-year-old had a precious conversation with the Creator of the Universe. She heard the message that all of us should purpose our lives after.

> *John 21:15*
> *"...Simon, son of John, do you love me more than these?" "Yes, Lord," Peter replied.*
> *"You know I love you." "Then feed my lambs," Jesus told him". NLT*

It amazes me how often our Lord speaks to children. They accept the Lord and Savior unconditionally. When we have the opportunity as a mother to witness what He can do in a child's
life, you can't help but live on the edge of expectation.

> *Mark 10:13-16*
> *"Then they brought little children to Him, that He might touch them; but the dis-
> ciples rebuked those who brought them. But when Jesus saw it, He was greatly
> displeased and said to them, "Let the little children come to Me, and do not
> forbid them; for of such is the kingdom of God. Assuredly I say to you, who-
> ever does not receive the kingdom of God as a little child will by no means
> enter it. And He took them up in His arms, laid His hands on them, and blessed
> them." NKJV*

Jacquelyn believed in Jesus that day. Who am I to even question her child-like faith when the
Master of the Universe says that this is how we should all come to Him? Think of the many
times we criticize our children when we see them do something out of the ordinary. Some
adults laugh and others think it not intelligent at all and it's just plain silly or ridiculous.
Jacquelyn didn't question the Lord. He questioned and she responded with a child-like faith.
She responded with simplicity and receptivity.

Jacquelyn learned to trust the Lord and listen to His voice. She had no preconceived notions.
She displayed trust and faith in Him that cold, sunny day in March and as a young adult today,
the benefits and results are astounding.

> *Mark 9:36-37*
> *"Then He took a little child and set him in the midst of them. And when He had
> taken him in His arms, He said to them," Whoever receives one of these little
> children in My name receives Me; and whoever receives Me, receives not Me,
> but Him who sent Me." NKJV*

Not only are we expected to treat children respectfully and well, but we are supposed to teach
them about Jesus. We need to teach them to await and expect His coming every day. As a parent,
we live on the edge of expectation, but sometimes for all the wrong reasons. When I watched,
and heard my daughter that day, I was reminded of all the days we invested into her eternal
future. We taught her the ways of the Lord and to expect His great and mighty return one day.
She was listening and in turn, responded to the Lord honestly and purely. One day we will all
be asked to face our true feelings for Him. We can only hope our response will be as honest
and pure as Jacquelyn's that day; humble with a child-like faith.

Jesus speaks frequently about having a child-like faith and attitude of trust in Him. We are more
stubborn as we get older, yet the receptiveness of a little child is precious and humble. They
don't have the worries of intellect or arrogance that stand in the way of living life on the edge
of expectation with a hopeful smile and a faith in Him. Jacquelyn approached the window, not
expecting to meet Jesus, but received Him by faith. I believe the Holy Spirit called her there
that very moment.

John 10:3-4
"...And the sheep recognize his voice and come to him. He calls his own sheep
by name and leads them out... and they follow him because they know his
voice." NLT

She heard and recognized His voice and that very day Jacquelyn showed the beginning signs of an attitude of service and trust. I knew then that she would grow to be a woman that would go beyond what any of us would ever expect.

March 6, 1999 was a day I will never forget. I saw, I heard, and I learned firsthand to live on the edge of expectation. I will and cannot underestimate the need to live expecting His prompting every day of my life, His conversations with our Spirit, and His coming once again, lest it be too late.

If you don't have Jesus as the center if your life, then you can ask Him right now. If you believe with all your heart and soul that He is Lord of all and acknowledge your need of a Savior and the forgiveness of your sins, He will be faithful and just to forgive you. Just ask... Tell Him that you will follow Him all the days of your life and you desire to live with Him eternally when that day comes. Let the Lord know you want this assurance and you will submit your life unto God. It is that easy. Just think of the legacy you will leave your children and others in and through your journey with Him when you make this life changing decision.

Choose to live on the edge of expectation. Await His coming, His prompting, and believe great and mighty things will happen. Jesus desires to talk to you, guide you, and protect you. Will you be expecting Him? Look for God; listen for Him, and tell Jesus you love Him.

Week 14/ Day 14: The Edge of Expectation

Think of a time you had an expectation of yourself or others. Was it too high or low? What happened?

_____

_____

_____

Have you ever approached your day living on the edge of expectation? How did it make you feel? Why?

_____

_____

_____

Have you ever approached your circumstances expecting great things from the Lord? What was that like?

_____

_____

_____

_____

What life lesson have you learned through this story?

_____

_____

_____

_____

_____

_____

A Priceless Purchase

"Here's a price tag Daddy. I'm for sale for $10.00," my 6-year-old daughter enthusiastically remarked as she stuck the price tag to her shirt. Daddy replied, "Oh Jacquelyn, you are worth more than that." "I am Daddy? How much am I worth Daddy?" "Jacquelyn, you are priceless. Remember, Jesus paid the price on the cross for you. He paid the ultimate price and because of His love for us, we are priceless. You, my little one, are a princess of the King." Before he knew it, Jacquelyn reached deep inside her toy box and pulled out a crown, confidently placing it on her head stating, "Look Daddy, I'm a princess!" What a priceless moment we all shared that day.

> *1 Corinthians 6:20*
> *"...You do not belong to yourself, for God bought you with a high price. So, you must honor God with your body." NLT*

How often do we put a price to something? I have had so many compliments over the years about my outfits and jewelry. In fact, I found myself replying, "Thank you, I got it for $7.00." Or I might reply, "Thanks, I got it on sale last week," as if someone would think differently of me if I paid full price. We constantly look for the best sales and bargains for our advantage, don't we? But, visualize for a moment... What if Jesus did the same? When it came time for Him to give his life for us, what if He decided not to pay full price? What if He died for only a few? What if only parts of us were worth dying for? Envision Jesus trying to dust you off and looking at you with hesitation, deciding whether you are worth the amount He is willing to pay for you.

People are always attaching a price tag to something. None of the items we ever buy are truly worth what we pay for it. Some feel your payment was overrated and others underrated. The fact is, whether you believe you are worth it or not, you really are worthy of your Father's love. He is your Savior and He paid the ultimate price for your life to be eternal with Him. Think a moment; every time we go to the sales rack, we pick and prod through everything until we get the best possible item. If it is worthy of our purchase, we buy it. We always have a choice to purchase the items of our fancy at full price or wait for the sale. Jesus did as the Father wanted and didn't wait for the perfect sale. When the time was perfect, He died for you and me. He died for all of us and Jesus paid full price.

> *Ephesians 1:7*
> *"He is so rich in kindness and grace that He purchased our freedom with the blood of His Son and forgave our sins." NLT*

You and I may fall short, but when we accept Jesus as our Lord and believe He died on the cross for us, paying the ultimate price for our sins; His forgiveness and love are priceless. The next time you question your worth, remember that God considers you highly valuable. We have great worth because we bear the image of God our Creator. God has declared how valuable we are to him and we are set free. Knowing that you are a special person of worth will undoubtedly help you love God, know him personally, and make a valuable contribution to all those around you.

Psalm 8:3-5
"When I look at the night sky and see the work of Your fingers, the moon and the stars You set in place, what are mere mortals that You should think about them, human beings that You should care for them? Yet you made them only a little lower than God and crowned them with glory and honor." NLT

The next time someone says, "Name your price," remember that the Savior of the World made a priceless purchase already. You tell them that they are right. You are worthy... **You are priceless!**

What will you do to find your worth? Will you believe Jesus paid the ultimate price for you? It's time to accept His payment in full and say, "Thank you!" Put some time aside and tell the Lord why you are so grateful. His payment in full provides you with a gift of salvation and a life eternally with Him. So, what are you waiting for? Acknowledge His payment and say thank you before it is too late!

Week 15/ Day 15: A Priceless Purchase

Before you read this story, did you know that Jesus paid the price for your life? Explain how your life was before and after you found this out.

_____

_____

_____

How have you or will you live your life differently?

_____

_____

_____

What have you done or still doing to find your worth? How has this decision affected your life?

_____

_____

_____

If you haven't accepted the Lord and what He did on the cross for you, what will it take for you to believe He paid the ultimate price for you?

_____

_____

_____

As a believer in Christ, Thank Him again for all He has done!

What life lesson have you learned through this story?

_____

_____

_____

Our One True Friend

What is a friend? Many individuals would say a friend is someone you can trust, someone who is a great listener, or someone who accepts you for who you are. As a matter of fact, if you asked several people, you would be amazed at their various responses. Everybody has their own definition of 'true friendship' and all their explanations are perfect, aren't they? Have you ever noticed that in most cases, an individual's response really embodies what they want or what they expect from a friendship? But the question remains; what is a friend?

As I look back at my life, I am reminded that I have been blessed with knowing hundreds of people. But, how many of these people were truly my friends and how many were mere acquaintances? Well, I could tell you a lot of stories, that's for sure. But I do remember having a few very close friends in my early childhood years and how difficult it was for me to share my friends due to the apprehension I would have if they would like another friend more than me. I was always afraid my friends would leave me because I wasn't as much fun and didn't have as many fancy things as the others. I remember being intimidated if I didn't feel as smart or pretty like my friends. I was never comfortable enough to give all of myself for fear that if I did, I would get hurt. What if they betrayed me? I didn't want to take the risk, yet deep down inside I still felt like I would be the best kind of friend anyone could have. I was loyal and integral, funny, athletic and artistic. I thought I was the perfect fit for a friend.

Sadly though, much of my childhood was spent with a quivering stomach, but I never told anybody. I was often unsettled, wondering if I was good enough or if my friends really cared for me. Every time one of my friends wanted to do something inappropriate, I got scared and concerned for them. I even lost friends or my relationships took on a new meaning because I was so anxious with their decisions and unfortunately, our relationships were not strong enough to endure the truth that needed to be spoken. I remember many times I would not only walk away from a friendship, but I never really gave them the common courtesy to explain 'why' because I was fearful of confrontation. I realize now, more than ever, that I was never taught how to be a good friend. I was never taught the importance of needing a good friend and how difficult it is to have a friendship. I was never taught the worth of working through tribulations even if you feel like you are the only one trying. I'm not sure I was really taught the value of friendship.

The things I liked most about my friendships though, was the feeling of trust; when you can tell someone the depths of your heart and you know it will only stay with them. I remember going to my dearest friend and telling her everything. I always remember the smiles we shared and the tears of joy and support we would have for one another. As a child, I never thought of thanking God for my friends. I wish I knew then what I know now because I would have done things so differently.

Prior to meeting my husband, I am reminded of how a dear friend of mine from high school was in a tragic auto accident. She and I parted ways due to her interest in using drugs, as well as our decision to go to different colleges. Our relationship changed drastically. Unfortunately, I was so saddened and embarrassed we were no longer in touch that when she died in a coma, I didn't attend the funeral. I was afraid of what the family would think when I wasn't in her life anymore and instead of going to pay my respects, I just sent a card. I lived with this regret in my heart for years. Consequently though, a question that has lingered in my mind all too often has been; who is really my one true friend?

There was another dear friend I had all during my early childhood years and we were insep-arable. We did everything together until we parted in high school. She went to a vocational school and our lives changed as we knew it. I didn't reach out as much and we found different friends to hang out with. I was angry and hurt because she didn't try to keep our relationship the way it used to be. As college days passed, I was ready to get married and choose my bridal party. Although we had very little contact, we decided as little girls that we would be in each other's wedding. I called my friend of years past and she accepted as my maid of honor. A year or two later I got an invitation to her wedding. What? This couldn't be! I was so upset that I wasn't a part of her wedding party. She said we were not as close as we used to be and had other friends to be in her wedding party. I respectfully declined. I was heartbroken and very upset. Rather than working through it, I looked at our relationship as another failure in my life. I decided to walk away from my friendship entirely. I sent her a card and haven't really seen her since.

What is a friend?

At the end of my college days, I remember a couple that were my friends and were there for me during my very sick days, as well as during the transition of some horrible 'boy-friend' rela-tionships. They let me stay at their house when I didn't have a place to lay my head down and gave me food when I worked tireless hours and didn't have dinner. I was hospitalized now and needed to go back home to my family for the summer to heal. I was out of touch with this kind couple and upon returning for my last semester, I met my husband. We didn't spend as much time with my friends, but we kept in touch. I remember feeling embarrassed every time I saw this couple or wrote them a letter because they knew the bad decisions I was making back then. Over time, I let my feelings drive me farther from my friendships. When we got together, I felt like I wasn't good enough because of my tainted past and it became a constant reminder every time we had contact. A few years later, I eventually let that relationship go as well. What is a friend? A friend is someone who sees beyond our failures and loves us unconditionally. I wish I knew then what I know now.

What do we do when we have a friend?

The first thing we all need to do is recognize that friends are a gift from God. We need to remember how careful we need to be when we treat the gifts that we receive, so why wouldn't we treat friends the same way? Realistically though, when we have that 'someone special' to share moments with, we often spend too much time gaining approval from them. We wait for the perfect response, when suddenly; we are all too disappointed when we don't receive what we are longing for. Think about how often we rely on the opinions of others, as if their reactions become our defining moments. Have you ever asked yourself what you are really looking for? And why do other's opinions matter so much? Is it truly possible to gain the unconditional love from our friends? Perhaps, but while we spend so much time depending on others, why don't we regard the unconditional acceptance of God and know His love and grace is sufficient? We certainly can't expect to get that from people all the time because people will fail us.

> Matthew 6:33
> "And He will give you all you need from day to day if you live for Him and make the Kingdom of God your primary concern." NLT

We are so quick to go to our friends for help and advice first, aren't we? We can feel them and see them immediately and why not believe our friends can help us with all the advice we need, right? When God says to seek the kingdom of heaven first, He means to turn toward Him first for help and to fill our thoughts and desires with Him. More importantly, to serve and obey Him in all we do. Unfortunately, through hurt, pain, gossip, broken down relationships, or distance, we often begin to treat God the way we do others. Sometimes we keep God at 'bay' like we might do a friend when we are afraid to call them, when we are embarrassed, or we feel they won't understand. We keep God at a distance like our friends when we think we might be complaining too much and what we must say isn't important. When we fall quarry to this way of thinking, eventually our hearts become hardened, bitter, and ultimately our friendship with others and God become strained, to the point of isolation. Now who suffers? You and I suffer, not to mention our relationship with the Lord. We must remember He loves us unconditionally and He is the One who will never leave you and will never leave me.

Don't get me wrong. God blesses us with wonderful friends and it is natural to turn immediately to that special person, but God wants us to turn to Him first for help and guidance. He doesn't want us to put friends before Him and compete for priority in our lives. We must remember that if we become so focused on other opinions and we aren't satisfied with the response, we tend to confuse the true meaning of friendship. We begin to question one another and it causes division. What if their advice is wrong? We begin to lose our trust in the very ones who were unable to guarantee the unchanging, unconditional love that only God can provide.

Let's face it, you and I will always experience some type of betrayal, miscommunication, and feelings of unworthiness in the name of friendship. So why would we spend so much time relying on those around us? If I relied on a friend's inability to put articles of clothing together, I'd be a fashion mess. If I relied on a friend to tell me not to apply for a job, I'd never take a risk. If I relied on a friend who tells me publishing a book is impossible, I wouldn't be sharing this with you now. I've learned over time that I can exhaust my friendships when I put all my confidence in them only. Inadvertently, I've noticed many of my discussions and concerns end up being all about me. I become the center of attention and there is nothing left for my friend. But when I go to my Heavenly Father with my matters, it is amazing the peace and clarity that will follow. My relationship is more fulfilled with my Daddy in heaven who wants to hear from me and in most cases, alleviates the motivation of going to a friend immediately for advice. I would prefer having my guidance come from my Heavenly Father and then the time with my friend can be a celebration of prayers answered and results shared. Do I call my friends and ask for prayer along the way; absolutely. But what a testimony it would be to share my situation with a true friend after I went to my Heavenly Father for guidance first.

> Romans 5:1-2
> *"Therefore, having been justified by faith, we have peace with God through our Lord Jesus Christ, through whom also we have access by faith into this grace in which we stand, and rejoice in hope of the glory of God." NKJV*

Not only has God declared us not guilty, He promised to draw us close to Him. We are not enemies of God; we are a friend of God.

> John 15:14-15
> *"You are My friends if you do whatever I command you. No longer do I call you servants, for a servant does not know what his master is doing; but I have called*

you friends, for all things that I heard from My Father I have made known to you." NKJV

How comforting this feels. He has reassured us that even though He should call you and me servants, we have the honor of being called 'Friend'.

Who is your true friend?

God will not condemn us. Contrary to worldly beliefs, He seeks to guide and support us through life's tragedies and triumphs. It's in God that we need to entrust our cares and concerns. He will give us the strength to carry on in all circumstances. Sure, I want to share my heart with my close friend and that is fine, but if there is one thing I learned over time is that we need to know when to go to our Lord and rest in Him because He will love us regardless of all the bandages, crutches, bruises, and emotional scars we have collected along the way. If we only rely on our friends to guide us, think of the unnecessary burden you put on their shoulders. It's time to call Jesus your 'friend'.

Matthew 11:28-30
"Come to Me, all you who labor and are heavy laden, and I will give you rest. Take My yoke upon you and learn from Me, for I am gentle and lowly at heart, and you will find rest for your souls. For My yoke is easy and my burden is light." NKJV

We may be carrying a heavy burden, sin or weariness, but Jesus wants to free you and me from all of that. Let's go to Him first. He is perfect and promises to love, heal, and bring us peace. Can our friends do all of this? What a heavy burden to place on them if we expect all of that from our dearest friends. He will know exactly what our needs are and will gladly set us on a path of righteousness. We just need to go to Him as a friend. He wants you and me to be His friend. Will you let Him into your life?

Who will you make your true friend? Will you rely on your earthly friends or will you rely on your heavenly friend, Jesus, who loved you first, unconditionally, and wants to hear, heal, and give you the desires of your heart? You decide!

Week 16/ Day 16: Our One True Friend

Define friendship:

_____

_____

_____

_____

Think of a dear close friend. Describe your relationship.

_____

_____

_____

_____

Has there been a time when your close friend could not reach your needs? Explain.

_____

_____

_____

_____

Write about a time a friend betrayed you. How did you deal with this situation and how did it make you feel?

_____

_____

_____

_____

_____

Have you ever given your circumstances to the Lord? Give an example of how this decision helped you.

_____

_____

_____

_____

This week, go to the Lord as a friend and try Him. Ask Him for His guidance and direction and see how the Lord can help. Write about your experience below.

_____

_____

_____

_____

What life lesson have you learned through this story?

_____

_____

_____

_____

_____

_____

_____

_____

_____

_____

Prepared to Give an Answer

I t was time to board the plane. I was heading to Texas for a homeschooling convention and this time I was traveling by myself. I gave my family a hug and a kiss and off I went. I have never traveled without my family and I must admit, I was a bit nervous.

Conventions are a lot of fun, but can be exhausting just the same. You are on your feet all day answering questions, selling curriculum, and presenting if you are fortunate enough to be chosen as a speaker. Even so, the three-day excursion was successful. My friend Ellen, walked me to the gate as I stood with a Starbuck's non-fat mocha in hand, waiting in anticipation of a direct flight home to Connecticut. It was August 11, 2001.

Strangely, as I stood waiting to board the plane, I noticed a gentleman glancing at me frequently. I was a bit uncomfortable, but dismissed it, knowing I would be boarding any minute.

My flight arrived and wouldn't you know; it was his flight too. The gentleman looked back at me as we both got in line. His seat assignment was in the front of the plane and for the first time, I was glad to sit in the back of the plane. I sat down and made myself at ease, turned off my cell phone and leaned back quietly. An attendant interrupted my relaxation, asking me if I wouldn't mind changing my seat. Certainly, I agreed and followed her to the front of the plane. I couldn't believe it! She showed me my new seat, right next to the same gentleman. He smiled at me as I hesitantly sat beside him.

"You have got to be kidding me Lord", I said to myself. "This is going to be a long trip. Please help me Lord. I hope he doesn't talk to me. What would I even say? I just want to be home with my family."

We quickly took flight and I decided to read my book authored by Max Lucado. "So, do you believe in that stuff?" he asks.

"Oh, here we go Lord. Now I must talk to him," I think abruptly to myself.

"Sure," I respond. "Faith can move mountains. It has in my life." He instantly changed the subject, wanting to know what brought me to Texas. I had to think carefully because I didn't want to give him my personal information, but he had one question after another. What convention were you at? What is the name of your book? You're a teacher; where? Where do you live?

"Lord," I thought silently to myself. "Please make him stop asking questions. I want to go home and I am just not prepared to give answers to this persistent man."

And then it hit me right away. The Lord revealed to my heart that we need to always be prepared to give an answer and I knew He was allowing this experience to happen for a reason. It was my time to turn my attitude around and see this man with the heart of the Lord.

Over the course of our three-hour flight or more, I learned that his name was Steve; he was involved in Karate, traveled between New York and Connecticut, had a challenging childhood, hated wars, cancer and the pain in this world and sadly didn't believe in a God who would allow this to happen. The more I listened to Steve's stories and complaints, the more compassion and concern I began to have for him. He was very angry and lost, but what do I say?

Steve kept referring to the book that lies in my lap and it was time to give an answer. "You are so sure of yourself. How can you have so much faith and assurance there is a God? Look at all the tragedies in the world. What kind of a God would allow famine, storms, wars, and diseases?" Our conversation immediately became one of life and death. On one hand Steve was angry and bitter and appeared unchangeable. On the other hand, I knew I had to treat his questioning as a cry for answers.

> *"Lord, what do I say? Please give me an answer that he will receive. What makes this so difficult is remembering that even though he keeps flirting with me, deep down inside he is prompted to ask relentless questions about You. What am I supposed to say? Steve, we live in a fallen world of sin. God has given us a free will to make the choice to follow Him or live a life filled with sin and no remorse. If we decide not to turn from our ways, we continually reap the wrath of our decisions called consequences. Sadly, there are famines, wars and diseases. Life and people can create the most horrible circumstances and as we move further away from the Creator of the Universe, the more devastating it will be on the face of this earth. God wants to reconcile us unto Himself, but it is our will that may prevent this result or it could be our faith that can draw us near to God so we can live through our circumstances, accept Him as our Lord and have life eternally with Him; putting an end to this fallen world, in His time. Well Lord, this is a start, but I think I'll be genuine and reveal my heart".*

Steve, I was at an all-time low during my college days. I dated the wrong guys; much like my earthly father, and made erroneous decisions. I was insecure with myself and my spirituality. For many years, I felt rejected stemming from my early childhood adoption and a volatile relationship with my adoptive father. In college, I stopped going to church, was stricken with pre-cervical cancer, an STD, and hospitalized with no insurance; alone and desperate for my family to love me and forgive me. During that tenuous time my father said he wished he never adopted me; words I have never forgotten to this day.

I had a lot of time to think during my time in that hospital room. My life hit 'rock bottom' and there were many lonely moments I heavily contemplated whether there was more to my existence than pain and suffering. Why would a God allow this to happen to me? I really began to panic about life more and started to fear death, especially after hearing the word 'cancer'. I figured I'd live hopelessly in fear, have some memorable moments and die some horrible death. My mind wandered thinking; surely there must be more to life than pain and suffering. There must be a Heaven. God loves people, right? He would never send anybody to hell. My father said we are living hell on earth. We live our lives, enjoy what we can, and then we die. But it just can't be... There must be more to life than this. There must be a God who loves and cares for me. There must be a purpose for my life, but what is it?

As you can only imagine, I struggled with my identity and my health. I remember humbly going home that summer to prepare for surgery, regain my composure, and heal from the sicknesses that came upon me. I talked with God and mentioned that if He was there for me, would He please take me off this path of destruction. Soon thereafter, I returned to college in the fall of 1988 and met my husband.

My husband and I brought a lot of hurt and personal pain to our young marriage. I was an elementary school teacher working ten hour days and working out at the gym daily and Hank was a sales representative, trying to work up the corporate ladder. I recollect my daily purpose was to stay physically fit and beautiful so my husband would only have eyes for me. My husband's career took off and he flew to Kansas City for three weeks of sales training and our relationship became strained. He didn't call regularly and when we did speak, our conversations were empty. I feared he was cheating on me, so I began starving myself so I could lose weight and look prettier. Unfortunately, I started to feel faint and became physically unstable. One day in my classroom a young girl named Natalia approached me saying, "Don't worry, Jesus loves you." I couldn't believe what I heard, but immediately I knew this young girl had something I didn't. She had peace, contentment, strength, courage, and confidence in God. But where is God? I felt miserable, scared, anxious, lonely, rejected, disappointed, and overweight. I couldn't help but wonder how an eight-year-old could have something I didn't.

"Steve, it was at this moment I realized I needed to see beyond my circumstances and by faith, receive the One who can make a profound difference in my life. It was obvious that my efforts were not good enough. I tried visualization, self-help books, counselors, anger, and bitterness. None of this helped. After building a trusting relationship with this family, my husband and I decided that timing was of the essence. We were seeking more to the meaning of life and over time, we agreed to walk by faith. Faith believes in what is not seen. Hope knows that there is more to life and that there is One bigger than our circumstances, wars, diseases, and famines.

Steve, I realize it is difficult to believe that God is good and God is real, but there was nothing left for me. I tried everything and when I heard that there was an open invitation for me to receive His gift of life eternally with Him, I took it. Eventually, the peace of God, the assurance that He is alive and forgives us of our sins, and the hope that He has gone before us to prepare a place for us to live eternally resonated in my soul. He knocks and waits at the door of our hearts, just waiting to bring us His promise we all intimately desire; drawing us closer to Him, comforting us and embracing our concerns."

"That sounds wonderful Kim, but I don't believe that for a second. I don't believe in God or a Heaven and I don't believe in hell. And if there is a hell, then fine, that's where I'm going".

I paused for awhile as my thoughts took me to a still, quiet place again.

> *"Lord, what have I done wrong? What do I say to this bitter, angry man who finds no use for you in this sick and dying world? Help me bring this conversation full circle before our flight comes to an abrupt stop and he is left to possibly die spiritually."*

I regained my composure and looked directly at Steve. Enough about me Steve; let me give you an illustration. I clenched my left fist and stated, "Okay, let's say this hand represents your beliefs and God doesn't exist and there isn't a heaven and hell is right here on earth. Then you lived your life, I lived my life, and we die and that's the end. But look at this other clenched hand. This hand represents the Word of God. What if I am right and you are wrong? What if the only way to Heaven is through Jesus Christ? And all those who believe upon His name shall be saved and have everlasting life. What if there is a hell where there is 'weeping and gnashing of teeth' to those who blatantly discredit and deny the Lord? The way I look at it is that I win either way. But if I am right Steve, where does that leave you?" What if I told you that it takes the faith of a tiny mustard seed and all you need to do is pray to the Lord and ask Him into your heart and He will forgive you of your sins? What if I told you that all you need to do is *believe* Jesus is the Son of God and through Him you have eternal life? Think about it Steve; you give so much time and effort to learning the art of karate, yet you won't give God any time or invite Him to change your circumstances. Why not seek God and see what He can do in your life or how He can see you through the pain and tragedy on this earth? Why not give Him the amount of time you give your talents and passions and see what the Lord can do?"

> Matthew 17:20
> *"Because you have so little faith; I tell you the truth, if you have faith as small as a mustard seed, you can say to this mountain, 'Move from here to there' and it will move. Nothing will be impossible for you." NIV*

Suddenly, the pilot's voice interrupted our conversation. "Ladies and gentlemen, we are experiencing some turbulence as we approach our landing. Please remain seated and buckled". The plane dropped instantly and Steve grabbed the arm rest tightly, as I calmly placed my arms across my chest. "You look a bit nervous Steve." "Aren't you concerned?" he asked. "No", I replied. "I know if the plane goes down, I'm going up. Where are you going?" "You have a point," he remarked with a smirk.

The plane successfully landed and we sat there, not a word to be spoken; not a word to be heard. We both looked out the window elated to be safely home again. "Is anyone waiting for you Steve?" "Yes, my girl-friend."

It was time to exit the plane and retrieve our luggage. Thereafter, our loved ones were waiting with smiles on their faces as we walked in opposite directions. Who knew, thereafter, if we would ever see each other again?

A month later, 9-11 arrived. Fear and anguish overwhelmed the United States of America that tragic day when the Towers were attacked and exploded, killing nearly 3,000 people. I remember standing in the library with my students, reminded of my conversation with Steve about life, death and unwarranted calamity. I instantly recollected how angry he was to think that a God would let tragedy like this happen, as if God is responsible for all evil in this world.

> *"Lord, you just dropped Steve's name into my heart. I don't know where he is Lord. I can only imagine how or what he is thinking right now. I know he works in New York sometimes, so I leave him with you. Please comfort him during this tragic and fearful time in America... Be with him Lord and reassure him he is not alone. Please reassure him that you are real. I pray he gives his heart to you before it's too late. Thank you, Jesus! Amen!"*

This was a profound moment in my life. God reminded me to pray for a stranger and by faith; I believe God heard my prayer that horrifying day. Maybe my prayer and conversation was a part of a life-changing decision for Steve. Maybe I will see Steve in Heaven one day. And at that very moment I realized how imperative it is to be prepared to give an answer, even to someone we would rather not speak with. Our selfless conversations can truly make a difference if we would just put ourselves aside and think of others.

What will you do to prepare yourself to give an answer? Will you find someone else to do it or will you have the confidence to be real and honest despite your challenges and fears? Will you be ready?

Week 17/ Day 17: Be Prepared to Give an Answer

Have you ever been placed in a situation you were uncomfortable with? Explain.

_____

_____

_____

_____

Explain the outcome and whether it could have been better? Why?

_____

_____

_____

_____

Have you ever been in a situation where you needed to defend your faith? Explain.

_____

_____

_____

_____

Could you have done anything differently? What or why?

_____

_____

_____

_____

_____

_____

What is the benefit of being prepared to give an answer about your faith? Why?

_____

_____

_____

_____

What will you do to prepare yourself to give an answer?

_____

_____

_____

_____

What life lesson did you learn through this story?

_____

_____

_____

_____

_____

_____

_____

_____

_____

_____

_____

_____

The Superman Ride of Steel

"Life isn't measured by the number of breaths we take, but by the moments that take our breath away." Anonymous

At the age of ten I asked my daughter what takes her breath away and she quickly mentioned roller coasters. The Superman Ride of Steel, at an amusement park in the Northeast, can certainly take your breath away, that's for sure. For years, I watched my husband and daughter run towards the fastest, highest and scariest roller coasters they could find while I stood on the sidelines holding their drinks and our family belongings; waiting for them to come back safely. Sometimes it was the longest wait of my life.

I asked Jacquelyn what intrigued her most about roller coasters and her response was typical; "I like them for the thrill, excitement and the cork screws too. They have big drops and the anticipation of the ride going up the hill is so exciting. You can catch the view on the way up and then suddenly things slow down at the top for a second and then swish... down the hill at high speed we all go with our hands in the air. It's a rush; especially when you are sitting in the front row with nothing in the way of your view. Coasters are a blast!"

Considering her emphatic answer, I had to ask, "Jacquelyn is there anything you don't like about coasters?" And without hesitation, she responded, "They are too short of a ride. The ride is over before you know it!"

Just my point, I thought quietly. So, I found myself continually asking the them both if this is the safest thing to do with their free time. Did it make sense that they should risk their lives on a high-speed roller coaster when they have their lives ahead of them to do great and mighty things for the Lord? "Oh mommy, why do you have to be so spiritual about coasters? It is fun to ride the roller coasters and you would love it too. Just come with us!" Jacquelyn would beg. Of course, she and Hank begged all they wanted, but I knew right then and there that I would not budge away from that fence or bench while I waited for their safe return. One thing was for sure; I was never a risk taker and I wasn't starting any time soon.

I have had many conversations like these over the years and they are memories I will laugh about for a long time, but Jacquelyn said something one day that has stayed with me until this very moment. She said, "Roller coasters are unpredictable mommy. You just never know what is coming next at such a high speed. Mommy, sometimes you go through dark tunnels really fast and I try to keep my eyes open, but it can be scary and fun all at the same time." Have you ever felt like that? Have you ever experienced unpredictable moments? You thought you planned everything, the seatbelts were secure, but life broad-sided you and swept you off the tracks, leaving you stunned, scared, unprotected or even out of control. Well, it happened to my family and even Superman couldn't fix this tragedy.

One sunny day in the spring of 2004, my family along with a friend and his daughter went to Six Flags New England for the day. The goal was to beat the crowd to the Superman Ride of Steel and then enjoy the other rides throughout the day. I agreed to stay with our friend's daughter and go on another ride because she wasn't tall enough to go on the coaster. Micaela and I knew it would be awhile, so we planned for a few different rides in the area and waited for a call when the others were off the coaster. Forty-five minutes passed as I anxiously awaited a call that Hank, Jacquelyn and Chris were safely done with the coaster. I intently watched Micaela, when suddenly; I heard the 'buzz' around the fence. "Did you hear what happened on the Superman ride? A man was killed and they had to stop the ride." My heart sank into my chest... To my right and left voices remarked; "I heard someone got hurt... I heard someone was killed... I heard the ride was stuck and they were waiting for assistance." I couldn't believe what I was hearing. I turned back toward the ride Micaela was on and was so stressed; I couldn't see her at all. Moments later I noticed her spinning past me on the ride and at least I knew she was fine.

As Micaela exited the ride, I signaled for her to join me. Immediately, my attention was diverted by the crowd around the entrance to the Superman ride and I shockingly noticed Hank waving his hat in a motion to come to him. I grabbed Micaela and we ran to the crowded Superman entrance surrounded by crying and commotion. I followed a line of people being led into another building and suddenly we were stopped and asked where we were going. I told the officer that my husband and daughter were ushered into the building and we are trying to join them. Hank appeared from behind the gentleman and reassured the officer I was his wife and they let us through the line. People were sitting in seats and being interviewed as Hank took my hand and joined Micaela and me with Jacquelyn and our friend Chris. Jacquelyn was crying and distressed and then I knew... Tragically, these people were all eye –witnesses to a roller coaster accident that claimed the life of a man named Stanley.

Per several eye-witnesses who were sitting close to Stanley, attendants did not check to see whether Stanley's lap restraint and seat belt were secure before the Superman ride left the loading dock. Stanley was seen popping in and out of his seat during the ride while others grabbed a hold of him. The G-force was too strong to aid their grip on Stanley around a sharp curve and instantly he was catapulted out of his seat, onto the rail and spun off like a Frisbee into the fence to his death. Our friend Chris was in the seat next to him. Hank and Jacquelyn were sitting behind Stanley and they saw everything. Dreadfully though, Hank also added that the attendants skipped the required safety check along the left side of the coaster after a seat switch and he had to secure our ten-year-old daughter and strap her in and push the bar down himself. My husband's parental concerns for our daughter's safety undoubtedly saved her life.

A Six Flags New England spokeswoman insisted that all operators of the Superman Ride of Steel go through rigorous training. She told the officers and reporters that they are trained to check the seat belt and lap-bar restraint of every guest, but unfortunately, rigorous training didn't help this man Stanley that fatal day.

Despondently, Stanley's death was being blamed on his wide girth, but according to several of the sixty-four eye-witnesses, many complained that the attendants did not perform the required safety check.

That day was heartbreaking for Stanley's family and all the eye-witnesses. Who knew that Stanley's life would be asked of him that critical day? Who knew that Chris, Hank, and Jacquelyn would be right in the center of this unpredictable circumstance? Like Jacquelyn said, "You just never know what is coming next at such a high speed." As I stood watching Micaela and waiting for my family to get off the coaster, I assumed the seat belts were secure. Just as a coaster ride can take you through dark tunnels and on new adventures around unexpected twists and turns, tragedies like this one can leave you stunned, feeling unprotected and even out of control.

Hank followed up the story by stating that employees and onlookers were slow to move to Stanley's aid and it infuriated him. He wanted to jump out and help, but he couldn't. He was locked in the coaster next to our daughter and all he could do was hold Jacquelyn's hand and tell her that God would see them through all of this. Hank called out for people to call 911 and help Stanley and an announcement over the loud speaker told people to stay where they were. Hank realized that all he could do is pray to God and hold Jacquelyn's hand. He couldn't change the circumstances, nor could he get out of his locked seat. The entire situation was in God's hands. As a father, Hank couldn't be Jacquelyn's Superman and save the day or protect his daughter. He couldn't protect her from the 'unpredictable' as life broad-sided them all to a stand-still on the tracks and spun Stanley to his death; but God can.

> Isaiah 40:29-31
> 'He gives power to those who are tired and worn out; He offers strength to the weak. Even youths will become exhausted, and young men will give up. But those who wait on the Lord will find new strength. They will run and not grow weary. They will walk and not faint." NLT

We can feel weak and unprotected sometimes when we don't put our faith and trust in God. It is God who gives power and strength to the weak; and His power will never diminish. His strength is our strength and God reminds us that He will see us through our circumstances if we call on Him. Hank's faith encouraged him to call upon the Lord at that moment sitting on the tracks and it was his faith in action that made all the difference for our daughter. Jacquelyn learned that Daddy was there to guide her in prayer and hold her tightly when she felt she was heading towards a dark tunnel. The spectacular thing though is that Jacquelyn never experienced any of those dark tunnels she described on some coaster rides. Praise the Lord she slept every night since and moved beyond this tragic event. Praise the Lord He was there to renew her strength when she needed Him most.

My husband is a minister and unexpectedly was asked to speak at Stanley's funeral. He remembered the countless comments made about Stanley and his joy and excitement for coasters. Stanley had been riding them his whole life and always shared the 'thrill' with others around him.

It took Hank and Jacquelyn almost two years before they got on another coaster, but they were determined to face any fear that may have crept in and they were resolute in finding the joy and excitement that once took their breath away. I love seeing the joy on Jacquelyn's face again after a coaster ride and although she is reminded that life is unpredictable, she realizes we need to still live our lives to the fullest. We need to remember that God is in control and He is there always and cares well beyond what we can understand or even imagine.

Where in your life do you feel you need to be Superwoman? Think of a time life swept you off track uncontrollably. What did you do? Do you believe God is bigger than your circumstances? Whatever the challenges or trials you have, give it all to Him and you will be glad you did!

Week 18/ Day 18: The Superman Ride of Steel

What takes your breath away? Explain.

_____

_____

_____

_____

Think of a tragedy you had no control over. What did you do to get through it? Did it help? Why or why not?

_____

_____

_____

_____

Why is it so important to put your trust and faith in God?

_____

_____

_____

_____

Where in life do you feel you need to be 'Superwoman'? Why?

_____

_____

_____

_____

_____

Explain how God is bigger than your circumstances. How do you know this?

_____

_____

_____

_____

What life lesson have you learned through this story?

_____

_____

_____

_____

_____

_____

_____

_____

_____

_____

_____

_____

_____

_____

_____

A Storm is Coming

"A storm is coming," the weatherman announced during a local morning news broadcast. I stopped everything to pay close attention; and this announcement got my attention. The weatherman proceeded to talk about a possible hurricane that would be coming our way. You could sense the apprehension on the announcer's face as the news cast interviewed several people in the local area to inform the public as to what a hurricane safety tip list would look like.

Hurricane Safety Tips

*Check that flashlights and radios are in good working condition
*Always have a stock of fresh drinking water, canned food, and warm blankets on hand
*If a hurricane is approaching, keep calm and stay with your family
*Listen to the radio or watch TV for storm conditions and evacuation details
*When officials tell you to evacuate, do it immediately
*Have supplies to survive for 72 hours after a hurricane strikes

The hurricane safety list was followed by the Mason Dixon Survey. This survey showed that 50% of people don't have major disaster plans or a survival kit. 30% say they won't prepare until there is a hurricane coming their way.

Several individuals were seen scurrying through stores to gather water jugs, duct tape, boards and more. Every channel dedicated time to informing the public about hurricanes and its powerful destruction. One of many documentaries I viewed that day were heart wrenching. Upon seeing the devastation of Hurricane Katrina, September 6, 2005, as well as other hurricanes across the States, most people in its path were left in complete despair. One woman stated, "How can this be? We prepared ourselves and did everything we were told to do and it didn't work." I pondered that comment deeply, hearing story after story. Conclusively I thought no matter what kind of storm; whether thunder and lightning, sleet, hail, tornadoes, or cyclones; they have something in common. Storms can uproot, dishevel, dismount, and destroy families, lives and homes.

Storms can leave our families barren, our homes withered, and our state of existence in absolute turmoil. We have become victims of natural disasters, day after day, month after month, and some year after year. The news affiliates relentlessly spoke about how to prepare for these natural disasters, such as hurricanes; a storm I am not naturally familiar with. However, it's hard to prepare for something you know nothing about. Unfortunately, the people who have endured such storms knew the steps they had to take to prepare themselves and often the results overshadowed their efforts. We can forecast some storms and have time to inform and prepare others, but we still aren't guaranteed we will survive the turbulence heading our direction. Consequently, there are people who live in fear of storms every day and there are others who don't pay attention until they are informed last minute. Some are proactive and have everything in place, while several just don't care. Many others just blame the ones around them as if it's their fault the storm raged upon them unannounced. And sadly, many individuals are left angrily asking why? Why did this happen to me and my family?

As the morning news continued with story after story, I was inspired when an older gentleman was interviewed after Hurricane Katrina leveled his neighborhood and yacht club. He was certainly distraught for himself, his family, as well as every individual around him. The cameras spanned the entire landscape and there was nothing but desolateness. Off in a distance a few birds were eagerly flapping their wings against the still horizon. It painted an image in my mind, when suddenly the gentleman spoke with a cracked voice saying, "I had two boats at the Yacht club right over there. Look, my boat is in shambles over here and the other boat is in more pieces than I can possibly count. I started to ask God why this happened. Why did this have to happen to me, my family and all of our neighbors?" The reporter questioned the gentleman asking him what he will do now that the storm is over. The man replied," I have decided that nothing is guaranteed except one thing and that is our faith and hope in God. I started to ask myself how I can pass on hope to others who will need to persevere. I asked God what I should do next and I felt He told me to use the wood from my demolished boats and turn the pieces into crosses for surrounding churches as a forthcoming message that there is a God who has suffered and walked the stormy seas of life and He will be there for us if we would just reach out and take His hands". The reporter was taken back by this man's response. "Well", the reporter says, "What about the people who have perished? Where was God then? And the gentleman remarked without hesitation, "God didn't bring the storm, but His Word says that He will carry us through the stormy seas of life and we can cast our worries and burdens upon Him. I pray for all the victims of this tragedy and we can only hope and pray that we as people start to prepare ourselves spiritually incase our lives are asked of us by the storms of this world. Making crosses out of the left-over pieces of wood is the least I could do to keep God's loving message alive. He will use me and I believe He will use you to keep that message of hope alive so we can all endure the next storm heading our way. And believe me, there will be another storm".

It amazes me the amount of faith that goes into believing the weatherman. He says there is a storm coming and we rush to the store and buy our supplies. We expect the weatherman to inform us and protect us. Some of these weathermen and women may even be new to the station, a stranger to you and me, and we still put all our confidence and faith in them. But as the gentleman alluded earlier, we need to be cognizant of who we choose to put our confidence in, to prepare ourselves for the storms that lie ahead.

It's important that we pay attention to the 'signs.' When you and I are tired, we sleep. When we are thirsty, we get a drink. When we are hungry, we eat. God has created our bodies with warning signs so we pay heed and take care of ourselves. Even storm trackers know to pay attention to the warnings. They take the storms head-on. When these pilots are tracking storms in a plane, the crew relies on the controls, but not always without a scare. The instruments may even go out of whack, leaving them dizzy, but the crews always fight to keep their hands and feet on the controls. There are times in the eye of the storm the crew will be tossed around so much, the instruments show one thing, but their body shows another. The pilots encourage one another to listen to their body, but to follow the instruments, even though they didn't feel right. Pilots know that for several uneasy minutes the instruments are correct. The instruments still do what they are suppose to do; measure temperature, and other conditions in the heart of the storm. Like the Lord in our lives, He is our instrument and He will meet us in the heart of the storm. He knows our condition and He measures our internal temperature during the raging storms of our life, no matter how uneasy we may feel.

Still dizzy though, every pilot knows there is only one way out of the hurricane. Pilots know all too well, they must go back through the windy eye wall and cross the stormy feeder bands to get to the other side. Yet, when all is said and done, the data helps scientists predict the hurricane's deadly path. Storm trackers help make these reports and warnings possible for you and for me. Are we listening? Are we watching?

> *John 14:6*
> *Jesus said to him, "I am the way, the truth, and the life. No one can come to the Father except through me." NLT*

I found it more interesting that giant storms start out at sea as weaker areas of circling winds. These winds are called tropical depressions. In our lives, it's not much different. You and I can think of times we were weak and depressed. When we don't turn to the Lord in times of trouble, the winds spin slowly and are spread out over a wider area; spilling over to other areas of our life. Just like storm trackers, they need to meet these first spinning winds head-on. You and I must do the same. We must focus our eyes on Jesus; the One and only who saves us from our wretched situation.

You may be thinking nine times out of ten, you can get out of your stormy situation without Godly intervention; the spinning winds just die out. Like a hurricane, if a tracker notices a tight, tiny hole in the storm, watch out! This means the winds may spin into a tropical storm. It happens one out of ten times and we must be prepared either way. Jesus wants us to follow Him and keep our eyes and ears open to the stormy warnings in our lives. We must remember that He is our instrument and we need to rely on Him before our lives spin out of control and it feels too late.

Hurricanes are hard to predict because of the crooked paths they take. The storms in our lives do the same. Our trials easily come from different directions and may even be for a time. Hurricanes have a beginning and an end. They can last approximately ten days before they run out of energy. Like a hurricane, when you and I lean on our own understanding, we run out of energy too. Did you know that hurricanes usually slow down when they hit land, especially mountains? Yet, when you and I are on the mountain tops, praising the Lord with our eyes upon Him, the storms begin to fade and the skies are clear again; our life's storms begin to slow down.

Our Lord has a sky-high view unlike no other. He watches over you and me. He is our satellite and He realizes the storms in our lives are significant. Unlike a satellite in 1969 that spotted Hurricane Camille in the Gulf of Mexico, the storm looked small from space and people didn't think much of it. On the contrary, God desires us to see the warnings and although we think our storms are too big or too small for God, His view isn't just from the sky. He sees into your life and mine. He can calm the storm and our troubled heart. God wants you and me to recognize the warning signs and He wants us to be prepared before it is too late.

Godly Safety Tips

*Give your heart to the Lord
*Ask Him for His forgiveness
*Turn away from your sins
*Recognize Him as your Lord and Savior
*Lean upon Him and His understanding
*Let the Lord be your instrument

*Let the Lord guide you every day of your life

> *Luke 8:25*
> *"Then He asked them, "Where is your faith?" The disciples were terrified and amazed. "Who is this man?" they asked each other. "When He gives a command, even the wind and waves obey Him." NLT*

Just as Jesus calms the wind and waves, He can calm whatever storms you may face. When we are caught in the storms of life, it is easy to think that God has lost control. It is easy to think we are at the mercy of the winds trying to change our direction. We must remember that we have a sovereign God. He is in control of our lives. Just as Jesus calmed the waves for the disciples when they were in fear, He can calm whatever storms you and I face. This week, what will you do to calm the raging storms in your life? How will you be prepared? Will you rely on God? Will He be your 'controls'? Are you ready for eternity if your life is asked of you by the next storm heading your way? Take this time seriously. A storm is coming, so be prepared.

> *"To realize the worth of the anchor, we need to feel the stress of the storm."*
> *Author Unknown*

Week 19/ Day 19: A Storm is Coming

Think of a storm that raged in your life. What was it and how did you handle it?

_____

_____

_____

_____

Perhaps you have heard not to ask God why something has happened, but rather what's next... Have you ever asked "why did this happen to me"? How did you deal with the answer?

_____

_____

_____

_____

Have you ever neglected the warning signs? What do you or can you do to pay attention to these signs?

_____

_____

_____

_____

Give an example of how God has calmed the storm in your life or someone you know.

_____

_____

_____

_____

_____

If you don't believe that Jesus can calm the storm (s) in your life, then today is the day to try Him. Give your circumstances to the Lord, rely on Him, and give Him the controls and watch what God will do. You need to be ready before the next storm comes. A storm is coming, so be prepared!

_____

_____

_____

_____

_____

What life lesson have you learned through this story?

_____

_____

_____

_____

_____

_____

_____

_____

_____

_____

_____

_____

_____

The Presence of Pain

There is much pain in the world we live in. We may experience it more than others and often wonder 'why'. Some of our pain is purposeful, perhaps brought upon ourselves because we weren't paying attention. Some of our pain may be accidental. Some of our pain may be circumstantial due to the diseased world we live in or some of our pain may be private and not foreseen by others. Women and mothers know all too well that they face a hurting world and it's their desire to protect the ones they love from needless hurt, pain, and suffering. It's their desire to show them how to survive and persevere when the pain floods in unexpectedly.

I have experienced a variety of pain throughout my life. Growing up and struggling with my identity, feelings of rejection and fear of failure were deeply rooted and manifested in and throughout many areas of my existence. It pained me to feel rejected and it affected the way I looked at people and how I believed they would perceive me. I had a very hard time trusting others for fear they were going to leave me. Therefore, I hid behind my incredible work ethic and ability to do well and achieve my goals. This kept me focused and was a part of me showing others that it was worth valuing me, when all along, I hadn't found self-worth or value in myself. I spent most of my life trying to please others and the returned favor let me down more times than I can count.

I can remember how challenging it was for me to cover up my insecurities every time I encountered a new situation or entered a crowded room. I would shake and struggle internally with the 'what if's.' What if they don't like me? What if they believe the rumor they just heard? What if I make a mistake? What if I must sit all alone? What if nobody talks to me? It didn't take long for me to develop many headaches and stomach aches. It was one painful experience after another and the remarkable irony is that I looked the confident part I wanted to portray. I hid my pain for a long time and my pain became bitter. And bitter isn't better, that's for sure.

However, over time, I was encouraged to face the truth and share my hurts and pains with other women. They were absolutely shocked to the point that many didn't believe me. "That's impossible", they would mutter. "You appear to have it all and most definitely have it all together. I didn't think a girl like you struggled, much less have insecurities. You just don't appear to be the kind of person who has problems. You are always put together", many would add. Although many women perceived me this way, they had no idea that their honesty made my pain worse. Often, I held myself together so well during trials and tribulations that I appeared to not need help after all. I tried to release my pain at home behind closed doors and publically hide my pain as I walked with confidence and sometimes a simulated joy for others to observe. But unfortunately, I felt all alone.

When I was simultaneously stricken with cervical cancer and a venereal disease, I experienced the worst pain in my life. I had cramping that doubled me over onto my college dorm floor, while gasping for breath as every inhale caused deeper pain that intently spread across my entire body. I was all alone and my roommate was nowhere to be found. As I lay there on the hard floor, I felt the open sores burning my genital area like fire. I felt as if I would regurgitate at any moment until the dizziness took over and the room began to spin. My roommate arrived and took me to the hospital where I was eventually taken care of. It was a physical pain I wanted to forget. It was a memory that stayed with me forever.

Although the physical pain at that time of my life was awful, in time, I healed. Yet, some of the worst pains I have endured were the rumors and gossip. Sometimes this private pain can last a very long time. During my career, I had to deal with jealousies and accusations that sent me over the edge on many occasions. The painful scars I have had over the years were not always physical. They were emotional and heart- felt. Whether I was at my job or even at church where I thought to be a place of comfort and support, I couldn't believe the painful experiences I had to go through.

We have all experienced the presence of pain in one way or another. The problem we have though is whether we choose to go through each painful moment with or without God. When I had cervical cancer, I experienced emotional trauma. I heard the 'c' word one day and realized cancer was not a good word. I needed to have surgery and eliminate the cancerous cells, but I was scared and felt all alone in my pain. How could this be? How could I possibly handle this and a venereal disease at the same time? I didn't have a relationship with the Lord. I was living my own life and didn't know God. I relied on myself and my emotions to get me through this terrifying experience. Unfortunately, that didn't work. I became more frustrated and bitter as time elapsed.

On the other hand, when I started my career with jealousies and accusations about me, I had the Lord in my life and although each circumstance had a meaning of its own, I knew the One I had to lean on for strength and guidance. I can openly say that the pain has subsided and the joy of the Lord came with each new day. Today I can face my accusers and not be reminded of the past because He threw it all into the sea of forgetfulness. My pain and sorrow has been covered and diminished. I gave it all to a God who loves and cares for me enough to bear my pain and sorrow and I know His endurance lasts forever in my heart.

> 1 Peter 5:7
> "Give all your worries and cares to God, for He cares about what happens
> to you." NLT

I have learned that carrying my pain, my baggage, and my personal struggles all by myself shows that I have not fully trusted God with my life. It was very hard to admit that I needed help when I wasn't walking with the Lord. Surprisingly, I also noticed many who do walk with the Lord still resist His help or even support from others in God's family. Sometimes we may purpose in our hearts that if it is pain we brought upon ourselves, it isn't God's concern. Perhaps we deserve it, right? I believe that when we turn our concerns over to God, He will bear our pain and sorrows. His desire is to actively, not passively control our circumstances, but unfortunately, we submit to them, thus, relying on ourselves.

Regrettably, in this fallen world, disability and disease is very common. We could contract an infection, have inadequate nutrition, or even be directly attacked by Satan. He is the author of evil, but the good news is that Jesus is more powerful than disease, pain and the evil one. We must believe that Jesus can bring physical and emotional healing in our lifetime and when He returns, there will be an end to all our pain and suffering.

When the presence of pain presents itself, we must be prepared to ask God for a healing. He is our Daddy and He cares for you and me. We must pray for the Lord's comfort and guidance. He wants us to live with peace in our heart, mind and soul. When I pray for His presence in my pain, I tell Him that I recognize His deity in my life. I ask Him to help me learn through my painful experience. Now and again I would spend time asking 'why' instead of 'what next'

Lord? I proactively changed my prayer to '*what next Lord* 'and didn't focus on the '*whys*', I felt comforted and directed. I realized more and more that He allowed certain pain in my life so I could seek ways to triumph in my tragedy. I learned to give Him all the glory for my healing and shared those results with others as much as possible. Often, I realized God used my pain to accomplish a meaningful purpose for those around me. A friend can help me pray through my pain, but imagine friends and strangers witnessing our healing and the joy that comes with it. Peter reminds us in the Bible about the inevitable result of living here on earth. Our bodies are weak and vulnerable. Our minds are easily coerced at times and our spirit longs for courage and strength to move on.

> *1 Peter 5:10*
> *"In His kindness, God called you to His eternal glory by means of Jesus Christ. After you have suffered a little while, he will restore, support, and strengthen you, and he will place you on firm foundation." NLT*

Realistically, we can get frustrated with "how" the healing process takes place, but when you and I are on the other side of the mountain; we can be assured the process was well worth it. When I learned that His strength is the most perfect thing in my weakness, I knew I had to stop worrying. If the pain doesn't change right away, I go back to the Lord in prayer and keep my requests in front of Him.

> *Philippians 4:6-7*
> *"Don't worry about anything. Tell God what you need, and thank him for all he has done. If you do this, you will experience God's peace, which is far more wonderful than the human mind can understand. His peace will guard your hearts and minds as you live in Christ Jesus." NLT*

I remember a time I was pained by not being offered the job I thought was for me, but my life lessons taught me to give it to God and trust His timing and choice is perfect. A few years ago, I was interviewed for what I thought was my dream job. I was told I had the job hands down by the woman orchestrating the interview and I felt quite confident. When I arrived at the interview, I was confused. The questions they directed towards me had nothing to do with the purpose of the interview. The 'bait and switch' made no sense at all. When I completed the interview, I sat in my car in total silence. I spoke a few moments later and asked God what just happened. I gave it to Him and positively moved on. I was eventually called back for a second interview and sure enough it was worse than the first. One of the ladies thought that it wasn't fair that I got this job so easily when so many others had to work harder and longer to achieve their desired job. She insisted that I reconsider my desires for working with this resource center, but would like a copy of my resume package to give to her daughter so she could use my ideas. I couldn't get out of that interview quick enough. It has been over eight years and they still haven't called me or acknowledged my follow up letters.

I was so deeply discouraged and the painful rejection hurt all over again. None of it made sense. When I was told I had the job and learned it was just a formality, I was heart- broken. The summer months passed and I discontentedly returned to my classroom in the fall, and to my surprise, I learned that I was chosen as one of the top twenty teachers in the United States by USA Today. Amazingly, I couldn't receive this award and honorarium unless I was teaching in the town I was nominated. God knew all along that job wasn't mine and now I tell this story to others when they are struggling with God's timing and the pain is so hurtful and confusing. Since I have been able to recognize the Lord's protection that summer, my pain has disappeared and yours will too, my friend.

I made it through that summer and it wasn't easy. But God knows what's best for you and me. He got me through that season and prepared me for the next one. No matter how much it hurts, how angry we are, or how much we are suffering, we can face the challenges and meet the presence of pain with confidence, strength, and His guidance.

> *Philippians 4:13-14*
> *"For I can do everything with the help of Christ who gives me the strength I need.*
> *But even so, you have done well to share with me in my present difficulty." NLT*

Rather than retreating from pain, we need to give it to God. We must bathe the painful parts in prayer and give it all to Him. Pain has a purpose. A purpose it doesn't have is to be ignored. We can't ignore the hurt and pain and expect it to go away. It's like a sliver. As soon as you remove it, the pain slowly disappears because the source of the pain has been removed. When I try to ignore the sliver, thinking it is too small, the skin grows over the sliver, but the dull pain still exists. Like anything, when we experience spiritual, physical or emotional pain, we need to acknowledge it's there, get to the source and do something about it before it's too late. But there's good news... God tells us He will never leave us. He tells us to cast all our hurts and pains upon Him and He will begin a healing, in His timing and in His way.

Who will you trust to meet your needs when your pain is too much? Pain and discomfort will always arise, but will you ask the Lord to strengthen and heal you or will you ignore Him like your pain sometimes? Give it to the One who has a purpose for your pain and see what the Lord will do. You will be glad you did and so will He.

Week 20/ Day 20: The Presence of Pain

Describe a painful time in your life. How did you cope with it?

_____

_____

_____

_____

How could you have coped with this painful time differently? If it worked out, why did it work so well?

_____

_____

_____

_____

If you didn't rely on the Lord, what is holding you back? If you did rely on the Lord, what advice would you give others?

_____

_____

_____

_____

Does carrying your pain by yourself benefit you or anybody? Why or why not?

_____

_____

_____

_____

In painful times, who do you trust to meet your needs? Why?

_____

_____

_____

_____

_____

What life lesson have you learned through this story?

_____

_____

_____

_____

_____

_____

_____

_____

_____

_____

_____

_____

_____

_____

_____

No Matter What

It was a somber and eye-opening walk down the sterile hallways at the Connecticut Children's Medical Center in October, 2006. Every floor was at capacity as doctors and nurses cared for various children with cancer and an array of medical needs. We whispered past a room as a nurse drew blood and gently stroked the forehead of a precious young girl. I couldn't help but gaze at a mother and father crying as they held their child's hand by the bed-side. The art director gently nudged me along and suggested we walk quickly and quietly through the corridor and give them their privacy. I completed my tour in about an hour and decided to sit with Susan and discuss the art reception I wanted to have at the end of the school year. I told her a little about a former student of mine named Danny. He has a rare blood disease and visits the Children's Medical Center every three to four weeks for a blood transfusion. I proceeded to tell her my desire to honor patients like Danny awaiting treatment by donating eleven canvas paintings of a story God inspired in me called <u>Wings of Faith</u>, and painted by my second-grade students and local artist. These paintings would adorn the walls in one of the cancer wings, along with twenty-one painted butterfly ceiling tiles that will grace the ceilings, guiding each patient to their next treatment. Before I knew it, the art reception: <u>Seeing from the Heart</u>, was birthed and we were on our way to creating what I thought was one of the most passionate and creative educational programs I have been blessed to implement in the public school.

The project was on its way and things seemed to be moving forward as expected until my phone rang a week later. My mother in-law called frantically concerned about my daughter. Linda noticed a shadow along Jacquelyn's neck and as she asked her to turn towards the light there appeared to be a lump. Before I got too upset, I reassured Linda that we would check Jacquelyn's neck and thanked her for her call. I called Jacquelyn over to me and told her about Grandma Linda's concern and asked her if she wouldn't mind me looking at her neck. Jacquelyn turned her neck slightly and to my surprise, Linda was correct. There was a lump and immediately my heart sank with panic. How could this be? Where did it come from and how could Hank and I miss something so obvious? We're her parents and parents should know every part of their child's body, right? I hugged Jacquelyn and thought if there was anything I knew about my daughter it was how emotional she would be if she senses anything out of the ordinary with me; so I hugged her again and smiled as I told her that *no matter what*, it will be fine and we will have daddy look at it when he gets home.

My husband was not in the house five minutes before I could break my silence and whisper into his ear about what we just recognized. Calmly, Hank called Jacquelyn over to get a look at her neck and unbelievably responded the way I did, reassuring her that no *matter what*, everything will be okay. Convinced, Jacquelyn went off to complete her homework as Hank and I sat and talked.

"Hank, your mother called and said as Jacquelyn turned her head, the light accentuated a growth in her neck that seemed to appear out of nowhere. How could a growth the size of a peach pit suddenly appear without notice?" Hank and I sat stunned... We wondered, what next Lord? Is it cancer? Is it a tumor? Will it be benign or malignant? Could it be as simple as a swollen gland? We were on the phone the very next day to set up what would the first of several appointments.

Over the course of six to eight weeks, Jacquelyn had an MRI, ultrasound and primary care visits to prepare for surgery. Not only was there a noticeably sized tumor, there was another in her thyroid that could only be detected with an ultrasound. The final decision was made and surgery was imminent.

During this long-awaited time, life went on *no matter* what. There were days Jacquelyn was strong and unwavering; there were other moments we all felt fear and concern. On one hand, we were blessed to have the top surgeon for her surgery and on the other hand, we were frustrated we had to wait so long for the outcome... would her tumors be malignant or benign?

Our lives changed instantly, but what amazed me even more was Jacquelyn's heart and example through this whole experience. She displayed such strength and courage during the moments I felt as if I had nothing left. I remember all the visits I was making back and forth to the Children's Medical Center for my program. Who knew that all those hours I spent learning about the hospital and the treatments given on each floor would be the very place God was preparing my daughter to be in the weeks to come. I began to feel that there were lessons to be learned if we could just keep our eyes off our circumstances and focus more on God. My whole family felt this way and immediately our prayer lives changed. We realized God was bigger than our circumstances, and through fervent faith-filled prayer we began to sense the peace of God. We tried to live our lives normally as possible. We had our moments of fear and frustrations, but our main goal was to walk through this trial so others could sense God's presence and know that *no matter what*, He is Lord of our lives and the God of our circumstances. I continued to teach, Hank continued to minister at our local church and Jacquelyn kept up with school and her voice classes each week, getting ready for a recital in January... or not?

> *"Lord, please hear our heart's cry. You know the outcome, so please give us the peace that surpasses all doubts. Lord, you know how close the second tumor is to Jacquelyn's vocal cords. Please let this surgery be a success. Please protect her vocal cords. Lord, she sings every day. What a testimony for Jacquelyn to come through the surgery and heal in time for her recital. Lord, we need you and can't do this without you Lord. Please hear our heart's cry."*

God continually showed Himself through cards, smiles of encouragement, prayers and phone calls. I'll never forget how Jacquelyn thanked God for her parents, friends and family support even if the tumors were malignant. I'll never forget how she prayed for the ones who could have malignant tumors and if she did as well, His will be done. Remarkably, one of her friends asked her mother if she would ever be as strong as Jacquelyn... she never cried in front of her friends, she never showed how scared she might have been, knowing she could have cancer and she always had a smile on her face. I shared this with Jacquelyn and my daughter responded, "Oh mommy, really? I'm going to cry." At that moment, I shared with Jacquelyn how we never know who might be watching us and we may never know how our trials or tribulations may affect others, including ourselves. What a blessing it was for Hank and me to hear one of the many ways the Lord was working in her life.

> *"Lord, please give us a sign. Speak to us Lord and guide us through the days ahead. We want to walk through this trial with You, but are afraid our only child could be asked of us. Lord, we are scared."*

Another dear family friend called and said, *"No matter what, no matter what*, remember that *no matter what*, God loves Jacquelyn more than you and Hank and she is in the palm of His hands. *No matter what* the circumstances, keep your eyes on Him and He will do the rest." A few days later I received a beautiful book, <u>I Will Hold you 'til You Sleep</u>, from a parent of one of my students who works at the Children's Medical Center. Amazingly, the dedication on the last page was written like this: For Klaus, *'no matter what'* happens. And not long after that, Jacquelyn was asked to sing a song for the recital with her father. Imagine that the title of the song that was chosen before the tumors were detected was titled, <u>*No Matter What*</u>.

> *"Lord, is this a sign that 'no matter what', you are in control?' No matter what', you will never leave us; 'No matter what', You will see us through? Lord, thank you for this sign because 'no matter what,' our faith is in You and You alone."*

Six to eight weeks passed and Jacquelyn had a successful surgery. The surgery was longer than anticipated, but the surgeon wanted to pay attention to locating the nerve to her vocal cords so it would not be damaged. We learned that the tumors were most likely benign and it would be five more days before the results were revealed. The assistant Pastor and Youth Pastor arrived at the hospital to wheel Jacquelyn through the corridors. Jacquelyn leaned back and looked up at the ceiling as a smile spread across her face. "Mommy, look at the painted butterflies on the ceiling. We can follow them right out the door."

> *"Thank you, Jesus! Who knew the ceiling tiles would be for my daughter too?"*

Within five days it was confirmed; her tumors were benign and the healing began. With each passing day, Jacquelyn's neck healed more and more. The pain subsided, her muscles regained strength and before we knew it, we were all back to a more normal schedule. One month later Jacquelyn and her father finally performed their song at the winter recital. It was simply a song about a father's love for her daughter, *no matter what!* The audience clapped with approval and I cried with pride and joy in my heart; knowing the pain and triumphant outcome my family just endured.

> *1 Peter 5:6-7*
> *"Therefore, humble yourselves under the mighty hand of God, that He may exalt you in due time, casting all your care upon Him, for He cares for you." NKJV*

We will all be faced with trials and unexpected journeys; but when we place our trust and faith in the Lord who cares for you and me; He will undoubtedly see us through until the end. *No matter* what the pain, God will assure we have a reason to hope and a reason to believe. He is bigger than our circumstances or any hopeless situations. What was meant for bad was turned to good and we are truly thankful.

No matter what your situation, trial, pain, or suffering, remember there is a God who loves and cares for you too. You must have the *faith* that God will see you through, the *courage* to look beyond yourself and the *perseverance* when you feel like giving up. It's when we are faced with adversity others will begin to see who we really are. Take a moment and think about a recent tribulation or one you may be encountering presently. What worries do you have? Write them down, pray, and tell the Lord. Cast all your cares and worries upon Him. Don't submit to your circumstances, but to the Lord who controls your circumstances and trust He will see you through them; *no matter what!*

Week 21/ Day 21: No Matter What

Write about a time you were overwhelmed by circumstances or setbacks.

_____

_____

_____

Was your faith in God in question or strengthened? Why or why not?

_____

_____

_____

Can you remember a time you had to wait awhile for results? How did you deal with this?

_____

_____

_____

How did God reveal Himself during this time? How did it make you feel? Explain!

_____

_____

_____

Have you or do you know anybody who experienced a healing? Write about it.

_____

_____

_____

_____

Perhaps you are experiencing a tribulation right now. Write your concerns down and tell the Lord. Join with a friend and pray and see what the Lord will do. Believe your circumstances are important to God, *no matter what!*

Dear Lord, these are my worries and concerns:

_____

_____

_____

_____

Please take them from me and help me get through my circumstances. Thank you, Jesus!

What life lessons have you learned through this story?

_____

_____

_____

_____

_____

_____

_____

_____

_____

_____

_____

_____

_____

_____

Peer Pressure

U nless we have Jesus in the center of our lives, I think peer pressure will be harder to evade. Peer pressure is no respecter of age or gender. It will present its' ugly head during any season of our lives and what we choose to do with it really is between ourselves and our Creator. It's time to be accountable to God; for if we don't follow 'something', we will fall for everything, right? Will there be peer pressure even when we have Christ in our lives; absolutely, but having the Lord to guide us during those challenging moments will make all the difference.

> *Hebrews 11:6*
> *"But without faith, it is impossible to please Him, for he who comes to God must believe that He is a rewarder of those who diligently seek Him." NKJV*

> *1 John 3:22 states...*
> *"Whatsoever we ask, we receive of him, because we keep his commandments and do those things that are pleasing in his sight." NKJV*

My daughter and I would often times sit and discuss new and old episodes on television together. There were many wonderful moments she and I would talk about the expectations God has for us, especially in those times of 'pressure' when those we do or don't know are watching. Sometimes, these 'heart to heart' discussions were some of the greatest life-defining moments for the both of us.

Although television is 'drama', there are various times when we can turn an episode into a 'teachable moment' and in the following account, that's just what we did.

Television Episode:

Emily adored her family. Dad made it to every game and mom always had the best meals for every occasion. Hospitality and love would spill out into the family and neighbors. Her mom and dad would feed the homeless and house strangers until they could get back on their feet. Emily was taught the ways of the Lord and the importance of living a life of truth. She knew the difference between right and wrong, but often were tempted by the world. One day Emily received one too many tardy slips and had to owe a detention after school. Now she was the basketball star and thought that if she could persuade her brother to tell mom and dad she didn't come right home after school because she was at an off-scheduled practice, surely, they wouldn't question why she was late. Her brother complied against his better judgment and no questions were asked. Emily entered the detention room and made her way to the back, as another teenage girl signaled for Emily to sit next to her. The young lady was known for her inappropriate ways in and out of school. As a matter of fact, she had a permanent seat in this detention room and Emily knew all about her. Emily took her place right next to this girl and their dialogues lead to Emily agreeing to go to the mall with this alluring teenager the very same night. When Emily returned home, her brother warned her not to spend time with a girl with a bad reputation, but Emily did not receive this advice at all. She thought it would be fun and temptation was luring her right to the mall against her brother's better judgment. As the night pressed on, Emily found that this reckless teenager wanted her to go to a fraternity party later that evening. All Emily had to do is sneak- out of her house after hours. She knew she needed her parent's permission, but Emily's appealing friend made it sound so exciting to 'not' feel like she had to do everything her parents said.

Emily arrived home and managed to sneak out after hours and left her younger sister to lie on her behalf. Emily quickly approaches the car and finds out that the young teenager has a dress for her to wear, but shoplifted it. Emily desperately puts the dress on and they head to the party. She thought it was a party with many guests, but it happens to be a blind date for Emily and her lying friend. Now Emily is left alone in an apartment with a girl who refuses to bring her home until she is done drinking with her boyfriend. Emily is all alone with a strange guy who wants to do more than 'talking'. It was obvious he wants to drink and have sexual relations. The pressure was mounting for Emily, but she privately gets to a phone to call her brother for a ride home and decided to deal with the consequences later.

Jacquelyn and I discussed Emily's resulting, yet fortunate consequences. I am sure we have heard many stories and have had various encounters of our own that did not end up as safely as Emily's. She succumbed to peer pressure and was lured to believe that sin was exciting and worth the decision. Sadly though, Emily knew from the start that she was wrong and unfortunately, she didn't go to God to help her make that decision.

"She was tempted by the tempter himself", I explained to Jacquelyn. "The tempter has come to devour and steal from us all and he will do whatever it takes to accomplish this goal. Emily focused on her own desires that day. She looked at this girl and wanted to experience something 'new'. She heard the message and made a conscious choice to participate. Eventually her sin was exposed and her consequences affected many others. Emily knew she was wrong and instead of listening to the truth of God, she missed His voice of truth", I continued.

Temptation has a place in God's plan, but Emily forgot that she has victory over temptation and so do we. We need to rely on Jesus and be lead by His Spirit. We must ask God to help us avoid temptation, and if we face it; ask Him to deliver us from evil. God wants to guide us and our children, but they must be taught daily to rely on Him.

It is important that we share stories like this with one another so we are all aware of the temptations that are in the world. Although this was a television episode, it was perfect timing for us to discuss the 'curiosity' that can cause us to stumble; but if we don't know more about these temptations and discuss ways to prevent them, our children will be blinded and so will we.

> *1 John 3:22*
> *"Whatsoever we ask, we receive of him, because we keep his commandments and do those things that are pleasing in his sight". NKJV*

Deep down inside, most of us want to do what is right when the peer pressure gets too intense. It's just hard to believe we don't. Moreover, some of us may surrender to the pressure's that surround us; but remember...

> *2 Peter 2:9*
> *"The Lord knows how to deliver the godless out of temptation;" NKJV*

Peer pressure may have tempted you and me, but know this, we need the Lord no matter what. He will help us make appropriate decisions in life and circumvent the pressure. If we make a mistake and are tempted, the Lord will give us a way out; even through the consequences. We know that temptation and peer pressure can be devastating, so here are some guidelines we can live with and share with our children:

1. <u>Flee temptation</u>; ask God to help you and pray for His guidance.
2. <u>Stay away from places, situations, and people who will tempt you.</u>

3. <u>Keep scripture nearby or memorized</u> so when you feel tempted, you can combat the root of it.
4. <u>Share with another believer</u> so you can pray and call when the temptation approaches you.
5. <u>Remember not to give up when the answer doesn't come right away</u>; trust in God's timing

The following is a poem written by my daughter March 29, 2007. Maybe you are a young mother and can relate or have a daughter who is experiencing some of the same things. Perhaps you are a teenager and see yourself. May these words be a blessing to you as it was for me.

Peer Pressure
Two words, so much meaning;
Influenced by the wrong crowd,
What an impact it has had on him.
What will he do? It's his choice. His decision;
He's dying to fit in. Dying to be cool;
He thinks he's not hurting anyone, but he would be hurting himself.

Peer Pressure
Two words, so much meaning;
She was an outcast. She was alone.
No one was ever seen with her and no one really cared;
This girl was made fun of constantly. She was rejected;
Just one sip, that's all she needed to make her "in" with the others.
One sip could change her life.

Peer Pressure
Two words, so much meaning;
He didn't study. Instead, he partied with his friends all night.
The teachers collected the tests in five minutes.
Not one question was answered.
No one will realize if he looks off to the next person.
It's not as if anyone can see him.
Little did he know God can see.

Peer Pressure
Two words, so much meaning;
Who are your real friends?
Those who make fun of others or those who care;
Those who tempt others or those who are there;
Those who deceive others or those who encourage;
Those who do not have faith or those who believe;
Who are your friends today?
Peer Pressure

Think back for a moment, about a time when peer pressure presented itself. What was your circumstance? How did you react? Was your choice worth it? What were the end results? Whether it is the workplace or school, I have found these moments of pressure to be easier when I asked the Lord what I can do to please Him.

When temptation is knocking at your door, who will you seek when the pressure is too much?

Week 22/ Day 22: Peer Pressure

Think of a time you were faced with peer pressure or temptation. What did you do? Explain.

_____

_____

_____

_____

Did you make the right decision? What were the consequences?

_____

_____

_____

_____

Who did you rely on to get you through? Why?

_____

_____

_____

_____

Why is it important to share about temptations and their consequences with others?

_____

_____

_____

_____

_____

_____

List the 5 guidelines you can follow to flee succumbing to temptation:

_____

_____

_____

_____

_____

What life lesson have you learned through this story?

_____

_____

_____

_____

_____

_____

_____

_____

_____

_____

_____

_____

_____

_____

A First Time for Everything

"**J**ust pull back on the throttle, step on the gas, and blaze the trail ahead. You will come upon tall grass in front of you and along the fence, but keep forging ahead until you see the dirt trail," the voice announced from behind me. Of course, I could barely see with dust flying in my eyes and the fear I would fall off the all terrain vehicle I was riding for the first time. Not only was this a 'first', I was the leader of three other experienced riders through the woods on a trail I have never blazed before. To top it off, I drive through a tic bed for the first time and hopefully the last. I had hundreds of tiny tics crawling from my ankles and up my legs. I immediately panicked, jumped off the vehicle, and ran back down the trail. I jumped over a fence and into my friend's Jacuzzi. Many tics rose to the surface, but that wasn't enough. I had to take a shower until I was sure they were all gone and since then, I have been disgusted with tics.

"And the National Environmental Teacher of the Year is Kim Waltmire. Please give her a hand as she approaches the podium. Before Kim speaks, we would like to apologize for not having the award video presentation for her program. This is the first time this has ever happened. Kim, we apologize and thought we would include a brief video clip of you typing in your office. Unfortunately, we have no sound or audio, but we can at least see you typing in your office." My heart sank and the convention hall fell to silence that night in Washington, DC as I stood in front of 100 environmentalists awaiting my inspirational speech and opportunity to receive $10,000.00 for my Intergenerational program. Immediately, it was my job to inspire the audience with a silent video footage of me typing in an office. Can you believe it? This would be my first-time meeting all these people and it was their first time meeting me; the first elementary school teacher to ever receive this award. I learned one thing that evening; never to take first impressions for granted.

Remember what it was like to be chosen first for something? Maybe you were chosen first for the kickball team. Were you ever spoiled as the first-born child? Perhaps you were chosen as the number one sales person in your company. Being first can truly be an amazing experience when God is in the center of it all. On the contrary, it can also be one of the most challenging and lonely experiences of your life.

I can undoubtedly say that being "first" has been an honor and challenge throughout my life and career. I have received over thirty awards, state and national honors, and have been blessed with over 100 news articles and various appearances on local, national and worldwide TV programs and documentaries such as CNN, Fox Reality- Real Heroes Among Us and OPRAH; not to mention being interviewed by Pat Williams, the Vice President of Orlando Magic NBA Basketball Team for his recently published book- Souls of Steel. My programs have even been recognized by two Connecticut State Governors and dignitaries, as well as one of America's First Ladies, Mrs. Laura Bush.

As I walked throughout my journey of 'firsts' during my career, I knew not to take the glory. I continually acknowledged the Lord, my students, colleagues, and administration upon receiving these incredible honors, as well as delighted in giving all my award monies back to the children and the community. I did not only have to learn how to handle first time moments, I learned quickly that many people were not interested in my accomplishments and sadly, it has been some of the loneliest experiences of my life. During these challenging experiences, I knew I had to believe in the gifts God has bestowed upon me and rely on the support of my dearest and closest friends and family members. I had to seek God for His strength and guidance. This allowed me to look at discouragement as only temporary. These "first time" moments were not always easy. I am a creative thinker and even my strategies were not easily accepted. But no matter what the reason was for being first, I knew I was on uncharted grounds and it indubitably left room in my life for perceived mistakes and personal growth. It left opportunities for others to criticize me and it left a void in my heart if I didn't seek God to carry me through it all.

What about our personal lives? I was stricken with pre-cervical cancer at age twenty. Unfortunately, I was unable to give the doctors my medical history because I was adopted and didn't have the necessary information. As far as I knew, I was the first in my family to have cancer. Medical history began with me. It was certainly a volatile time in my life and I had nobody but my adoptive mother to lean on at the time. I was extremely lonely and quite scared during this season. Maybe you can relate in some way. Sometimes it's not easy being first.

Believe it or not, there is one woman we can relate to though. Her name is Eve. The Book of Genesis introduces her as the first woman, first wife, first to fail, and the first mother without epidurals. We can only imagine the joy and peace she felt in the Garden or the failure and separation Eve felt when she was lured by the serpent's temptations. There is a first time for everything and the consequences can be unfathomable.

Being the first to fail was always frightening to me. I have feared failure most of my life. Upon my adoption, I felt rejected from birth. This rejection manifested itself into a "fear of failure." It equated to be something like this; if I fail, I'll be rejected. Then I will be separated from those who say they love me. Can you remember the first time you were rejected? Have you ever feared failure? Eve never knew these emotions until she made a '*wrong*' choice for the first time. Although her good and bad choices all had consequences, Eve's sin separated her from God for the first time. For the first time, she needed to accept her mistakes and the consequences to follow. Eve had many new and first-time moments like us. She learned from her experiences and Eve passed her legacy onto us, but will we choose to learn from her life lessons or will we repeat the same mistakes?

When I became pregnant, I was about to be a mother for the first time. I couldn't talk to my adoptive mother about the details because she was unable to bare children. Now imagine Eve for a moment. She was a first-time mother. She didn't have a mother to talk, laugh or cry with. She didn't have a Lamaze class, a female coach, nurse or doctor. What's a girl to do? Eve had to rely on the one and only God of the Universe. Now there is nothing more comforting than that; not even epidurals.

If we were to study Eve's life lessons, we would recognize she shared the image of God and complete oneness with Him. She shared her commitment to others, along with her companionship for the first time. Eve reflected God's glory. Whether she failed as a wife and a mother at times, her lack of hope never negated God's goodness and mercy in her life.

> *Psalm 30:5*
> *"For His anger is but for a moment, His favor is for life; Weeping may endure for a night, but joy comes in the morning." NKJV*

Whether it is your first time with pain, loss, failed grades, hurts, or even celebrations, there is nothing more comforting than knowing you are not alone. There will always be someone you can relate with, but when those 'first-time' moments appear knocking your way, you first need to rely on the One who can see you through. It is hard for any of us who are not walking by faith and don't have a hope in Jesus because *our faith is often driven by our sight.* Our attention is drawn away from the godly abundance that many of us have because we think we need more and when we are in pain or at a loss in our lives, we don't seek the One who can bring us joy and healing.

> *Philippians 4:4*
> *"Rejoice in the Lord always. Again, I say rejoice!" NKJV*

We need to remember that no matter what happens; God is with us. Ultimately, joy comes from Christ dwelling within us. It is so easy to get discouraged about the unpleasant circumstances or distracted by the pleasant ones in our lives, especially when we experience them for the first time. God sent His first and only Son to be sacrificed for you and for me. He understands what it means to be first. God's mercy is new every morning and He wants you to have it. He wants you and me to reach out to Him and think of Him first. He wants us to rely on Him before we make any decision. Sometimes we may make impulsive decisions and will be swayed at times and our first-time experiences end up lonely and frightening. Thank God; thank Him that we are not alone.

Eve was content and knew she was not alone. She lived in the Garden of Eden with Adam. It is said that the Garden of Eden was like heaven. It was perfect and for a time, without sin. "She was the first co-manager of the garden thriving with beauty. She was the first female to share a special relationship with God. Then Satan approached Eve and questioned her contentment. He convinced her that God was withholding her true happiness from partaking of the tree of knowledge of good and evil. Satan wanted Eve to doubt God's goodness". NKJV He wanted her to focus on the one thing she couldn't have. Her doubts began to lead her into sin for the first time; the first wife, first mother and first female allowed herself to be undermined and drawn away from the One who should be a part of every decision she made. Her relationship was compromised with God. She sinned for the first time. She not only sinned, but she shared her sin with Adam and had no problem blaming him as well.

Sometimes first time moments can be detrimental without God. Imagine living in the Garden with God and turning your back on Him after all the mercy and goodness He lavished on you. Imagine Eve after she sinned. She was convinced for the first time that she could be more like God if she partook of the tree. She learned all too quickly that when she left God out of her plans, she really placed herself above God. A decision like this may be anyone's first and Eve did something all of us have done at some point in our lives; she looked. The first thing she did was look. How many of us have lost battles by just considering the eyes of temptation first? We see something and then we want it. Looking is the first step toward sin, right?

After all that Eve had gone through; yes, she and Adam had consequences, but there was and is a God of mercy and goodness that wanted to be there for them even though they made the wrong decisions. Their decisions warranted a price and so goes the fallen world we live in today.

We have a God who is merciful and good.

Colossians 1:15
"... He existed before anything was created and is supreme over all creation, for through Him God created everything." NLT

He will forgive us our sins and He will also show us His mercy and goodness, even if we are first timers. But we must be reminded that He who lives in us will fulfill His final purpose in us, but not without a cost. There is always a consequence, but His mercy is new in the morning. God wants you and me to rely on Him first so He can guide us and help us through all our decisions whether it is our first time or not. There is a first time for everything, so why not rely on Him; first?

If this is your first time recognizing your need of a loving Savior, then stop right now and tell Him. You have plenty of first-time moments to come, so why not experience those moments with a God who loves and cares for you?

Will you recognize God's mercy and goodness? Will you remember you reflect His glory? Will you rely on Him for the first time and before every new decision? There's a first time for everything, so rely on Him first. You will be glad you did!

Week 23 / Day 23: A First Time for Everything

Think of a "first-time" moment in your life. Write about it.

_____

_____

_____

Was God a part of this experience? Why or why not?

_____

_____

_____

Think of a first-time moment that you can thank God for.

Dear Lord,

_____

_____

_____

Will you rely on God for every decision? Why? If not, what is holding you back?

_____

_____

_____

What lesson have you learned through this story?

_____

_____

_____

The Harvest is Plenty- The Workers are Few

Every weekend service I would see the most beautiful girl go to the altar. I was always so drawn to her. There was something about the way she humbly walked and her tone of voice was so sweet. Often, I would find Heather with tears streaming down her soft cheeks. Whether she was standing, kneeling or embracing another, Heather had such a compassionate heart that I would begin to cry as well. Whenever I saw her approach the altar, I would wait to feel the tug of approval from the Lord in my heart and I would go sit beside her or hold her hand. Sometimes her sweetness and sincerity were worth watching, despite the hurt and obvious pain she may have been feeling deep inside; for whenever we spoke to one another, all I wanted Heather to know is that she is a beautiful girl who has so much to give in this world. She would hang her head in disbelief and I would give her a hug and whisper in her ear the words I think God would want me to say and that was, "God loves you Heather and knows your heart. Give it all to Him." And Heather would weep even more.

This would go on for quite awhile. I always found myself looking for her at our church altar or in the crowded hallways just to ask her how she was doing. For years, I could hear the pain and the insecurity in her voice. I just wish she could know the value she has in the Lord and to others around her. I wish she would realize that her beauty and sweet sensitive spirit comforts many and her presence makes the world a better place.

I felt God may be using me in a small way to be there for Heather during those few quiet moments. Every conversation I have ever had with her ended with a precious smile and a promise to see each other again soon. But it wasn't until this present season that I would be taken back breathlessly by a decision Heather would make that would change her life and bless others, forever.

I will never forget the day Heather told me she was going away; that she was called to go to Guatemala for the summer months. I was thrilled and stunned at the same time. God transformed this young lady from insecure to confident, from disillusioned to purposeful, from weak to strong. She told me with confidence and assurance this was for certain. My admiration for her grew immensely. I was so proud of Heather for hearing the voice of the Lord and the call in her life and honestly, a smile swept across both our faces simultaneously. What an honor to serve the Lord and know in your heart it was time to step out of the comfort zone and go to a foreign land where the needs far outweigh any of the trials some of us would ever encounter here in the States. She was ready and I knew at that very moment, 'for such a time as this,' Heather's life will undoubtedly change forever.

> *A letter from Heather:*
> *I have so much to say, but first I want to give God praise. He is worthy of all praise, all glory and all honor. There is none who compares with our God. I am very excited because I know that God is working beyond what I can understand right now. The Bible says that 'His ways are not our ways and that His thoughts are higher than our thoughts.' I am certain that it is His will for me to be here and no matter what the difficulty may be, there is no place I'd rather be than in the center of His will. Everything pales in comparison to Jesus. Yo quiero mas.*

God has made the way for me to be here. He has used brothers and sisters in Christ to make it possible. Thank you, guys! Initially I had no clue how this was all going to happen, but I was determined to go through the opened door by faith. Four months before my appointed departure God provided a new job with the Village for Families and Children. At first I thought I would have to give up my apartment, but the pay increase helped tremendously. I also thought when I was offered the job that I would have to turn it down because of the length of the trip. God gave me a Christian supervisor who advocated for me to have these two months off. God also gave me Christian landlords who are very supportive of mission's work. They have been my most generous sponsors giving close to $1000 and are holding the condo for me. Glory to God! Thank you all so much. XOXOX.

God is doing many wonderful things here. The church is seeking a revival or "avivemento". I must say from watching, it has begun. There are many manifestations of the power of God taking place. It is at times frightening and exciting. During services the altars are filled with people crying out to God. I have never experienced anything like it before. People were jumping, screaming, laying on the ground with the spirit interceding through them. I am not talking about a couple of people here and there; I am talking about most people at the altar. In all honesty, it has been at times overwhelming being that I don't understand Spanish, but I feel the presence of God. I never thought I was a conservative Christian, but my level of freedom and comfort is being stretched. One night I was at the altar seeking God and wanting more of Him. We were asked to take someone's hand next to us as a point of contact. Suddenly, I felt the lady to my right collapse, so I let go. I opened my eyes and everyone to my right was on the ground. So, I closed my eyes and then I felt everyone to my left collapse. I was the only person in the row still standing; that was until the row in front of me came crashing down on top of me. Fortunately, the altar workers saw that I was buried alive and dug me out. It was hilarious, well not exactly at that moment. I know that we must be like little children with faith, but I feel like an obstinate toddler. I am working on that. I think I am a little afraid. 'The spirit is indeed willing' and the flesh, on the other hand has its own agenda.

Hi Everyone,
In my first letter, I mentioned working in the bilingual Christian school. This is the pastor's vision; to develop a high-quality school for an affordable price. The public education system here is very poor. So far, the school is affordable, but they need help to achieve its goals. I have been observing in the classrooms. Last week we coordinated a meeting with all the bilingual teachers, the pastor, principal and administrative staff to begin talking about some of the strengths and weaknesses in the public educational system. The meeting seemed to go very well. We designated a team leader who will coordinate the bilingual grades through regular biweekly meetings. This area really needs attention and the teachers do not get paid much and without support, won't last. They are looking for correspondence from the states. They are also looking for teachers who are willing to come here and help train teachers and demonstrate lesson plans. If anyone is interested, please let me know.
Anyhow, I know I am going on and on. I would love to hear from you all.

Lots of Love,
Heather

Heather,
I am more blessed than you can imagine. Your heart and willingness to serve the Lord is astounding and I am a better person having known you. I love hearing what the Lord is doing in and through you. Keep writing and keep a journal of your emails to others. It is a book in the making and a legacy to leave for your loved ones. God has a plan for your life Heather and it is mighty. I love you Heather and I am so honored and blessed to read about your experiences. Keep your letters coming and know you are not alone.

By the way, Hank is preaching 6 weeks out of the summer. I am so happy to see him serving the Lord during this new season in our lives. God is providing and we are so blessed.

Write again soon,
Kim

Hello Everyone,
I survived my first week in the mountains. Glory...Hallelujah...I am alive!! The first few nights were horrifying. I encountered a couple of tarantulas, well THREE to be exact, and a scorpion living in the house with us. I didn't sleep very well and I wanted to come home. In the evenings when the family turned the generator off my room was pitch black. I couldn't even see my hand in front of my face. It was moist and dank. I felt like I was in the abyss. I thought I couldn't breath. I was thinking, "Oh God, I can't do this". I didn't realize how heavy the curtains in my room were. And once the power was off I was too scared to move. I was wondering where in the world the moon and the stars were. I knew that the Bible said they existed to light the night. On about the third day I opened my curtains and there was light. Thank God.

To make matters worse, the first night, in the middle of the night, I heard some-thing fall and I could hear movement. It sounded too close and all I could do is pray and hope whatever it was couldn't see me. In the morning, I saw that something had knocked over the brass candle stick on my night stand. I never found out what it was and I am glad for it. However, I did find that we had a problem with rats. And because the roof is made from tin or metal, you could hear them very loudly. I am happy to say that we no longer have that problem. We could help by buying garbage cans with lids and garbage bags.

Yes, I wanted to come home, that is, until I saw the children. Hopefully I'll be able to successfully send pictures along with this email. I am proud to say that we have been helping to provide more nutritious meals for the students of two schools on the mountain. We serve them breakfast and lunch every day. Many of the children are malnourished, so we had to be careful how and what we introduce to their diets. For breakfast, they have been eating items such as black beans, eggs, cheese, tortillas, mush (some oatmeal stuff) and juice. For lunch tomorrow, they're going to have chicken and rice soup. We've also been providing treats like cookies and marshmallows. Many of the mothers of the children have been happy to help prepare the food. I tried making tortillas and it's much better when they do it.

My trip back to Honduras was packed with events. I didn't have anytime to use the computer; if we weren't on the bus traveling from place to place then we were ministering somewhere. Okay we shopped and went to the beach too. It was wonderful. We went to church and the center of the town and prayed for the city of Honduras. It was in the newspaper here. We also held a women's conference, visited the prison and the school. We also ministered to the pastor's family and ministered to the leadership of the church, along with leading a couple of services. It was a great time.

I am back in Equiplulas, Guatemala and this Saturday we are holding a special service for the students and their families. I will be the speaker. This will be my first time and I really appreciate your prayers. I am not sure what it is that God wants me to say yet and I am afraid that I am going to be all over the place. Glory to God!! More of a reason for Him to get all the credit! Anyhow we will be providing a healthy meal for the families with chicken, rice, beans and salad. We would also like to send families home with a small basket of food. Initially we were hoping to raise $5,000.00 but I only raised $3,000.00. I am hoping to raise more money for this project. For those of you who asked me if I needed anything, I am fine, but if you have it in your heart to give, please give to the Kitchen of Love Ministry. Father you're able!!!

God has been bringing me to Isaiah 58 and I would like to share it with you as well.

XOXO
Heather

Please forward

I have too much to say.
Sorry it took me so long to write back to you. I have been a little all over the place and when I get on the computer I have limited time. There is no such thing as knowing anything in advance here. My ability to communicate is extremely limited and it doesn't stop people from trying to talk to me. I get tired and frustrated at times. Today is one of those days where I would like to be home. Tomorrow I am supposed to speak to the families of the mountains and I don't know what to say. Sunday I leave the mountains and head to Guatemala City where the other Kitchen of Love is located, Pastor José's family is coming tonight. His children speak English so that will help make my last week be a little easier and his daughter is close to my age. I still don't understand the bigger picture. I don't really understand why God brought me here.
Anyhow, thank you so much for your encouragement. I am blessed to hear God moving in your family's life. I know when you step out in faith, faith is all you have. God honors that and indefinitely follows behind. Praise God for His faithfulness.

Lots of love to you Kim...
Heather

Dear Family and Friends,
I am in Guatemala City now. I will be spending the last week here. Last night
we stayed at the beach in Puerto, San Jose. I will send pictures. The sand is
black and it's neat.

It all went well Saturday. We handed invitations to the children in the schools
on Thursday to take home. We gave out 60 invitations. Somewhere around 300
to 350 people showed up. We could provide them with lunch, chicken and salsa
with pasta and tortillas (a little change in the menu) and a bag of food that
contained mush, rice, a small bottle of oil, salt, sugar, noodles, and spaghetti.
The Cocina de Amor crew brought toys for the children and some school sup-
plies from the missionaries in Texas.

The service went well. They told me ahead of time that the people are attentive,
but not participatory. During worship, no one moved. Even with lots of encour-
agement it was difficult to keep the people standing. After worship, the pastor
of the Cocina del Amor in Guatemala City opened. I spoke and he did the altar
call. Karla lead the children in some worship activities and we served lunch,
gave out gifts, bags of food, and called it a day.

Praise God many women along with their children responded to the altar call,
Hallelujah!!! Many people raised their hands to receive Christ into their heart.
I was very blessed. I really enjoyed watching the activities with the children.
It blessed my soul. They were very open and cooperative, learning to worship.
They were not afraid to come to the front. I was so blessed and I know that
God was too. It was beautiful to see them. Their little faces are etched in my
heart forever.

Some person gave me a word while I was in Honduras that God was preparing
me during this time and that He would ask me to return and that I would know
when. All I know right now is I just need my apartment back, hallelujah, for hot
water. We live in a great nation.

Thanks for your emails. Lots of love to you all, Heather

These are just a few letters from a friend I am proud to know and pray for. Heather made
herself willing and available for the Lord and now, my once shy and insecure friend has been
strengthened and encouraged to step out in faith. Honestly, I don't think I could sleep with
tarantulas in a dark, dank home infested with rats, but glory to God, Heather can. Who would
have ever thought after all these years God was preparing her for such a time as this.

Heather's recent experiences caused me to reflect on my life and I realized even more that life
isn't worth living if we are not willing to step out of our comfort zone and take risks.

Matthew 9:37-38
"Then He said to His disciples, "The harvest truly is plentiful, but the laborers
are few. Therefore, pray the Lord of the Harvest to send out laborers into His
harvest. NKJV

Maybe you and I aren't called to Guatemala like Heather, but have you ever asked the Lord for His will in your life? Do you have any idea what harvest field He has planted you in? When Jesus speaks of the ripened harvest, He is referring to people. There are so many people, adults and children, who don't know His truth about the gift of salvation that He wants to give us all. Whether they refuse to hear God's truth or haven't heard because they live in the forgotten areas of the world, people like Heather, you and I can make a difference. God wants to answer our prayers and guide us in His direction. He needs workers and wants to use us to lead others into His Eternal Kingdom of glory. Are you ready to ask Him?

What harvest field will you focus on; your home, neighborhood, work, school or abroad? Ask God to lead you and give you the strength and courage to step out of your comfort zone. People are waiting; the time has come; the time is now!

Week 24/ Day 24: The Harvest is Plenty- The Workers are Few

Have you ever asked the Lord for His will in your life? Explain.

_____

_____

_____

What harvest fields are you planted in now? Describe one and what God is calling you to do.

_____

_____

_____

Has there been a time you felt the need or were called to step out of your comfort zone? What happened?

_____

_____

_____

Who did you rely on? Why? Explain.

_____

_____

_____

What life lesson have you learned through this story?

_____

_____

_____

His Size Fits All

When you walk into my closet, you will find at least ten pairs of jeans. Over the years, either my weight has changed or the style has changed, but unfortunately, my closet didn't get any bigger. Interestingly, I don't usually give my jeans away just in case I may need that size again. Perhaps the style may come back. You know what I mean... skinny flair, boot cut, low- waist, and stretch, comfortable, relaxed fit, straight legged... As a matter of fact, there are so many kinds of jeans; I can't keep up with the changes, especially in the dressing room. Some jeans slip on easily and others not at all. Some jeans fit in the bottom, but not at the waist line. Some jeans are too close to the ankle and others are so wide, I think I'll fly away with the next windstorm. Every time I visit the mall, I find myself looking for a new pair of jeans that *fit just right*. Is there such a thing? I am not kidding you. Every time I try on a pair of jeans at the store, I would look at myself in their full-length mirror and after trying on several styles, I would finally do a little "pose" and that was it. I was convinced I had the perfect pair of jeans. Of course, I would buy my new jeans and as soon as I got home and put them on and looked in *my* mirror, they didn't look or feel the same. Immediately, I would be frustrated because not all jeans are inexpensive. It amazes me how I can look at other women in jeans and no matter what size they are, I am certain everyone else looks great, except me.

No matter how difficult it was for me to find a perfect pair of jeans, I was constantly reminded that nothing is perfect. So why do I try so hard? Why is it when I look in the mirror for the first time in a new pair of jeans, they look great, but when I get home to wear them, I don't like what I see. Why is it that my jeans fit so well in the morning and as the day progresses they stretch and get too baggy, reminding me of the jeans I left behind on the shelf?

We spend so much time looking at ourselves and trying to see the perfect size. We are constantly comparing ourselves to everyone around us. Their dark jeans look better than mine. Her skinny jeans make her look skinny, but my stomach hangs over mine. It appears to be a chore keeping up with the newest and latest fashions. If the manikin looks great, then why can't it be that easy for us?

Have you ever bought a pair of jeans that were so tight that you had no room to breathe, grow or make a mistake? You know what I mean. You look unbelievable in the mirror and your image reflects an incredibly curvy, perfect fit, right? Surprise! However, God calls us to be spiritually fit first; not necessarily physically fit. The difference is that He wants us to have room to grow and of course, make mistakes. If we start off with a perfect fit, we have nowhere else to go but the scale to measure our "growth" based on worldly standards. Subsequently, we are frustrated with every part of our day because we can't stand the chance of getting bloated or gaining too much weight due to the excess caloric intake.

Have you ever felt trapped? Sometimes I feel trapped in the same "one size fits all" instead of the "His size fits all." The basic question is; which would you prefer? Do you want to spend the entire day worrying about sucking in your stomach and controlling your waist line or do you want to be relaxed and let Him be in control? Are you going to worry about your *weight* or are you going to *wait* on Him every day?

I have drawn closer to realizing that a perfect pair of jeans comes in all shapes and sizes much like us. We spend a great deal of time looking for the perfect "fit" when God might be "stretching" our size to fit His style all along. The more we resist the changes we see or feel, the more difficult it will be to understand what "*style*" God may see fit for us.

> 1 Timothy 4:8-10
> "For bodily exercise profits a little, but godliness is profitable for all things, having promise of the life that now is and of that which is to come. This is a faithful saying and worthy of all acceptance. For to this end we both labor and suffer reproach, because we trust in the living God, who is the savior of all men, especially of those who believe". NKJV

God is calling us to be spiritually fit and we need to give ourselves over to His conditioning and let God get shape our lives, not our jeans. It's time to work those spiritual muscles...Believe it or not; putting our lives in spiritual order has a much higher priority than being perfectly fit. When our lives are in spiritual order, we will see things differently. Think about it, when you are shopping for a pair of jeans in a blissful mood, you aren't bothered by the several styles leaping off the shelf saying, "I'm just the fit you want." When we are comfortable and relaxed with whom we are inside; the jeans don't matter anymore. The clothes we adorn our bodies with take on a new meaning. The jeans don't define us, but rather enhance us a little bit. And that's okay. It's when we spend too much time looking for perfection; the realities begin to fail us. Nothing is perfect except the One who created you and me. We must remember He sees our persistence, not our perfection. He sees us the way He created us; in the image of God, not Calvin Klein. Whether you are over- weight, under- weight, short, skinny or tall; remember there is a God who created you perfectly and uniquely. His size fits all.

So, your closet is organized with jean sizes 2-22. Make the adjustments needed and wear what fits best. Wear your jeans in style and confidence, but be prepared; God just might be ready to stretch your size throughout the day when you least expect it. Will you let the Lord stretch you?

"I may not be perfect, but Jesus thinks I am to die for." Author unknown

Week 25/ Day 25: His Size Fits All

Do you worry about being physically fit? Why or why not?

_____

_____

_____

Would you describe your life as more in physical or spiritual order? Explain what this looks like.

_____

_____

_____

What do you do or should you do to keep your life in spiritual order?

_____

_____

_____

Do you recall an area God stretched you? What were the results?

_____

_____

_____

What life lesson have you learned through this story?

_____

_____

_____

_____

_____

The Naked Truth

Has there ever been a time you have arrived somewhere naked? Now, I'm not talking about one of those strange dreams you and I have experienced. You know, the ones where we show up at work with just our under-garments; partially naked. On the contrary, I am asking if you have ever arrived somewhere naked. I certainly have; spiritually naked that is...

I have spent many mornings getting myself prepared and dressed. I would begin my day with a quiet devotion and a cup of coffee; eat my breakfast, get dressed, complete my make-up, and have a family prayer before I left for work. Sounds like a normal routine, right? I thought I was prepared for my day and would leave most mornings with a smile on my face. But there is one thing I must tell you. It's a little secret between my husband and me.

During a season of time, I let my husband dress me. I know... He insisted. Sounds like fun, doesn't it? Every morning, just before I would leave for work, my husband would spiritually dress me. He always referred to Ephesians 6:13-17 which reminds us to wear every piece of God's armor. "Now Hank", I reminded him, armor doesn't sound too attractive for my figure," and we laughed.

> Ephesians 6:13-17
> v.13 Therefore, take up the whole armor of God... v.14 Stand therefore, having girded your waist with truth, having put on the breastplate of righteousness, v.15 and having shod your feet with the preparation of the gospel of peace; v.16 above all, taking the shield of faith with which you will be able to quench all the fiery darts of the wicked one. V.17 And take the helmet of salvation, and the sword of the spirit, which is the word of God... NKJV

Imagine my husband on his knees in front of me, placing on my shoes shod with peace. He would rise to his feet and position around my waist a belt of truth and of course my body armor for protection. He would pretend to rest a shield of faith on my arm and secured my suit of armor with my helmet of salvation. Of course, I wouldn't let him touch my hair. Next, my husband would move across the room and simulate fiery darts being thrown at me while I was encouraged to "play along" and raise my shield of faith to repel any illusions or distractions coming my way, insisting this would truly prepare me for the day ahead. As I was ready to step foot out of the door, Hank would approach me saying, "Here, don't forget your sword of the spirit. You will need the word of God, so don't leave without it". How many husbands are willing to take the time to see that their wives are properly dressed for the day, right?

Truthfully, what really amazed me were the simple things during our morning routine. My husband wouldn't complain if the coffee was too dark, the bagel was too light, or if I woke him up too early. He would say "I love you" in a sweet spirited way. What mattered most to him was his excitement to show me he cared for his one true love; me! Hank wanted his most prized possession to always be encouraged, uplifted, loved and protected. He also wanted to show me, in an affectionate way every morning, how to be spiritually dressed for the day ahead. Instantly, I believed my day would be different and I left my home with confidence, assurance, and peace in the Lord.

For certain, on many occasions, I have left the house spiritually dressed and ready for my day. Unfortunately, it was the car ride that would undoubtedly change everything. Who would think it would be so easy to get undressed in the car. Why is that? How is it possible that I could start my morning spiritually dressed and twenty-five minutes later find myself spiritually naked and quite vulnerable? Sadly, there have been days when I have worried about important decisions, stressed about the schedule ahead of me, thought about someone who didn't treat me nicely, or just looked in my rear -view mirror only to find a few blemishes I forgot to cover before I left for the day. I would spend twenty- five minutes undoing what God had already begun in me to the point of arriving at school spiritually naked and sometimes utterly exhausted. Until one day... during my half hour drive, I suddenly felt a faint tug on my heart and I sensed the Lord whisper to me "Kim, you spend so much time looking through the rear- view mirror and worrying about the past, when you need to be focusing on what lies ahead; my eternal direction for you." I knew that moment I wasn't fixed on the things of the Lord. Surely, I allowed my husband to "dress me", but it was time to dress myself. It was time to take accountability for my actions and my thoughts. The only one who could keep me dressed was my Lord, not my husband.

From that moment, God consistently reminded me to change my thinking so I could change my current situation. I replaced the complacent moments of idle and destructive thoughts with worship music. It helped me fill the silent void and prompted my spirit to bask in His presence on my way to work. Now I spend more time praising the Lord during my early morning drive and arrive at my destination spiritually dressed for the day. Intently, with my focus on Him, the Lord continually reminds me that the armor of God doesn't always protect us from what we think others will do to us, but more importantly, it protects us from our own self sabotaging that happens more often than we would like to admit.

We need to spend more time dressing ourselves and less time spiritually undressing ourselves. We need to think upon the Lord more often and thank Him for His protection. We must wear our suit of armor with righteous pride and lay aside the falsehood of delusions and distractions; for it is these negative elements that will undoubtedly guide us along the paths of unrighteous thoughts and experiences.

Whether it is the fun of having your husband help you get dressed or taking the time to gird yourself entirely, let the God of creation speak to your soul and bring you comfort and direction. Let God encourage, uplift, love and protect you. Rely on Him and He will draw close to you!

How will you get dressed for now on? Will you dress yourself in God's spiritual armor or will you arrive at your next destination 'naked'? Will you rely on the delusions and worldly distractions that whirl around you or will you rely on His truth and protection? Decide today 'what' or 'whom' you will rely on for your protection because your self-doubt and sabotaging will only leave your spirit cold, vulnerable, and exposed. If you choose the later of the two, you might want to bring a coat just in case.

Week 26/ Day 26: The Naked Truth

Can you remember a time you became emotionally or spiritually undressed and vulnerable? Explain.

_____

_____

_____

Have you ever dwelt so much on past circumstances that it prevented you from living out the day or the moment? Give an example.

_____

_____

_____

If you have recognized this has happened throughout your life journey, what can you do to get properly dressed or prepared for the day?

_____

_____

_____

Why is it beneficial to get dressed in God's spiritual armor daily? Explain how it can benefit you and others.

_____

_____

_____

What life lesson have you learned through this story?

_____

_____

_____

Masterpiece or Mistake

Take a moment and look at a beautiful picture of a woman. It could be someone you know, a painting, another photograph. What are you thinking right now? What do you see? Soft skin, peaceful eyes, beautiful hair, perfect teeth, a perfect friend... When you look in the mirror every day, what do YOU see? What does your reflection tell you? Have you ever heard, "I have so many wrinkles, my face looks like a road map;" "I'm sure this pimple will arrive before I do;" "Hey, I thought bags were for shopping."

Let's think back to our childhood and young adulthood. I remember glancing into my mirror and saying:

> *"God, can you make me into a princess like Barbie? God, I want to be beautiful. Please God. Make me captivating, so others will notice me too.*

Does your mirror reflect similar conversations? Unfortunately, I didn't see a beautiful reflection in my mirror and the same conversations remained with me for years. The next thing I knew, I began to isolate myself against failure. I believed it was better to withdraw myself from situations and people so I wouldn't be disappointed in myself or others wouldn't be disappointed in me. And of course, the reflection in my mirror as a child always seemed to nod back at me, confirming I'm just a mistake.

Over time, I realized I spent most of it denying the way God made me. I'm afraid not to please others for fear of being rejected; afraid to ask questions of myself, for fear that I wouldn't find or like the answers; and concerned because one wrong move could ruin everything from relationships to career decisions. I just wanted to be desirable and beautiful more than anything.

I don't think this story is much different than yours. I truly believe that we all long to be beautiful because it is a part of our design as women. God designed us this way for a purpose. We often long to be beautiful, yet the world does a wonderful job of squelching this desire and tries to destroy God's plan for you and me, doesn't it? You know what I'm talking about... Commercials, magazines, movies and billboards surround us every day. After the world is done with us, you are probably thinking, "I'm just a mistake." Can you relate with me on this? Well which is it? When you look in your mirror, do you see your imperfections or God's reflection? Do you see a masterpiece or do you see a mistake?

Unfortunately, our reflection gives us a limited view, doesn't it? We consider the mirror every day and allow the mirror to give us a sense of our own self-worth. What we see can easily become what we choose to believe. What do you choose to believe when you look at your reflection? What pictures have you painted of yourself? If God painted a picture of you, what would it look like? Would it be the same? Of course not; would a creator reject his own masterpiece? No, because it is not a mistake. It's a work of art.

> *We are His masterpiece.*

A lined drawing gives us a limited view. It's a lifeless, flat example of how we sometimes choose to see ourselves. Visualize the initial contour of a masterpiece. Do you see flaws, inconsistencies or imperfections? Perhaps, but the masterpiece is not complete. It's a work in progress.

We are all a work in progress. If that is all God sees, imagine how limited His view of us would be. Why would we limit ourselves to a one-dimensional view? We think that what we see in our reflection is the only thing God notices. We must remember; God sees the end in mind.

Masterpiece or mistake you ask...

Our first mistake is *we study the mirror to see our rejection and not God's reflection*. Let's face it, I have rejected my hair color for years. I have more color in my hair now; I can't even remember its original color. But, God remembers. He created beauty. My daughter asked me one day, "Mommy, what is the color of your hair?" I responded, "Jacquelyn, I can't even remember." That tells you that I must not have liked it; I changed it so many times.

I was walking across the classroom the other day and totally forgot why I was standing at the cabinet. "What do I need in this cabinet?" I asked myself out loud, as I absent mindedly stare at the cabinet. Breaking my concentration, one of my students muttered, "I know Mrs. Waltmire; you are there because you are getting drawing paper. I heard you talking out loud across the room." How funny was that? I was even talking out loud and still forgot. I may reject myself because I forgot a few details, but God knows my thoughts. He created me and He remembers every detail.

His esteem for you and I is immeasurable. So why do we spend so much time measuring ourselves against our failures, frustrations or rejections and not against God's immeasurable reflection?

Masterpiece or mistake you ask...

Our second mistake is *we sometimes believe we are not women of value when we are weak or see flaws in ourselves.* This is when we call ourselves names; convinced we are not beautiful, tell ourselves we are ugly, too fat and not good enough at something. What I learned over the years though, is that it is my definition of self-esteem that was flawed. I always figured if I am a person of value then I don't make mistakes and others won't see my flaws. I was wrong. If I didn't feel valued, then my self-esteem was flawed and tattered and life was a constant struggle. If I am not sure about my value, then I will ride the emotional roller coaster, thinking I'm fine one day and not so fine the next. We shouldn't live this way and God doesn't want us to live this way either. It's too exhausting, but we do it anyway. He wants us to be secure in Him, period! When we look at our self-worth from an earthly woman's perspective, we will never be satisfied. But if we would measure our value against God's infinite reflection, we will have all the value we need to live life like a masterpiece and not a mistake.

We spend too much time looking at our flaws and weaknesses, blemishes and wrinkles. We may feel good about ourselves one day and terrible the next, but God created us in His power and through Him so we can do all things.

Philippians 3:14
"We can do all things through Christ who strengthens us." NLT

I realize more and more that when my self-esteem is not secure in Christ, I dwell upon some things unnecessarily. When I am secure in Christ, I will be better able to leave my failures in God's hands, the hands of our Creator; knowing that it is His strength at work in my life and not my own. He can work all things for His glory, despite my personal weaknesses.

Masterpiece or mistake you ask…

The third mistake is that *we let our own estimation of value limit God's eternal purpose for our lives.* Have you ever heard, "Just be yourself?" But to do that, we must accept ourselves the way God made us, believing that if God wanted us to be a different kind of woman; He would have created us that way.

Although I still feel insecure and inadequate in certain situations, let me share an experience that went a long way towards helping me work through this issue. This is when I think of God as the potter and myself as the clay. I only wished He molded me a little less around the hips and more in other areas, if you know what I mean. Unfortunately, though, I grew up looking in the mirror and thinking I was not thin or pretty. And sadly, my adoptive father helped create this inferior complex due to the hundreds of pornographic magazines he read and kept in the house. I saw every one of those magazines as a young child and my unhealthy image of a woman was formed. The magazines and media tell us that we must have a perfect body to match a perfect personality because this is what men want. No doubt that many of the women in the movies, magazines, and commercials made me feel uncomfortable because I judged my worth by comparing myself to them. I never thought I could measure up to their beauty, poise, and figures and thus, my self-esteem suffered. Still there are visuals that evoke those same childhood insecurities.

But praise God! I have decided to change the mirror and maybe you need to change your mirror too. I realized that I needed to begin my day with God and not my mirror. I needed to begin my day with His reflection and not my imperfections. Think about how many times you and I look in the rear-view mirror when we are driving. Of course, we are driving forward, but often time's key into what we just passed or left behind us. God wants you and me to stop focusing on the past or what is left behind. God is calling us to look ahead.

Masterpiece or mistake you ask…

The fourth mistake is that *we don't accept we are different by design and created by the same designer.* Imagine looking at a partially painted portrait. As an artist, we begin to add color to our canvas, but God says that we are a work in progress, working through our insecurities, flaws, disappointments, and blemishes. The masterpiece is not complete. What does His word tell us?

"My grace is sufficient, for my power is made perfect in weakness." 2 Cor. 12:9 NLT

Sure, we can learn skills to make ourselves more effective in life, whether it's painting, making new friends, or dressing in colors that bring out the best in us. Each of us can be strengthened in areas of weakness. Remember though, it's not only futile, but wrong to try and change ourselves into what we are not, so you need to let God use the raw materials He created in you to accomplish His purpose in your life.

Our Creator is so creative, isn't He? I have come to believe that creativity isn't optional. Creativity came from our Creator. Let's face it, I had to keep reminding myself that although I may not feel smart or pretty, I am creative; that's who I am and I am a gift from God. When I accept this gift from God, I realize that creativity is a daily part of our lives, no matter our age, background or abilities. It's the gift that enables us to build a new high-riser, solve our problems, or start a new path. Creativity can produce a five- layered chocolate cake, an innovative bobsled, or a new business. Creativity can shape our lives. It's allowing God to rearrange the raw materials of your life into something new. Some of you are thinking, "Wow, am I raw then, because there are so many raw materials in my possessions, there isn't an attic big enough to store them". But God is saying, "Yahoo, more to work with."

When we stare at the mirror, we need to remember the work of art He is in our lives; the masterpiece no less, that He wants to create in you and me. God wants to speak to us through the masterpiece He made for Himself. If we reject ourselves, then we reject Him. This reminds me of the countless times I have said negative things about myself and my husband saying to me, "Where's my wife? That's not my wife. Kim, every time you say something negative about your life, you are rejecting God and who He created you to be."

Every artist likes to choose the frame that best displays his work. With the same notion, God chose my frame and He chose your frame and we are not a mistake. We are the canvas on which God wants to display his beauty, and we are the frame for the artist's work. Who knows, maybe it is the very thing we dislike most about ourselves which is the canvas God needed all along for the beautiful work of art He plans to create out of our lives. But unfortunately, we tend to look too far into the mirror and see nothing but flaws, insecurities, weaknesses, and fall prey into believing that we are a mistake. We look so deep to find the gnawing feeling that God made a mistake when He created you and me. More importantly, this feeling affects everything we do, as well as our attitude toward God, whom we won't see as a loving and perfect Father. How could He be perfect if He made mistakes in you and me, right? This mind-set is not from God.

Masterpiece or mistake you ask...

The fifth mistake is that *we allowed the ugly mirror to be purchased in the first place.* When we glance into the mirror we must look at ourselves in an entirely new way. God knows this won't be easy, particularly if we disliked something about ourselves for years, but if we shift our perspective and see ourselves through God's reflection, we might be surprised by what we see. Now don't you want that mirror? It's time to buy a new mirror because we might be surprised by what we see and hear... "You are my child, beautifully sculpted and created for my purpose. You are always loved through your feelings of inadequacies. You are my canvas, my work of art and I love you!"

> *2 Corinthians 12:9*
> *"Each time He said, "My grace is all you need. My power works best in weakness"*
> *so now I am glad to boast about my weaknesses, so that the power of Christ can*
> *work through me... v. 10 For when I am weak, then I am strong." NLT*

God wants to take your shattered life and broken heart and create out of it a work of art that will bring Him glory. In your failures and imperfections God's radiant glory can be shown; so, remember, God can take your suffering and turn it into a blessing for yourself and others.

Will you let Him mend you?

It's time to take your eyes of yourself and remember that nothing can keep God from turning your life into the beautiful masterpiece He intended it to be. No matter whom you are today in the mirror, or what you were yesterday in your rear-view mirror, you are not a mistake. You are a work of art in which God wants to reveal His power, love, and creativity. So, let Him sculpt your life into the masterpiece He has planned for you.

Every circumstance will move you to your destination. Is your destination with God or not? Every response you make adds another brush-stroke to the final picture. You are God's masterpiece. The moment your canvas was placed before Him, He smiled over the purpose and plans He has for you. Don't miss God's path and truth for your life; buy a new mirror. I promise you; when you purchase God's mirror, you will learn to trust in His paintbrush because He will make your colors sing. You will learn to trust in God's pen because it will make your lines dance. So why would you hold anything back from a loving Creator. Why would you hold anything back from your Eternal Daddy? If you are truly a masterpiece, then you are NOT a mistake.

Rest in God's grace and stop looking in the mirror through your eyes and begin looking through His eyes. We may not always have the same attention- getting appearance we once had. We may still have insecurities or see flaws now and again and we may not deserve his love, but what we feel about ourselves has nothing to do with the fact that He loves us and always will. There's no greater self-esteem than that. So, our goal in life should not be to pursue what the world says is valuable, but to strive to be what God says is valuable. We don't even have to put a price tag on our valuable masterpiece because God paid an enormous price out of His love for us when He gave us the life of His Only Son, Jesus Christ.

> *Ephesians 2:10*
> *"For we are God's masterpiece; He has created us anew in Christ Jesus, so we can do the good things He planned for us long ago." NLT*

Let God sculpt you, mold you and paint you through eternity. His love for you is immeasurable, so let Him continue to create a work of art in your life. Remember, paint can be removed, but His brush strokes will last forever.

God's desire is to reshape you within your frailties, faults, and imperfections… He won't throw the clay away. God will reshape you into His masterpiece, but when you are hardened by your imperfections, you will be harder to reshape. What will you offer God; soft clay or hard clay?

You are a masterpiece, not a mistake. Take a moment and reflect upon your life and what your mirror is saying to you. Give all your thoughts to God and let Him mend your precious heart and life and I promise you, your life will change forever when you see His reflection and not your rejection. Will you buy a new mirror?

> *"Beauty is a blessing when used to bless another's life."*
> *Author Unknown*

Week 27/ Day 27: Masterpiece or Mistake

What does your reflection tell you?

_____

_____

_____

Do you understand why your reflection gives you a limited view? Give examples.

_____

_____

_____

If you asked God to change one thing about you, what would it be? Explain.

_____

_____

_____

Why do you think you need or want to change this area of your life?

_____

_____

_____

Do you believe God's grace is sufficient in your weakness? Why or why not?

_____

_____

_____

_____

What can you do to change this limited view of yourself?

_____

_____

_____

Do you believe you are a masterpiece or a mistake? Why?

_____

_____

_____

Can you think of a time you began to look through God's eyes? Share your results and how it made you or others feel.

_____

_____

_____

What life lesson have you learned through this story?

_____

_____

_____

_____

_____

_____

_____

_____

The Power of One

How many times have you ever wanted an answer to a question and mom would be the best one to answer it? How many times have you struggled with mechanical injustice around the house and dad was the only one to fix it? How many times have you been frustrated with a heavy item or something out of reach and your brother or husband was stronger and taller to take care of it? How many times have you endured challenges at work or in a relationship and you thought you were the only one to turn it around? How many times have you cried out for help; your health is failing, you are scared, or all alone, and your friend was the only one to make it all better?

These situations happen to us every day and there is no discrimination of race, ethnicity, gender, or age. It doesn't matter who we are or where we are. Often, we rely on that *one* person for help. We are willing to wait for that perfect gesture, listening ear and unwavering answer as if there is no other. Sometimes we are willing to wait forever until that *one* person meets our needs. Unfortunately, though, many times the power of *one's* opinion crushes our spirit and knocks us over, causing you and me to stumble. Our faith gets challenged or our self-esteem shatters. Who knew the power of *one* could be so powerful?

This reminds me of a time when I was simultaneously diagnosed with pre-cervical cancer and a sexually transmitted disease. I was scared and desperate before anyone would learn of my heart-break. How could I ever share this situation with anyone? They could never understand my pain or embarrassment. I felt I was the only one who could change my circumstances. I turned inward, relying on myself and visualization strategies. I imagined beautiful butterflies taking the cancerous cells away and unfortunately, the cells remained untouched. I imagined the open sores dissolving, but they worsened by the day. I was left dejected and lonely; hopeless, and empty. You could say I felt powerless. I didn't know who I could share my pain with. I was convinced that I would never be able to have children and fear rose out of me like a vengeance. I couldn't control the diagnoses so I succumbed to the feelings of unworthiness. I contemplated that if there was a God, He wouldn't care and if I had a boy-friend, he wouldn't last, so why bother? Rejection was a familiar territory for me; I guess you could say *it was my comfort zone.*

Similarly, I look back at my teaching career and can't help but think about the various decisions I had to make, particularly during the incidents when I thought the situations would have a successful outcome if only there were more people that would take a stand. Sometimes we think there is 'power in numbers', but when the final decision time appears, we are usually the only ones left standing. Incidentally, we think perhaps if our voice is loud enough or strong enough in the gap, it will make a difference. But it wasn't until I realized *who* the power of one was supposed to be; that made all the difference in the world.

No matter what the circumstance, trial or tribulation, I have learned that I have *one* choice; and although there is nothing wrong with sharing our concerns with that special 'someone', clearly, God revealed to me that the power of O*ne* is in Him.

11 Chronicles 14:11
"And Asa cried out to the Lord his God, and said," Lord, it is nothing for You to
help, whether with many or with those who have no power; help us, O Lord our
God, for we rest on You, and in Your name, we go against this multitude.

Lord, you are our God; do not let man prevail against you!" NKJV

Asa had battles. His army was out- numbered and he felt powerless, but Asa prayed to God and the Ethiopians were defeated and chased away. It wasn't until Asa recognized his limitations did God's power encase his enemies and calm the confusion. It wasn't until Asa recognized his limitations did God reduce his enemies' resources and vindicate Asa's victory.

If we face adversity, battles, even experience struggles we know we can't accomplish, then we better recognize our limitations. There are hordes of enemies and frustrations lurking throughout our lives and we must recognize our powerlessness without the Lord before it's too late. It is in these very moments that God has shown me that the power of *One* is in Him. He is our triune God. There is one Father, one Son and one Holy Spirit. This is where God works His power through those who truly recognize they need it. We can rely on friends, neighbors, family, loved ones all we want, but unfortunately people can fail us. And unfortunately, it will be those who think they can do it in and of themselves who are in the greatest danger.

Another lesson we can learn through Asa's paradigm is that he sought wise counsel with those who had a close relationship with the Lord. We need to keep in close contact with people who are filled with God's Spirit. It is then we will learn His counsel. We must spend ordinary time in conversation and prayer with godly counsel so we can hear and apply His significance to our lives. We need to recognize the power is in One; the Lord.

Psalm 20:6-8
"Now I know that the Lord saves His anointed; He will answer him from His
holy heaven with the saving strength of His right hand. Some trust in chariots,
and some in horses; but we will remember the name of the Lord our God. They
have bowed down and have fallen; but we have risen and stand upright." NKJV

The real power comes from the saving strength of our Lord and the transforming power from His Holy Spirit. As long as there have been trials, tribulations, famines and wars, everybody at some point have boasted about their power within; but this self-indulgent power will not last. It's a slow fade and over time, the self-reliant power we think we must change our circumstances will vanish and where will we be left then? Our trust must be in God's power before it is too late.

When I realized the transforming power of the Holy Spirit is what I needed to rely on, my worries withered away and my trials turned to triumphs. When I realized He died with His arms opened wide for me on that blood-stained cross, who better to rely on than the One with the power to resurrect Himself to a heavenly realm, as well as resurrect us out of the powerless situations we find ourselves in every day.

We have a choice to either rely on the One with the power or ourselves and others who remain powerless. What voice should we be listening for over the roar of confusion and decision making? It's the Lord. God has given us His one and only Son, Jesus, who intercedes on our behalf. His Holy Spirit wants to live in you and me. He wants to guide us, so why won't we patiently wait for His answer and comfort as we would our friends and loved ones? Are we going to seek others first or will we acknowledge the power of One? Will we listen for the familiar voices pulling us in the direction that is not God's will, or will we listen for that One voice above all others?

When I made God my first choice, my power of One helped me to conquer things I thought I would never be able to achieve. My power of One was mighty enough for me to walk through trials with His strength and confidence… and He has the power to do that for you as well.

This reminds me of a quote from Michael Jackson's memorial; "There's nothing that can't be done if we raise our voice <u>as</u> one." I'd like to change that quote to sound something like this," There's nothing that can't be done without the power of One." God is not limited by our resources and worldly counsel. He will work His power through ordinary people and it is up to us to give Him the attention He deserves. God created you and me from the inner depths of his heart and love, so why wouldn't we rely on Him as our power? Don't focus on your problems; focus on His power in your life. When we focus on what bothers us, *we* stumble, but when we focus on the power of One; God, what bothers us won't stumble us.

Let me leave you with one thought… While watching Michael Jackson's memorial, they paused during the ceremony for the world to hear his voice one more time and Michael said these lasting words:

> *" In my darkest hour, in my deepest despair, will you still care? Will you be there? In my trials, through my tribulations, through my doubts and frustrations, in my violence and in my turbulence, through my fear and my confessions, my anguish and my pain, through my joy and my sorrow, and the promise of tomorrow…I will never let you part, for you're always in my heart."*

I cried with sadness when I heard these pain-filled words. Were these authentic thoughts intended for the world? Was Michael feeling so powerless he wanted the world to love him through all these emotions? Was he seeking the approval and acceptance from the world that would chew him up and spit him out in a moment? "Oh Michael," I thought. "Did you turn to God during these times of despair and anguish? Did the King of Pop rely on his power that the world exalted him for, or did he rely on the risen King of glory and power?"

Let's look past the old cliché, 'There's power in numbers" and rely on the power of One. Numbers can fail us, but the power of One can change us. Do you believe God's power can overcome your powerless circumstances? Do you believe God's power can overcome your outnumbered enemies? Do you believe God's power can overcome your trials? Do you believe God's power is not limited by your resources? It is time to rely on His power and not everybody else.

Week 28/ Day 28: The Power of One

Describe a time you relied on one person to see you through your circumstance.

_____

_____

_____

_____

Describe a time you relied on God to see you through a situation in your life.

_____

_____

_____

_____

What commonalities do you notice when people don't rely on God to see them through their struggles?

_____

_____

_____

_____

Why is it so important to recognize the power of God in all your circumstances?

_____

_____

_____

_____

_____

Do you believe God is limited by your resources? _____

When you decide to rely on God as your power and strength, what steps do you or can you take to walk along His path?

_____

_____

_____

_____

_____

What life lesson have you learned through this story?

_____

_____

_____

_____

_____

_____

_____

_____

_____

_____

_____

_____

_____

_____

Groaning to Gratitude

My husband and I watched a documentary about a gentleman who received the first double hand transplant in the United States. This middle-aged man expressed some discontent with the way he was forced to live. Because he missed the opportunities to touch, hold his wife's hand, feel his children's faces, and wished he could cook again. He admitted the challenges overtook his emotions and caused him to focus on his circumstances, but more exigent was the waiting. The doctors implied that it would be at least two years before they believe he would have a wider range of movement and sensitivity. "Sometimes it is harder to wait than to deal with the physical pain," the gentleman reminded the interviewer. But with all the pain and suffering this man endured, he mentioned one thing; "With my wife and family by my side helping and loving me every step of the way, I can't help but be grateful for them and, in turn, makes the waiting much easier. I am truly grateful to the surgeons and this new technology."

When I hear stories of gratitude like this one, it takes my breath away and breaks my heart at the same time. There have been countless moments I have felt gratitude and expressed my feelings with a phone call, a letter, a special meal or flowers. Inadvertently though, there have been many moments I found myself focusing only on my circumstances as if they would never get better. There have been countless moments I have hit 'rock-bottom' with no place to look but 'up". The gratitude he expressed far outweighed the groaning he endured throughout this interview and if this man can muster up the courage needed to circumvent the pain and agony he has felt, then certainly I can press on too.

How often do we thank the people around us for adding to our lives? How often do we recognize God through our circumstances or thank Him for our physical or spiritual healing? What gives us grief and what are we doing about it? It isn't until we are struck with dire conditions, that we are often reminded of what we have had all along. It is when we show our gratitude and remember those along the way that it expands our love and spiritual healing; inside and out.

I am not sure what caused this man to have a double hand transplant, but the message that rung in my mind that day was the gratitude he had for special ones in his life and the reminder to all of us not to take life for granted because it can change at any moment. Furthermore, throughout the rest of the interview, he expressed the struggles he has living with this challenge. He articulated the details of pain that surged through his body and the bitterness that followed before he accepted the physical outcome. He expressed how much of an inconvenience his circumstances were and how many times he wanted to give up completely, had it not been for his loved ones and competent and caring surgeons. Interestingly though, at the end of his interview, I noticed he never once mentioned God, yet still expressed his gratitude for his family and surgeons for their love and support. If he could show this type of gratitude without mentioning the Lord, then all the more reason for Christians to rely on God and thank Him during our challenges as well. Whether diseased by the physical 'plagues' of this world or set-back with confrontational situations; we must be very grateful for our lives because we never know when portions of our time and life may be asked of us.

When we are living ungratefully, often discomfort, discontentment, disappointment, and disruption infiltrate our existence, causing us to grumble about both God and our present circumstances. In many cases, resentment follows and we must beware! If we frequently exhibit constant dissatisfaction and resentment with our present situations, our attitudes will eventually lead to rebellion and separation from God. And any choice to walk away from God is a step in the loneliest direction of our lives.

The easiest way to fall away from God and His life-sustaining guidance is to look at our present circumstances and think we can handle them on our own. Subsequently, another way to fall away from His life-sustaining guidance is to mistakenly exaggerate them. Have you ever thought about that? Have you ever taken the time to reflect on whether your current 'condition' is really the way it happened or really the way it is? Have you ever tried to analyze the purpose of 'why' you are in the situation you are in and not give God a second thought; or perhaps, questioned God about your lack of blessing or why the pain must be so deep? I ask this because I know how easy it is to lose your perspective when you take your eyes off God and focus on your problems. I know what it is like to go through the 'fire' and then be reminded that someone else's problem is far worse than mine. It's in times like these when we clearly miss the blessings and are left carrying the burdens. We can't let our difficulties cause us to lose sight of God's direction or purpose for our lives, but unfortunately, it is so easy to do.

> 1 Timothy 6:6
> *"Now godliness with contentment is great gain." NKJV*

This scripture is part of the foundation to my spiritual growth and personal success, but God didn't say it would be easy. Let me be transparent for a moment. I have gone through many trials, but this recent one has hurt to the core, and since this transition began over the past few years, I have learned so much about myself and those around me. Before I share my heart, I need you to know that there are not enough pages to account for the various lessons I have gained through my discontentment, however, I have finally come through my sensitive season and I'm continually trying to hear and feel God's grace and I hope you can too.

Over twenty years ago, my husband and I were called into the ministry. Neither one of us felt worthy enough to live out the call, but by faith we accepted the Lord into our hearts and chose to live out the biblical truths revealed from Genesis to Revelation. Throughout our Christian journey, we grew quickly into leadership and thereafter, my husband was honored with the opportunity to serve full-time on a church staff as one of six associate pastors. We spent many years erecting new walls and foundations through various building campaigns, as well as writing, and teaching classes for the Bible Institute and adult classes, overseeing multiple front-line ministries, banquets, pastoral care, leading the senior citizen bible studies, officiating weddings, funerals, as well as counseling sessions. We were in the choir, lead the nursing home ministry, church trips, and volunteered with the church musical productions. Even hosting in the new café ministry was time-consuming when you live far away, but by the grace of God we managed to meet most of the needs of others if we forgone our own family time and friends. To top it all off though, my husband was getting his Masters Degree an hour and ten minutes away and our daughter was going to a Christian school near the church and was involved in various children's ministries. Unfortunately, we lived forty minutes from her school and thirty -five minutes from church, which placed us on the highway so many times during the week and weekends that we often kept a bag of clothes in the car just in case we needed to visit a friend and rest before the next church service or school event. Thereafter, during our tireless commute and dedication, God finally gave us a reprieve and allowed us to move one mile from the church; making this one of the most pleasurable transitions of our lives.

As I continued working as a full-time teacher, driving back to our recent home-town and managing my church loyalties, Hank was excited about the church expansion. He was excited to grow various ministries, work on his seminary classes, as well as enjoyed the respite from traveling. Even our daughter became more connected with her new high school and extra-curricular activities. She could visit all her local friends and Hank and I were thrilled to be able to do the same. Everything appeared to be just as we prayed until one Christmas morning; God undoubtedly had a message for Hank. My husband placed his head on the kitchen table during breakfast and softly said, "I have been so busy, I missed Christmas." My mother, mother-n-law, Jacquelyn, and I stared at Hank as he lifted his head with tears softly dripping from his eyes. I indisputably knew we were about to make a transition that would impact the family, but undeniably would affect so many other people; I just didn't realize the entire impact it would have on our lives.

A transition was inevitable. Don't get me wrong; we did not transition out of this church because Hank and I were asked to leave. We transitioned out of church ministry because we sensed that our 'season' came to an end. Only God can define the reasons and His timing, but remember, when we live in a fallen world of human frailties and attitudes, sometimes our transitions can leave unnecessary wounds and room for doubt and judgment by others; even by the ones who you thought were your friends.

During our transition, God provided my husband with a job too rare to get when you have been out of the business industry for nine years. Moreover, Hank and I were taken back by the various doors that God kept opening and closing as well. Unfortunately, our transition had some incredible highlights and not so good ones. You could say that the moment of our departure was equated to a thank you card on Hank's desk. Sadly, when we finally thought we would have the opportunity to finally address the congregation and thank them for our eighteen years of service and their support, the weekend we transitioned out of ministry never went the way we had planned. Sorrowfully, we didn't have the opportunity to share the details about why we were not transitioning into another ministry like pastors naturally do, and before you knew it, several congregation members questioned the message of our departure. Some were frustrated without preparation or an explanation from us. We felt our integrity was at stake given all the confusion and we lost all of our friends with the exception of a few that you could count on one hand. I felt all of what we gave to the church was compromised and the truth was brought to light, in my opinion, when so many didn't even show that they cared since we left. You can say that in moments like these, you learn who your real friends are and it took three more years before we heard or saw many of our friends again. In retrospect, we didn't know how difficult it would be leaving the role of leadership and spiritual influence without moving out of our community, especially when we only live five minutes from the church.

The first year of our departure was the hardest experience of my life and a few years to follow would be the loneliest. My husband left the business world years ago, as a district sales manager within the pharmaceutical industry, only to come back for a season as a sales representative in the pharmaceutical industry; a blessing no doubt, but this job transition brought us back to the beginning days of our marriage and felt as if our eighteen years of ministry was being erased. It felt like a demotion on many levels. Hank's pharmaceutical friends are now CEO's, vice presidents, and national account managers. It is difficult especially when you pass familiar people in local doctor offices that recognize that you were one of their pastors serving God in their church community and now are waiting on doctors, nurses and secretaries. You could see the question in their eyes as they wrestled with our quick departure. Hank would often be addressed, insensitively speaking; "Oh, you are selling drugs now" to "Hey, you even look like a drug rep" to "Speaking of the devil, what are you doing carrying that brief case?" It saddened my husband immensely because nobody really took the time to call or care to ask him how our new ministry opportunities were going other than one of his friends. He felt he was being perceived as a minister who fell away from God's grace, and as people began to inadequately fill in the blanks about our departure, in these inconsiderate moments, the unfounded truths were very hard to accept without bitterness and resentment.

Hank and I clearly knew we were on a two -year plan before we would aggressively start seeking full-time ministry again and we knew how difficult it would be to forge ahead under the radar of insensitive comments or complete silence with no support from friends. We were working full-time, encouraging our high school aged daughter to look forward without her friends and reestablish herself in other extra- curricular events and a new youth group, while her daddy took three classes a semester to complete his 93 credit Masters in Divinity, as well as consult on staff as a non-paid Associate Pastor in a small church community. Imagine driving by the church you served for eighteen years every day and week, wondering why we have had to feel rejected by all those we have known for our entire Christian walk? Where is everybody in my time of need, I asked. Who is there for me?

> *"Lord, one friend from church was there for me when I needed to talk or cry and even then, I was fearful to share my heart. Dear Lord, the burden I must have placed on her, yet she was the one willing to let me express my pain and sorrow countless times. How can I thank her? Lord, I need to thank you. I need to thank you for sending me one friend I could trust. Lord, forgive me for not expressing my gratefulness to you for all the times you gave me a smile and hope to get through the next day. Forgive me for all the times you were performing tiny miracles along the way and I didn't notice them because I was so focused on my pain and discontentment.*
>
> *Oh, but Lord, the decision to transition affected our daughter, family, and how we would emotionally respond to others. Lord, you saw me and heard my crying for a full year. Did our serving mean anything Lord? Were lives touched at all? Despite our transition, will the congregation ever know how much we have given, how much we cared for them, and how hurtful it was to leave the way we did? How will they ever know how we feel if we don't even have a relationship with the congregation anymore? Lord, help me get past the heartache and pain. This has been the loneliest and hardest walk of my life. My family has been hurt deeply and I can't hear your voice sometimes. Will we be back in ministry again soon? When? How long will we have to wait? Will I ever be ready for ministry again? Lord, help me to take my eyes off my circumstances. If the man with a double hand transplant can smile through his trying ordeal, then what is my excuse Lord? Forgive me Father".*

Whenever you experience an emotional transition, with little to no support, it is very easy to groan and not grow. It is very easy to 'spill over' every sentiment towards anybody who will listen, that is, until we realize that our identity isn't in people or in this case, church ministry. Our identity is in Christ alone and it is Him we need to turn to, not to those around us. We finally realized after all these years of service just how easy it was to lose our identity amongst the congregation and in the ministries, we were serving. *It was time that our groaning turned into growing.* And eventually, in our loneliness with nobody to lean on, it was time to give it all to the Lord.

When we are at a crossroads in our lives, it is so important to take inventory of our resources. Our tumultuous transition caused us to do just that and what appeared to be a burden, soon turned into a blessing. Usually it is when we are being tested that we are forced to take a rest and reevaluate our physical and spiritual condition.

Maybe you can relate to a transition out of or into a work place, school, marriage, relationship, or even the death of a loved one. Maybe you know what it is like to have little or no support during your trying ordeal. Perhaps you have been dissatisfied, discontent and those around you disillusioned by your circumstances. What I do know is when you transition out of serving a congregation in leadership for eighteen years with no true recognition, not moving out of your community, and with no 'friendly' support, you feel like you have been dropped in the middle of the widest and driest desert, parched, dried up, all alone, and starving to be loved and fed. It reminds me of the Israelites who wanted more water, food, and rest. They wanted the Promised Land immediately and they were more concerned about their physical condition, rather than their spiritual condition. They were dissatisfied and discontent with how long it was taking them to get to the Promised Land, that they ignored the blessings God provided along the way. Instead, they grumbled about their circumstances and disobeyed God while more problems erupted. Unlike the Israelites, if we would just pay close attention to all the signs of God's presence in our own lives, our feelings of dissatisfaction and discontentment would diminish, right?

On the contrary, this was one of my painful dilemmas. Waiting to hear God's voice and direction; waiting to feel His strength and power over my bitterness, hostility, and resentment so I could understand His purpose was one of the hardest lessons for me to learn. The deafening silence and loneliness was challenging for me at times, but slowly I began to pray again through my circumstances and for the needs of others. Slowly I began to thirst after God's grace and view our transition as a miracle in the making. Slowly I smiled again and looked at my discomfort as an opportunity and a catalyst for change. Slowly I recognized this situation as a need to share with others when they feel all alone. Slowly, I realized I had another grateful chance to experience the presence of God; a God who loves and cares for my every need.

How often do we stop and recognize God's provision in our lives during the high and low moments? Repeatedly, the Israelites expressed grumbling in exchange for gratitude. The wilderness was hostile, infuriating and extremely hot; God provided a cloud covering. Food was scarce and water not to be found, but God provided manna with dew and drinking water from the rocks like rain. God met their needs His way, but the Israelite's selfish desires, greed and rights overshadowed God's miracles and blessings because all they could focus on were their problems. We must be careful not to be preoccupied with our circumstances so our perspective on everything else changes. You see, although my family despised being alone for those few years, it was a blessing all around because a complaining, ungrateful spirit is contagious. How would any of us benefit or heal if all we did was talk about the pain rather than how to heal through it? The Lord is all we need during our discomfort! He alone needs to hear about our concerns and yes; God will take care of the rest if we would just let Him.

No matter how difficult our lives may be, there is always someone struggling more or longer than you and me. Furthermore, when we run from God, we inevitably run into more problems. We need to take a heart-felt moment and stop and wait upon the Lord for His life-sustaining guidance. We need to trust with all our heart and soul that He has our pain, frustration, dissatisfaction, disappointment, disillusionment, discontentment, and discomfort in the folds of his loving arms if we would just let Him embrace us. It's time to take our eyes off our problems and set them on the possibilities.

> Romans 8:35,37-38
> *"Can anything ever separate us from Christ's love? Does it mean He no longer loves us if we have trouble or calamity, or are persecuted, or in danger or threatened with death? No, despite all these things, overwhelming victory is ours through Christ, who loved us. And I am convinced that nothing can separate us from his love." NLT*

Bill Crowder was once quoted saying..." King David experienced hopeless despair as he struggled with his own failures, the attacks of others and the disappointments of life. The depth of his sorrow and loss drove him to heartache, but in that grief, he turned to the God of comfort".

I promise you; in your own disappointment, you too can find comfort in God who cares for your broken heart. What or who is keeping you as a groaning prisoner? Will you transcend whatever is holding you back from showing your gratitude and begin to trust that God will see you through the eye of your storm? Your faith and trust in Him will bring you joy through your pain if you can see beyond your circumstances. You can be confident that your trials and problems will enhance your strength over time. So, don't let this expectation disappoint you.

> Romans 5:5
> *"For we know how dearly God loves us, because he has given us the Holy Spirit to fill our hearts with his love." NLT*

Will you change your groaning to gratitude? Is there someone you can thank through your tribulations? God is waiting. Will you respond?

Week 29/ Day 29: Groaning to Gratitude

Think of a time when you realized you focused too much on your circumstances and not the needs of others. How did you feel? What will you do to change this?

_____

_____

_____

Are you a groaner? Describe a time you complained too much. How did it make you or others feel?

_____

_____

_____

Have you expressed gratitude? Describe a few experiences that brought you or somebody else gratitude?

_____

_____

_____

How do you find your contentment? Would God approve or disapprove? Why?

_____

_____

_____

Think of an area in your life you are groaning and not growing the way you would like. What is holding you back from successfully living in gratitude?

_____

_____

_____

When we run from God, we inevitably run into problems. Are you willing to transcend whatever is holding you back from showing your gratitude and begin trusting God will see you through it all?_____

What will you do to involve the Lord and replace your groaning for gratitude?

_____

_____

_____

_____

What life lesson have you learned through this story?

_____

_____

_____

_____

_____

_____

_____

_____

_____

_____

_____

_____

_____

_____

The Gift that Keeps on Giving

T he summer of 1965 was no different than any other summer, except for Doug and Sharon. Doug was the most handsome seventeen-year old boy and every girl knew it. All the girls talked about him, wanted to date him, and so did another seventeen -year old girl named Sharon. They noticed each other at football games, began dating, and as time passed, Sharon was convinced she loved him. But who knew a decision she and Doug made that unforgettable summer would absolutely change everything.

"Doug, I'm pregnant", revealed Sharon. She was terrified and he didn't want to know. He was too young and had his whole life ahead of him. "You need to get rid of it," he demanded. "I'll pay for half of the abortion and you pay the rest." Sharon was confused, hurt, and scared. Doug didn't seem to care about the implications at the time and she knew she had to tell her mother, but how will she take the news?

"You are a disgrace to the family Sharon", her mother insisted. Soon thereafter, she found a quarter placed on top of her suitcase, packed and waiting for her at the front door. "Call your father in Connecticut and take care of things there. You are not welcome in this house." Sharon found herself at the local corner store waiting for her father to arrive. Sharon's pregnant 42 -year old mother voiced her opinion that volatile day and with no remorse, sent her daughter on her way to figure *things* out on her own.

Sharon's father was living with her wealthy Aunt Gene in Westport, Connecticut. Upon her arrival, it was evident that Sharon felt ashamed and lonely. Her heart said to keep the baby, but her mother and family made her feel that the decision to keep the baby would ruin her life. Aunt Gene told Sharon that she could live on the streets or she would live out her pregnancy in a home for teenage pregnant unwed mothers. Sharon was expected to give birth, give the baby up for adoption, and come back to live with her Aunt who would support her schooling so she could get a business degree and make something of her life.

Sharon followed her Aunt's suggestion to give the baby up for adoption. Unfortunately, she was encouraged to lie about the timing of her pregnancy so she could get into the facility. You had to be pregnant four months or less to receive care. Somehow and unexpectedly, Sharon could transition into the facility. Interestingly though, all she could remember at that time was the exchange of a large sum of money; and is unsure to this day what it was used for. Nonetheless, as uncomfortable as Sharon may have felt beginning her abandoned journey alone, it didn't matter what the cost; her decision was made and it was time to press on and deal with the consequences.

When Sharon arrived at this special home, she found it to be the most unfriendly and lonely place. "It's like a prison here," she stated. The girls roomed together and were advised not to share last names or personal information. Some of the young ladies were still getting an education and all the girls were expected to clean, scrub the floors, keep their rooms tidy and follow every rule. Sharon felt as if she signed up for the military, having to follow every drill with perfection; something she has fallen short of all her life. Moreover, Sharon knew all too well that the girls were there for one reason; punishment for what they did. This experience was not to be fun. This was a place for these girls to learn a lesson and if their experience is difficult, perhaps they will think twice before they make the same decision that put them there in the first place.

The days and months were agonizing for Sharon. She had few to no visitors and she felt ostracized by the very one she fell in love with. Her mother didn't care. "Where is my family when I need them?" she frequently thought.

Watching her young body change over the months was extremely difficult, but waiting for delivery would be the worst. One would think eating and socializing with the girls would be encouraging and help alleviate the anxiety that comes from early pregnancy, but not in this facility. The girls ate three meals a day at a community table and sat per their expected delivery date. They were told not to share stories or personal information; just eat and go back to their chores or studies. A head mistress sat at the head of the table and the girls knew all too well, that the closer they anxiously sat to her, the closer they were to their impending due date. They were constantly reminded that once they gave birth, they would never see one another again. You would give birth, go back to the facility, pick up your belongings, and move on. Sadly though, most of the girls had no idea what was waiting for them on the other side of the door.

Sharon approached her final hours of labor. According to her supposed due date, the mistress felt Sharon could not have been in labor; but they had no idea at the time that she lied about the date all along. Her water broke and she was immediately reminded that it was her responsibility to clean up after herself. She was taken to the hospital and typically, once the nurses discovered the young girls were from the home for teenage pregnant unwed mothers, they were treated as second class citizens. As Sharon spoke of that emotional day, she recalls the unfriendly nurses telling her to push through the pain for a natural childbirth, but it was nothing short of natural on all levels. Her tired 18- year old body was stretched and stressed until nearing the end of her labor, when finally, her body couldn't take the pain anymore. Immediately, the nurses and doctor gave her a spinal. "If only they gave me relief from this labor earlier," Sharon sadly thought.

Through all the pain and suffering, Sharon's baby was born healthy. Regretfully, at that moment, Sharon wished she didn't give her baby up for adoption. Not only was she giving her baby girl away; she wasn't even able to see or touch her. Fortunately, Sharon found out that her own father was waiting all along and able to hold her baby just before she was handed off, most likely to never be seen again. Sharon stayed in the hospital for a few more days due to some complications and then was discharged back to the facility to gather her belongings and transition for good.

Sharon's Aunt kept her word and housed Sharon, as well as paid for her schooling until she graduated with a business degree. After graduation, Sharon worked at a laboratory in Stamford, CT while her sister informed the family that she and her brother were relocating to CT as well. Sharon realized her mother was left raising a baby all alone in New York and decided to go back home and live with her mother and found herself caring for her mother's baby; her little half sister. Although Sharon agonized over this decision, for years she helped raise her little sister. You can only imagine how hard it was to have a baby of your own, give it away, and then raise another baby in the home where you were unwelcome, but what was she to do?

Sharon could remember all the family gatherings like they were yesterday. She thought half of her was gone. Everybody would be happy, but Sharon couldn't stop thinking about what life would have been like if she had kept her baby. "Everyone was happy, except me. I had a daughter and she wasn't with me. Half of me was missing and there was nothing I could do about it," she sullenly commented.

Sharon lived with regret in her heart for years. There were even moments she was so convinced that her little sister could possibly be her baby all along and nobody had the heart to tell her. She spent so much time raising her sister, even others wondered. But unfortunately, it was the guilt, shame, and confusion that were too much for her to bear; so Sharon did what she had to do in order to survive. It didn't matter what her mother thought or demanded of her. She raised her little sister, worked, learned to cook, and managed the family responsibilities the best she could; there was no other choice.

For many years, Sharon struggled with her decisions and more importantly, where her daughter might be. Was she alive, hurt, scared, or possibly angry with being given away for adoption? What does she look like? Will she ever meet her? What would Sharon say if they did meet? For years, Sharon wondered about the answers to these questions and more. She even paid for a private investigator to help her find her daughter multiple times, but to no avail, her daughter was never found; not until 41 years later.

Sharon received a phone call one August day in the summer of 2007. A strange woman on the line asked if her name was Sharon and revealed to her that her daughter was found. Sharon thought that it had to be an insensitive joke, but eventually learned that the woman from Connecticut was real and her daughter was alive and well. Her 41- year old daughter was ME.

At the time, my daughter Jacquelyn had surgery on her neck and my husband and I felt it was time to get my medical history. I contacted a local Adoption Agency and eventually spoke to a woman who could locate my personal files. Upon returning from a family trip to Colorado, the most amazing voice mail was waiting for me. "Kim, I found your mother. Call me as soon as you can." I couldn't believe the message. Could it be possible that I will be reunited with my birth mother?

I opted to pen a letter to Sharon, rather than speak on the phone for our first communication. I was so excited to tell her that I am healthy, doing well, and that there are no hard feelings about her decision to give me up for adoption. I expressed the importance of her knowing that she doesn't have to live another day with regret and that she can be free from the pain and emotional suffering that she may have endured over all these years.

Soon thereafter, I received a phone call from my husband while I was teaching. "Kim, right now I am looking at an envelope; a letter from Sharon, your birth mother and I am also looking at another envelope signed by a man named Doug. I wonder if it is your birth father... Would you like me to open it and tell you if it is?" my husband asked. Tears streamed down my face. Of course, I wanted to be the one to open the letters, but I anxiously wanted to know who Doug was. "Open the letter for me," I blurted. "Kim, oh my goodness, it's your birth father. You got a letter from both of your parents on the same day." I couldn't believe it. I had to tell my students why I was crying happy tears and instantly they all got up out of their seats to hug me. I called the Principal and requested a substitute for the remainder of the day. I prayed to God all the way home and honestly, I don't remember one exit along the way. I remember calling my dear friend Cheryl to meet me at the house and as soon as she arrived, we sat at my kitchen table and cried as I read the letters aloud.

Here is a letter from my birth mother:
9/17/07

Dear Kim,

You can't imagine how wonderful it was to receive your letter. Throughout the years, I have made numerous attempts to locate you, going as far as hiring a private detective, all to no avail. Since receiving your letter, I have been dealing with a wide range of emotions from wondrous joy to a hurtful sorrow, knowing what I have missed out on over the past 41 years. I want to thank you for telling me that you do not harbor any bitterness or anger towards me. Thank you from the bottom of my heart for taking the time to say that to me.

From looking at your pictures and enjoying again and again reading your eloquent letter, I seem to have some sense of peace knowing that your adoptive parents raised you with much love and encouragement. I would like to say "thank you" to both of them for the tremendous job they did! You look to be happy and you have a wonderful looking family. Your daughter is stunning. I am looking forward to our reunion and can hardly wait to meet you in person along with Jacquelyn, your husband Hank, and of course your adoptive mother. I was sorry to hear of the loss of your adoptive father. That must have been a very devastating loss for you. I myself am a widow having lost my husband to adult onset leukemia 3 years ago. We never had any children together; however, I do have 3 adult step children with families of their own.

I want you to know that I have given your address to your biological father. He will be writing you his own letter, but he has told me that he is married and has 2 adult sons; your half brothers. Although Doug has been somewhat receptive to discussing with me what we were going to do if this day ever arrived, his wife has not been.

I have enclosed a couple of pictures of myself and Doug. My family says that you look just like me. As far as my family is concerned, you have 2 aunts (one in N.Y. and one in CT.) and one Uncle residing in MD, along with many cousins. I have also included a picture of your relatives. Your grandmother is still alive, however, your grandfather passed away 7 years ago.

I don't know what information you were given about me. I too am musically inclined, having played the flute and piccolo, performing in my high school marching band and orchestra. In fact, I played a flute solo at graduation. I was also fortunate enough to perform numerous solos, sang alto with the All-State choir and had the opportunity to practice with the Norwalk Symphony Orchestra in CT. After graduating from high school with honors, belonging to the National Honor Society, and after your birth, I was fortunate enough to attend college, receiving an associate's degree in Business. I am not very artistic, but love interior decorating, having just completed redoing my home. My friends and family tell me I am a great cook and have made an award-winning clam chowder. I own my home and hopefully you and your family can come to NY and see my home in the very near future.

I am very fortunate having enjoyed a long career with Bristol-Myers Squibb Company spanning 27 years. Although I find myself busier being retired than when I was working, it gives me the freedom to pack up and go whenever I want. I am only four hours away from you and can be there to meet with you and your family when you decide the time is appropriate. I am looking forward to meeting you (the sooner the better) so please feel free to call at any time. Again, thank you for letting me into your life.

Your Biological-Mom,
Sharon

Sharon and I reunited in October 2007 at her home in N.Y. My family walked through the door and into her kitchen surrounded by several women. I recognized Sharon right away, approached her and gave her a hug. We had a heart-warming day together, sharing pictures and talking about family. It wasn't until Sharon visited our family in CT a few months later, that I heard her story. What a remarkable day we had at a local restaurant as she shared the details of her life and what lead to her decision to give me up for adoption.

Recently, I asked Sharon if she had any regrets. She responded...

"In the beginning, I truly felt I made the wrong decision giving you up for adoption. My family insisted that it was impossible for me to raise you and I needed to think about what life would be like. I lived with this regret for 41 years, but now that I have met you, I know I made the right decision. I look at you and you are the gift that keeps on giving. Giving you away for adoption became a gift for a woman who couldn't have children. Being united 41 years later, I can see the gift you are to the world; your teaching, kindness, making a difference in the lives of others, a pastor's wife, and a beautiful mother. Your mother Sally gave me a gift too; a gift of acceptance and love by taking care of my only child and supporting this opportunity to finally meet you."

Our conversation continued as I asked if she had any advice for a young woman deciding whether to choose life or death for their baby. Sharon quickly mentioned...

"Don't take the life of your baby...choose life! You will never know what you are taking away from the world if you choose death. If I aborted my daughter, I wouldn't know about God or a chance to do for others. Since I met my daughter, I found my husband Fred, I am free from guilt, I witnessed the gift she is to other's lives because I chose life for her, and I could meet the four most wonderful people in the world; Kim, Hank, Jacquelyn, and Sally. When I met Sally, I was so thankful. I felt proud that she would come to my home and care enough to meet me, the one who gave my daughter away. Because I chose life, I gave a gift to the world, you Kim, and another gift to your adoptive parents when they couldn't have any children of their own. I would tell any girl facing this heart-wrenching decision to choose life and not death."

Sharon, I noticed you mentioned that you know God now. Did you believe in God all these years?

"I went to church when I was younger, but I didn't think God could love me for conceiving you and then giving you away for adoption. I lived with this guilt for

> *41 years, but talking with and meeting you has helped me to realize there is a*
> *God who has been watching over me all along and He used my husband Fred*
> *and your letter to also show me His love and forgiveness. "*

Sharon may not have realized at the time, but it is amazing that she was willing to make the tough sacrifices to accomplish what was right; to save my life. It wasn't easy, nor was it comfortable. She experienced pain, fear and abandonment from her mother and friends, and she did it anyway. "The hardship of gaining approval from our earthly families contrasts the joy of adoption by God. You see, we often succumb to negative thoughts and frustrations with our broken families, but those adopted by God enjoy all the liberties and privileges of being in God's family. How many of us have had mothers or fathers leave, ridicule and offend us?" NLT Although her mother or even my birth father offended her, Sharon realized over time that forgiving an offender doesn't deny the pain or cost; it acknowledges it and releases it. It took many years for Sharon to resolve in her heart the importance of forgiveness of herself and others, even though offenses and sins hurt. But we need to remember that Jesus died on the cross and He didn't take it lightly for us either and nor should we. He gave His life so we may have life, so who are we to take it away? To think if I was aborted, I would not be writing this story. If you were aborted, you wouldn't be reading my story, now would you? I am so grateful Sharon chose life and not death.

> *Galatians 1:15*
> *But even before I was born, God chose me and called me by His mar-*
> *velous grace.NLT*

I can't help but think how her body and heart were broken at such a young age, but Sharon is reminded today that God was always there for her and His love for her never changed. He loved Sharon despite her decisions and He loves you too. Although Sharon hated herself for years, as I am sure some of you may have felt when you were faced with difficult decisions; please remember that there is a God who loves you, knows your pain and cares deeply about the circumstances you are in. You are here for His purpose and glory. It's not about what "you" did, but rather, what was done for "you". When you realize this, your life will change. But the only way it will truly change is if you choose 'life' and life in Him!

God wants to free you from your guilt and shame, so He lovingly sent His Only Son to the cross to be crucified for you and me because nobody else could do it. Our impending death awaited us all until Jesus died in our place to give us life. If you believe Jesus died for you and you ask Him into your heart and for His forgiveness of your sins, you are adopted into the Kingdom of Heaven and you will have life eternally with Him. He wants you to choose life and to know that your life matters to Him. Will you choose life today?

Our parents may die or even reject us or turn against us, but Christians can never be orphans. I was immediately freed in my spirit when I realized that I will never be alone if I accept the Lord in my heart and more importantly, be adopted into the Kingdom of Heaven. My identity is in Him, not my earthly parents. For some it seems that life on earth is simply one amazing accident. Life is not an accident; you are not an accident. Your life is a gift from God and that's all that matters.

So, what will it be? Everybody will be faced with this question if they are on this Earth. What will you do with Jesus? Will you accept Him and be adopted into the Kingdom of Heaven despite who has wronged you or will you deny Him? Will you choose life or death? God has a gift for you that will keep on giving; will you accept it?

> *"If Jesus died for you, you must live for Him. Give your life to Jesus and you will live forever." Author Unknown*

My first Mother's Day letter to Sharon-
May 8, 2008... my Birthday!!

Dear Sharon,

Happy Mother's Day! It is amazing to think we can celebrate 42 years later.

Sharon, I thank you for sharing your story with me. I can only imagine how painful and difficult it must have been to relive the past and I truly appreciate the time you spent to help me understand what happened.

There have been various emotions and I can only believe God will wash away our tears of reconciliation; bringing us to a place where we are comfortable and more open with one another.

Time may have appeared against us causing us to ask why? When? How could this happen? But what I do know is that you don't have to worry another day Sharon. This opportunity is a gift you can receive openly. All I desire is to relish in the time ahead and know that you are never alone. For all those times you were in pain, turmoil, felt confused, worthless, fearful or even hopeless...there is a God who loved you all along and He will continue to fill that void through the rest of your journey.

God made me and the delicate inner parts of my body. He knit me together in your womb and I thank Him for making me so wonderfully and complexly. God's workmanship is marvelous and I know this now. He watched me as I was formed in utter seclusion and He knew you while you suffered with giving life as well as the death of giving me away, out of sight for 42 years. He wove me together in the dark of your womb and saw me before I was born. I believe with all my faith and hope that God saw me before I was born and every moment was laid out before a single day has passed.

Sharon, your decision to choose life on May 8, 1966 changed my life forever! Thank you for making such a heroic decision. When the world was speaking louder than even the still soft whisper of God, your spirit remained strong. God was there that day when you cried out in pain, felt helpless, and scared. He knew your pain because He walked that journey 2000 years ago. And for the first time, having heard your story, I began to realize God loved me enough that He chose me to be born in exchange for the pain and suffering you endured. And through that suffering, you still chose life for me. Moreover, God allowed me to be placed with a family safely and He journeyed with me all along, but little did you know that He walked with you all along as well.

God chose death so you and I could have life eternally... you chose adoption so I could have life beyond your circumstances. Thank you, Sharon! I am so glad

God is bigger than all our circumstances. It is so refreshing for me to look back and be reminded of all the lives God has touched through me, especially with my teaching. I have become a gift that keeps on giving.

May this Mother's Day have a sweet impression upon your heart and the hurtful memories be washed away by God's ebb and flow of mercy and grace. I pray His light shines upon you and His embrace comfort you. Believe God's enduring promises and always realize that you are uniquely and wonderfully created; you are my birth mother.

Happy Mother's Day!
Love,

Kim

Week 30/ Day 30: The Gift that Keeps on Giving

Have you or do you know someone who has given up something precious and had to live with the guilt/regret? Describe the situation.

_____

_____

_____

_____

How are you or this person dealing with the guilt or shame?

_____

_____

_____

_____

Is it working? Why? If it is not working, what could you or they do differently?

_____

_____

_____

_____

How has God helped you through this trial? And if you haven't allowed the Lord to guide you, why haven't you?

_____

_____

_____

_____

Whether we have felt guilty for a decision or felt rejected by another, we are never alone. God loves us all despite our failures. You were created in your mother's womb and God is the source of our identity. Explain how <u>you</u> know this and how this can change the way you look at your life?

_____

_____

_____

_____

What life lesson have you learned through this story?

_____

_____

_____

_____

_____

_____

_____

_____

_____

_____

_____

_____

_____

_____

Life in the Balance

How do you balance your life every day in school or motherhood, work, marriage, or even in your relationships? How do we study, volunteer, meet new neighbors, shop for groceries, and plan for weekly meals? How do we find the time for household chores, projects, favorite hobbies and still have date night with our boy friend, spouse, go to our children's games and have lunch with a dear friend? How do we manage our time and our lives and still make it all work as a biblically guided woman? Is your life in the balance or not?

God's word promises we are individually and uniquely made in His image. We as women are built with a specific design and calling. He designed us to have a life in the balance according to His purpose, but often times though, life will cause us to feel as if we are breaking down if we are choosing to do the things that we aren't necessarily designed to do. If we can learn early on that God can supply all we need to live our lives in the balance, we will be less fitting to live our lives in the shadows of exhaustion.

I have had more pots than I have had burners and I have been burnt-out more times than I would like to mention. We gave countless hours to a church we were a part of for 18 years and the travel alone was time consuming because we did not live in the same town. My husband was a full-time minister on staff and between the hours, evening commitments, my master's program, his seminary classes, and our daughter attending a school outside our community as well, we found ourselves traveling so much, we needed a change of clothes, a place to take a nap, and a fast food restaurant during every transition. Coupled with me teaching full-time and keeping up with serving at church, taking classes and supporting my husband in the ministry, I became tired very easily. Unfortunately, my father died years ago, which left my mother with barely enough to live, so we offered to care for my mom and provide her with a home as well. We tried to keep up with relationships and this was a challenge on all levels. The ministry is all about people and many times we were 'peopled out'. Between me writing weekly lesson plans, creating projects and always fighting traffic to get home and care for the family, house chores and be there for my mother, we tried to steal time from other areas so we could rest, regroup and head off to the next event. The relationships that suffered in our lives were our family and friends. Sadly, we missed many events over the years due to church commitments, busyness, and distance. We knew then our lives were not in a balance, but everything 'else' seemed to be important at the time.

I can't tell you how many times I have taken on experiences or expectations I really wasn't equipped to manage. Many times, I have said 'yes' when I should have said 'no', for the sake of what others may think or say? I have wrongly prioritized things in my life because I thought I was the only one to get the job done, I didn't want to bother someone else, or I felt it was my only way to connect or reconnect with others. I think part of my problem was that I was so busy accomplishing goals and tasks, I missed many opportunities to listen to God and understand His purpose for me as a wife, mother, family member, teacher, and a friend. No matter how I labeled it, I have experienced this life style and have confused this simulated balance with God's design for my life. Has my life been in the balance you ask; sometimes, but not always.

When I am not living my life in a melodious balance, I feel as if I am in a game of pick- up sticks. Have you played that game too? You hold the colorful sticks upright with a firm grip and let them all scatter onto the table or floor; some landing crisscrossed or piled on top of each other.

It's just a mess. We purpose to strategically lift one stick at a time so we don't move another out of its place, else we lose points. Talk about stress. It is so difficult to figure out which stick to move. One mistake and the rest of the sticks will reposition and you never gain the points you set out to reach in the first place. Then you wait for your next turn. Of course, the one who maneuvers the best without too many mistakes wins the game. And if you are a perfectionist like me, you won't like this game very much.

As I mentioned, sometimes my life feels like a game of pick-up sticks. One day, in the middle of one of my melt-downs, my husband decided to illustrate the situation for me. He ran to the closet to retrieve a broom. Hank stood along the counter in the kitchen and said, "Now Kim, bare with me a moment. Here is a stick and let's call this teaching, this one relationships, this one publishing your book, this one meeting with a lawyer, this one meeting with the company, this one being a mother, this one being my wife, this one church, this one chores, this one grocery shopping and so on… Okay, hold onto the meeting with the lawyer. See the other sticks all over the floor? Watch me… I am going to sweep the rest under this rug. You don't see them right now. They are still there, but you don't have to focus on them right now. When your meeting with the lawyer is all set, then take out the next important stick." We laughed awhile and Hank followed up the illustration with validation which always helps. "Kim, I admit there is a lot on your plate, but you need to prioritize. Every one of the things you mentioned are all important, but you can't do it all. It's like writing a letter on behalf of a lawyer, but you aren't a lawyer. That's what lawyers get paid to do. It's the same thing with God. God is our sustainer, our provider, our help in situations like this one and you need Him to help you prioritize these things. We can't do it on our own."

> 1 Peter 5:7
> *"Give all your worries and cares to God, for He cares about you."* NLT

Hank is right! God has created us to fulfill a purpose; His purpose. He planted a purpose deep within us, but without a connection with Him, our lives will be out of balance. It's obvious that frustration has paralyzed me from accomplishing what God has planned for my life, whether it's a dream, daily tasks, or projects. They seem unattainable sometimes and I want to give it all up… and why; because I didn't prioritize. My time-table spins out of control and it feels impossible to progress because it wasn't God's timing or direction. Why is that we think the only way to survive is to do it our way? God is telling us to let go and let him lead. He warns us that our lives are out of balance, but promises He will be there to guide us… Are we listening? His perspective is unlimited, but we are limited by our fear and control. Will we ask for help?

The key to a healthy life in the balance is connecting to our Lord. Only He can nourish us when we are tired, withered and weary. Sure, we were at church all the time, but we needed to take the time to abide in Christ even more and often we were on the run being there for everybody else and not ourselves. Have you ever experienced that? Have you ever felt like all you do is give, give, give and people just take, take, and take? Instead of slowing down and spiritually refreshing ourselves, we would continue adding more projects and expectations to our lives and so goes our life right out of balance.

In order for us to thrive, we must live a life in the balance, not on a see-saw teetering back and forth. There have been many moments throughout the years that I have felt the world closing in on me and my peripheral vision skewed with the stress of 'balancing' everything. I have come to realize that some things I engaged in seemed to be more important than the 'last' and before I knew it; my sense of balance was unstable. Unfortunately, I became more and more unproductive as the days and months progressed. I tried to manage my life better, praying to God, having devotions, writing a 'to do list' or reminders on sticky notes. I even tried to delegate projects and found that the projects were not done the way I needed them to be and before I knew it, I took all those important 'things' back' and was out of balance all over again. Interestingly, the common denominator in the last few sentences I shared with you was the word 'I'. Where is God in all of this? Sometimes I just didn't ask.

> *"Lord, who knew these sticks would be so heavy. I can't pick them up on my own. Father, I need your help. I need you to sort them out and help me prioritize which one is a necessity and point me towards a more balanced way of living. Lord, I desire to make Kingdom choices and the load is too heavy for me to carry. Forgive me for thinking I can balance so many things. Forgive me for not always going to you first; for it's in You I will find my life in the balance".*

Our busyness ends up being a distraction and it is difficult to hear God when we are too tired or not available, but when I slow down and seek His plan and purpose for my life, I begin to see His priorities. When I share my deepest and more passionate concerns, I feel His presence and direction for my life and that is the beginning of a perfect balance.

> *John 19:28*
> *"Jesus knew that His mission was now finished, and to fulfill Scripture He said, "I am thirsty." NLT*

Even Jesus knew that when He had a need it was time to ask. We must do the same and surrender our Pick-Up Sticks unto Him. Let God label them, position them, pick them up, and sequence them in order of importance so that you can have a clear direction through the clouds of confusion.

> *Luke 23:46*
> *"Then Jesus shouted, "Father, I entrust My spirit into Your hands." NLT*

Are you tired of juggling everything in your life to the point of confusion and exhaustion? Jesus knew when and how to surrender and now it's your turn. Think of the various situations or projects knocking on your door. Ask God to label and prioritize your sticks. List your priorities and do one thing at a time. Create a check list for your accomplished goals and thank God for every single one of them. Surrender your circumstances unto the Lord and watch what happens to your life. Something tells me you're going to love it!

Week 31/ Day 31: Life in the Balance

Busyness can become a distraction. Write about a time your life was out of balance and you felt as if you were breaking down.

_____

_____

_____

What steps did you take to adjust your life and keep your balance?

_____

_____

_____

How was God a part of this process and if He wasn't, why not?

_____

_____

_____

What is the key to a healthy life in the balance? Why?

If you can label your projects right now, what are they? List them by priority by asking the Lord to guide you with the appropriate expectations. Try 3-4 on a list at a time, so as not to get too overwhelmed. Create a check list for your accomplished goals and thank God for every single one of them. Surrender your circumstances, projects and concerns unto Him and watch what happens to your life.

My Priority List	Accomplished	Date
1. Give my list to the Lord	X	__/__/__
2._____		
3._____		
4._____		

What life lesson have you learned through this story?

_____

_____

_____

_____

_____

_____

_____

_____

_____

_____

_____

_____

_____

_____

_____

_____

_____

_____

_____

_____

_____

Creative Courage

I thank God daily for giving me creative opportunities to think outside the box, even in times of testing- when God may seem distant. Creativity is part of what lies within me. It takes courage for me to think creatively and journey outside the "normal standards". And it takes courage to resist the pressures of those who demand I do things a certain way. It takes courage to do what is right and sometimes *creative courage* to stand alone when it is not the most popular choice. How many times have you wanted to try something new, but feared what others may think or say? Mom, how many times have you discouraged your daughter from her creative thinking? Girls, how many times have you unintentionally journeyed away from the world's normal expectations? How many of us have refused to walk in faith, dared to dream or wasn't willing to have the courage to experience the *unexpected* because we could not see it?

You need to remember that God has created you uniquely to change your circumstances and influence those around you. This is where courage can drive your faith. It is the willingness to move forward and creatively find ways to get there, without really knowing how to reach the outcome.

This reminds me of a time at Kids Camp when the counselors wanted to teach a lesson about faith. They created an obstacle course in the woods. The objective was to work alongside another person to guide the child who was blind-folded through the obstacle course, relying on just their *voice*. When you walked the course, another person hit a tin can to cause a distraction. What a creative lesson. The youth experienced so many emotions. Some were bold, some were timid, others were confident, some fell, some quit and others watched the experience from the side-lines. The tears were emotive as a few of the youth reflected on how scary it was not being able to see their 'guide' and having to rely on someone else giving directions. I heard one person share how they couldn't believe that they were guided by a person they despised. I was so touched by the *creativity* and uniqueness that went into such an incredible life lesson that day; a lesson that will undoubtedly impact their lives for a very long time.

> Hebrews 11:13
> "... *They did not receive what was promised, but they saw it all from a distance and welcomed It*" ...NLT

Honestly, I felt it had to take courage to not only think of this lesson, but to participate when you feel defenseless without distinct sight or being able to hear clearly. Isn't that just like life? How many times have we felt defenseless, scared, fearful, distracted, or even faithless? How many of us have refused to be courageous and move ahead through our circumstances? "Faith is like a rope; God lowers it down to His people, enabling us to firmly grasp it and hold on until we join Him in heaven. Our grip on faith may loosen, but God's grip on us will not." NLT

> Act 3:11
> "*Peter took the lame man by the right hand and helped him up. And as he did, the man's feet and ankles were instantly healed and strengthened.*" NKJV

In Acts chapter 3, Peter and John were going to the temple. They entered the gate called Beautiful. This was a favored entrance and many people passed through this gate to worship. A lame man creatively positioned himself where he would be seen by most people because he knew it was praiseworthy in the Jewish religion to give to beggars. Peter and John entered the gate and did not give the lame man money. Paul gave him something healthier... you guessed it; the use of his new legs! The lame man stood that day and began to jump and praise God for his healing. This defenseless man thought he was creative, but God creatively granted him a healing that undoubtedly surpassed this man's understanding. What courage it took to sit there day after day, waiting for help. What courage it took to stand up, walk, and leap for joy. And think of the courage it took for Peter to grab a hold of the lame man's hand, expecting a miracle. This experience became a teachable moment for an audience of onlookers that day who took walking for granted, yet Peter's courage had astounding results.

> Esther 3:2
> "All the king's officials would bow down before Haman to show him respect whenever he passed by, for so the king had commanded. But Mordecai refused to bow down or show him respect." NLT

In the story of Esther, Mordecai and his family were deported to the Babylonian empire. At one time, he overheard the plans to assassinate Ahasuerus, reported the plot, and saved the king's life. Mordecai's providential life was more than coincidental. God was clearly in the details and filled Mordecai with courage that definitively changed an unpredictable event. As the story unfolds, Mordecai adopted a young cousin named Esther. He took care of her and continued to advise Esther even when she was drafted into Ahasuerus's harem and chosen to be Queen. Shortly after, Mordecai found himself in conflict with Hamen, second in command. Modecai refused to worship the king's representative and soon Hamen plotted to kill all the Jews, including Mordecai. Mordecai had the courage to stand alone and refuse to bow to the king. But it took an amazing act of God who creatively wove into action the plot that would quickly bring Hamen down, expose him for who he really was and eventually save Mordecai's life, Queen Esther, and all the Jews.

In Esther's case, an opportunity slowly unfolded that put her in a place of influence that ultimately helped her people. God revealed a creative plan to Esther, who had the courage to step out in faith even though her life was at risk. "She recognized why God promoted her and used her influence accordingly. When Esther discovered the plot against her people, she knew the right thing to do: creatively and courageously tell the king and ask for his intervention. But asking an ancient Near Eastern king for favors was risky- even for a queen." *NLT*

God doesn't change, but we do. We may feel as if we have no power to effect change, but He is creatively working out our circumstances to complete His plan for our lives. Do you have the courage to step out in faith? He uses our circumstances to creatively weave a pattern of godliness into our lives. Remember, the opportunities we have are more important than the ones we wish we had. It's time to have creative courage and step out in faith... So, what is holding *you* back?

God loves creativity. He didn't let anything get in His way when he created the World. He added such miraculous beauty and intrigue for you and me to be inspired. When was the last time you appreciated the creativity of your existence? You are uniquely and creatively designed, inside and out. *It's time to embrace your personal creativity and take courage.* It's time to share with one another the faith walk you will embark on and no matter what the result, believe the journey will be worth it. You must believe that no matter what the cost, no matter what obstacles or distractions are in your way, you need to take your eyes off your circumstances and creatively think about the impact you can have on those around you. You must believe that unexpected creative changes can lead to many brilliant and godly opportunities. So, take hold of courage and be creative.

You have a purpose and your life can radiate the light that can make a difference in the world around you; your family, neighborhood, workplace, projects and relationships. God uses the weak and the powerless today to change the world. All He requires is a willing heart and obedience. If you place yourself in His hands, He can creatively use you in ways you may never expect. Your life is like a work of art, so be creative and have courage to reshape your circumstances. That's when others will begin to see the real you. It's time to unleash the courageous creativity within you. What will you do to creatively change your life?

Week 32/ Day 32: Creative Courage

How many times have you wanted to try something new, but feared what others may think or say? Describe an experience.

_____

_____

_____

How did you choose to deal with it?

Have you ever refused or feared walking in faith? Why? Tell about this time.

_____

_____

_____

What would it take to creatively change your world or mind-set? If you were to pray to God about your passion, what would it sound like?

_____

_____

_____

It's time to have courage and step out in faith; so, what is holding you back and why? If nothing is holding you back, what action steps can you take to make this a reality?

_____

_____

_____

What life lesson have you learned through this story?

_____

_____

Second Chances

The 2010 Tournament of Roses Parade in Pasadena, California reflected the most stunning floral displays. The puppetry, dances, and music were vibrant and ushered in such a sense of cultural expression. Onlookers eagerly waited with each passing exhibit welcoming the throngs of crowds with New Year resolutions and hopeful memories of days' past. Suddenly, the musical interludes changed and so did the tone of the crowds when an exquisite 'Donate Life' float captivated the multitudes responding with a standing ovation. Tears fell from my eyes as the announcer spoke of 'second chances' and the life- giving miracle of organ donors. With each passing side of the float, a precious face was carved out of unique floral arrangements representing individuals who gave their organs to save the lives of others. The donor recipients were sitting along the edges of the float, smiling with appreciation, grateful for a second chance at life.

> *John 15:13*
> *"There is no greater love than to lay down one's life for one's friends." NLT*

The Lord delivered a heart-felt message to Brad Barrows on February 16, 1998. Brad remembers this moment. "I remember checking the time… it was approximately 11:15p.m. I was praying and asking the Lord how I could be *loving* in a profound way that would change someone's life. I told the Lord I would donate a kidney to anyone He would bring. I trusted Him that He would know who needed it." Brad explained (Pentecostal Evangel; January 24, 1999).

Brad wasn't your typical organ donor. He didn't have a family member or close friend who needed a kidney. Clearly, the message that Brad received that night from the Lord was for him to give his kidney to a total stranger. What is even more amazing about this story is that my dear friend is physically blind, yet his spiritual 'sight' surpasses what many of us can ever imagine seeing with our own eyes.

> *1 Corinthians 13:7*
> *"Love never gives up, never loses faith, is always hopeful, and endures through*
> *every circumstance." NLT*

Brad is one of those individuals who will lead his life with a heart after God and not his own sight. His Godly insight brings him peace and confidence when others are in need and Jose, a 12 -year old from Connecticut would finally sense that peace and hope too; when at last he came face to face with a loving stranger. He would no longer struggle with renal failure or several daily hours on dialysis in his bedroom because on July 16, 1998 Jose received a life-saving kidney by a 37- year old blind stranger; now called a friend.

I'll never forget the photograph of Jose waving to Brad as he was being wheeled into surgery. Jose finally met Brad and could thank the man who would donate a kidney to save his life. And although Brad couldn't see Jose or him waving that day, Brad knew in his heart that God would give him a heavenly glimpse of his new friend when the time was right. Remarkably though, Brad's blood and tissue was an incredible match for Jose and presently, gave him a second chance at life.

Upon watching the act of love from a stranger, Jose's mother, Sandra, rededicated her life to the God about the time of surgery. Praise the Lord! It reminds me of how powerful an act of kindness and love like this can be when it penetrates and spills over into the lives of others. How kind it is when we lay our lives down for another and trust God for the rest.

Jesus Christ is the perfect example of love and kindness. Jesus loved the Father and His people with perfect holy affection. He selflessly laid down His life for all of us and He asked the Father to forgive all those who persecuted Him. He was wounded for all our transgressions. He spilled His blood upon the cross and took the sins of the world upon himself so we may live. This is the utmost display of kindness and it is His love for us all that allows us to love and show kindness to others, just as Brad did for Jose.

I remember watching the Chef Jeff Project on the Food Network station. He spent years in prison and learned to be a fabulous cook while he worked out his sentence. When he reentered society, he decided to give young adults with similar addictions and challenges a second chance at life. He innovatively had a hand in a vision that the Food Network supported and gave these young people the leadership, mentorship, encouragement, coaching, inspiration, tools, management, love, and kindness to become the best that they can be in the culinary arts.

Every one of the participants on his show had a chance to display leadership, face daily challenges and adversity while they persevered through commitment and hard work. He showed that he valued each of them and his act of kindness began to melt away their fear and anxiety of addictions that have been tempting them all along. They each had an equal opportunity to try something new to better themselves and why; because Chef Jeff gave them a second chance. He asked himself how he could make a difference in others lives, as well as do whatever it takes to make other's dreams a reality. He valued them, loved them, and encouraged excellence in everything they did. It wasn't about whether the show would be a success or popular to thousands of viewers; in my opinion, it was all about investing in people and adding value to their lives so that they, too, can make a difference in the world around them. Finally, someone cared enough to take the time to invest in their lives and now they can't wait to do the same thing through their acts of random kindness towards others. Now that's what I call a second chance.

> Romans 12:8
> "If your gift is to encourage others, be encouraging. If it is giving, give generously.
> If God has given you leadership ability, take the responsibility seriously. And if
> you have a gift for showing kindness to others, do it gladly." NLT

I was loading my car with clothes I had hoped to donate at a local consignment shop when a red van pulled up beside me. A woman got out of the van, puzzled, yet half smiling and commented as to why I was putting clothes back into my car when it should be the other way around. I laughed half-heartedly, telling her that they thought the clothes were outdated. Instantly, she became frustrated, assuming the same thing would happen to her. "You don't understand; my daughter has cancer and doesn't wear these clothes anymore and I hoped to get as much money possible for these clothes to go back into our cancer fund. We are starting to sell everything so we can raise enough money to afford more treatments". I gently put my hand on her shoulder and reassured her that I would be praying for her family and daughter. As I got to know this woman who undoubtedly needed someone to share her pain with, I shared the Lord and His enduring love for her and I prayed for her in the parking lot as well. I reached into my car and pulled out all the clothes and gave them to her to sell at a yard sale, which seemed to be the next thing on her "to do list' and she was so happy. "You are so kind to me. How could

I ever repay you?" I carefully put her concerns at ease and tried to remind this lovely woman that there is no need to do anything for me, but believe in a God who cares and loves her and wants to help her through this tragedy. Immediately, she reached for her wrist and took off her bracelet. "Here, I want you to have this bracelet. The clasp comes apart at times, but the words are meaningful and perfect for you. I held the bracelet and the charms said love, hope, peace, and joy. I may not remember this stranger's name now, but her act of kindness towards me will be remembered for a life-time.

"Lord, I was not expecting to be on the receiving end of such kindness. This woman's generosity during her pain was so precious. Please bless her wherever she is today. Lord, please bring a healing to her daughter and the entire family. Please give them all a second chance in your name Jesus. Amen!"

> *"Kindness has a way of inviting honesty."*
> Max Lucado

My daughter and I were waiting outside the front entrance of the grocery store as my husband ran in to get a few quick items. Jacquelyn and I turned up the radio and started singing and having a blast. While we were singing, I noticed a very old man trying to hold back a grocery cart along the walk- way as he struggled to open his umbrella. It was pouring immensely and as this man continued to struggle, nobody stopped to help him. Various people hurried by this man not to give him a second look. Our hearts sank as Jacquelyn quickly got out of the car and ran over to the gentleman. Tears streamed down my face as I watched my daughter show tremendous kindness and gentleness towards this stranger. I wiped away my tears and noticed the umbrella up in the air while the old man nuzzled underneath closely to Jacquelyn with a precious smile on his face. "You are so kind and there should be more people like you in this world," he delightfully remarked. Another woman stopped Jacquelyn on her way back to the car and mentioned that was the nicest act of kindness she has seen in a long time, especially in the pouring rain. Jacquelyn got back in the car and started to cry. "Oh mommy, he was so sweet and nobody stopped to help him." We both talked about how kindness is love in action and love is kindness in action and when we do what is nice and good for others, God manages to bless us in the process.

Jacquelyn's act of kindness that rainy day allowed an old gentleman a second chance at believing that there are still kind people in our world. Love, self-sacrifice and kindness are the essence of life and without it our world is hurting and individuals are dying. We need to remember that our gentleness and compassion can change the world, one person, and one situation at a time.

When was the last time you served someone else other than yourself? How did it make you feel? Can you recall a time you were given a second chance? How did it make a difference in your life? You may not be called to donate a kidney or mentor addicts. You may not be called to donate clothes to strangers or help the elderly. If you want to influence others around you and touch their lives, you must love God, serve others, and give from your heart expecting nothing in return.

Jesus gave you and me a second chance, now it's our turn to accept His gift of Life and give back to others. What will you do to make a difference in someone's life?

Week 33 / Day 33: Second Chances

When was the last time you served someone other than yourself? Write about this moment.

_____

_____

_____

How did this experience change you or make you feel? Why?

_____

_____

_____

Can you recall a time you or someone else was given a second chance? Explain.

_____

_____

_____

Did it make a difference in your life? How?

_____

_____

_____

Remember, Jesus gave us a second chance; now it's our turn to accept His gift of life and give back to others.

We must:
1. Love God
2. Find the greatest need in others
3. Serve them
4. Give from our hearts expecting nothing in return

Think about how you influence others. What can you do to make a difference in their lives?

_____

_____

_____

_____

What life lesson have you learned through this story?

_____

_____

_____

_____

> *"Ask for forgiveness and God will give second chances in His timing."*
> *Author Unknown*

> *"If you have a gift for showing kindness to others, do it gladly."* NLT

_____

_____

_____

_____

_____

_____

_____

_____

_____

_____

On the Heels of Hatred

On January 8, 2011, tragedy consumed the airwaves as hatred filled the heart of a twenty -two-year-old that intentionally shot several people and killed six unsuspecting individuals. "Congresswoman Gabrielle Giffords, 40, whom the authorities called the target of the attack, was in critical condition Sunday morning at the University Medical Center in Tucson, where she was greeted by a team of neurosurgeons." Dr. Peter Rhee, medical director of the hospital's Trauma and Critical Care Unit said Saturday that she had been shot once in the head and straight through her brain and out the other side." *The New York Times; January 8, 2011* Every news station continued reporting their perspective of this tragic incident and many questions remained; will she survive? Where was she and who did this unspeakable act?

"I saw the Congresswoman talking to two people and then this man suddenly came up and shot her in the head and then shot other people," said Dr. Steven Ragle, a witness to the shootings. Every news station revealed various photographs and video footage capturing the calamity, heroes, tears, survivors and critically injured people as our Nation stood in disbelief. Apparently, Gabrielle was holding a town meeting to answer questions and concerns of her neighbors. She was quoted as, "doing what she always enjoyed." Even President Obama was quoted saying," Gabby is an extraordinary public servant." But the same question still lingers in our minds; how can something like this happen?

Rabbi Stephanie Aaron articulated that the Congresswoman never expressed concerns about her safety. "No fear. I've only seen the bravest possible, most intelligent young congresswoman. It's one of those "things" seemingly coming out of nowhere."

From blogs, to YouTube; news media to Facebook, it appeared that many people were trying to get on the 'cutting edge' of the story. What appeared to be a normal morning for Giffords and the others, turned into tragedy without warning; and still, many questions remained; what is the background of this person and could this have been prevented?

According to the *New York Times; January 8, 2011*, "The attacker became increasingly erratic in recent months, so much that others around him began to worry (sign number 1). He acted oddly during classes causing unease among other students (sign number 2). Although there was evidence and various reports suggesting his increasing alienation from society, confusion, anger, as well as foreboding his life could soon end (sign number 3); others characterized Jared as a troubled man; emotionally underdeveloped and quite reclusive (sign number 4)." Unfortunately, there appeared to be NO explicit threat of violence. Yet, more questions exist; have these concerns been reported? With this much evidence, could something have been done to prevent such a heinous act? Why does something so tragic have to happen for the 'authorities' to 'wake-up' and finally realize that there were signs all along and something could have been done? Why is it that unless it is a literal detailed threat as to 'how' it will occur, we disassociate or pretend it's no big deal? Whether it is murder, sexual assault, robbery and more; the common rhetoric is, 'There is no evident sign of a literal threat, therefore, there is nothing we can do.'

On the heels of hatred since this tragic weekend, the very same day I received a heart-wrenching message on Facebook. Thankfully it was not posted on my home page. First, let me start by saying; my entire family can affirm that I'm not the best when it comes to being updated on technology. The running joke when I experience technological difficulties is the response to my request for help; "Did you turn the computer on Kim?" That may sound familiar to some of you too, but in lieu of this running joke, I did turn the computer on January 10, 2011 with no problem and what I read was no joking matter. Immediately, I noticed that Facebook sent me an email stating that there was a message for me from a person named Michael. The name was familiar and I clicked on the message to reveal who he was. To my surprise, it was a message from one of my former students titled: Remember Me? At first I remembered the name, but couldn't place his age. I began to read the message and I froze. My jaw dropped and I believe my heart stopped beating for a moment as well. The entire message was filled with profanity and anger. He proceeded to tell me that I was the teacher that sent him to the office in 2nd grade for saying "shoot" and this has scarred him for life. He said that he hears about how great a teacher I am, but it's time the whole nation knows the truth. He stated he knows that I am really a horrible teacher and he has been waiting for years to tell me this. He also added that the music I played was awful and the only good thing I ever did for him was pay for his breakfast when he didn't have money. Every other word was profanity and he described what I could do to myself in a horrific way. I was completely devastated. I have never experienced anything like this. What was I to do? Then I asked God the very question I have learned not to ask; "Lord, why me? What have I done to deserve this?"

I felt so violated and harassed. Can he get away with this? How old is he? How dare he do this? How did he leave me a message? My mind was in a whirlwind and finally I had to tell my husband. "Calm down Kim! We will get to the bottom of it; one thing at a time", Hank responded. We contacted Facebook to report the vile message and have him blocked. We checked my settings and realized we forgot to check the message box which meant anybody could leave a message. We fixed the immediate problem, but unfortunately, we needed to resolve the major issue and decide who to report to next.

I reported the incident to my school principal and she made the necessary contacts to find out the appropriate protocol. The local Police Resource Officer stated that they would keep this information, and although I felt threatened and scared, it wasn't a literal threat, and therefore, nothing can be done. Thereafter, the next best thing was to locate Michael's school records. We could place him in his twenties. Why, after all these years, would he be contacting me like this? It's out of nowhere. It just doesn't make sense!

I read the files and interestingly his parents wrote a letter stating that he had the best year and hoped that his third- grade experience would be the same. I read my comments and noticed that he had difficulty with authority, frequently used profanity, and had challenges with socialization. He seemed to progress throughout the year and I know for sure I would never have sent him to the office if he used the word "shoot" in the manner he referred to.

> "Lord, why would he single me out after all these years? I am scared Lord. Why now? This doesn't make sense. I wouldn't send a child to the office for saying that word, unless he said he was going to "shoot" someone. How can anybody feel this way and say such a thing after all these years? His words were filled with hatred and anger. Lord, please help me pray for him. On the heels of what happened with Gabrielle Giffords this weekend, the timing couldn't be worse. What if he is after me? What if he wants to attack me? He was so vile and expressed such animosity. Lord, please protect me."

Why is it that I feel his rights are protected and mine aren't? The resource officer stated that it is *freedom of speech*. "He didn't actually say he was going to kill you, even if you feel threatened; it's not a real threat. If he threatens you, then we can do something about it. "The principal also conveyed to me that the High School Principal wanted to reassure me that he gets hundreds of letters like this and not to worry. "Tell her that's what kids do."

'That's what kids do' and 'freedom of speech'; are you kidding me? What is wrong with this world? There are no appropriate consequences anymore and sadly, a moral compass is non-existent. With freedom comes responsibility and it is not being reinforced. To this day, I would like to contact Michael's parents, but to hold him accountable for what? Most likely nothing would be done or even worse, perhaps it could have angered him more.

> *True Freedom*
> *Is not in having your own way, but in yielding to God's way.–Unknown*

As for Giffords and the other victims, their attacker had all of what 'freedom of speech' had to offer and look what it did. Per a recent quote in *The New York Times,* it was mentioned that "the rambling, disconnected writings, and videos on the internet are consistent with the delusions produced by a psychotic illness like schizophrenia, which develops often in the teens or twenties". Again, Giffords' attacker wasn't stopped and he shot and killed people for his cause. Michael is the same age...It's just wrong!

People like Michael and Jared can be called all kinds of names for their behavior; wicked, vile, despicable, a disgrace or evil; but we need to be reminded that vengeance is not ours. These words will not bring back the lives of those victims, nor will it help the pain, distrust and anger go away. Trust me, I wanted to yell at Michael and I wanted to yell at Jared for what he did to those people and again I was reminded that sometimes horrible things happen to good people and we will not always have the answers. As hard as it is for some people, we need to remember that the same God of the Old and New Testament will ...

> *Matthew 5:45*
> *"...rain on the just and unjust." NLT*

God tells us to love our enemies and pray for those who persecute us. It's not easy sometimes, but as a believer in Christ, the Holy Spirit nudged me on January 10, 2011 and reminded me to keep Michael in prayer and so I have. I have shared my concerns with some close friends and family and I have expressed my need for others to join me in prayer. I've asked many to pray against the fear that has pressed its way into my thoughts as well as for Michael and his salvation.

> *"Lord, I don't understand why you allowed this to happen, but I do know that I am to pray for Michael. You know why he did this and more importantly, you know how I will choose to respond. So, please help me to respond out of faith and not fear. Please take away the fear that I have been feeling and help me to remember...*

> *2 Timothy 1:7*
> *"For God has not given us a spirit of fear and timidity; but of power, love, and self-discipline." NLT*

You created Michael and know his ways and the choices he has made. Lord,
please place a Christian in his path; someone to reveal the truth to set him on
a journey to salvation. I pray that your love will replace the hatred in his heart
and he would come to know You before it is too late. Thank you, Jesus!"

I prayed for Michael and asked God for His continual protection in my life. After a week of relentlessly listening to the news updates about the tragedy in Tucson, Arizona, anger still found its way into my life, so I decided to turn off the television and pray more fervently for the survivors and the injured. I decided to pray for Michael whenever his name crossed my heart and suddenly my fear turned to peace. I wasn't looking out every window wondering if Michael was there to attack me. God's peace flooded my soul and I found myself pouring my love and compassion into those around me that were struggling with their own situations. Soon thereafter, the focus was off my circumstances and placed right where it needed to be; on others. It was when I stopped reveling in the details of the news or rereading the horrible message left on Facebook, did I start to give all my heart-aches and concerns back to the Lord where it belongs and it made all the difference in the world.

I don't claim to know where you are in life and what anger or animosity has come your way, but I know this; we will all experience it at some time and we need to know how to respond when it floods into our world. Tragedies will inevitably occur. Life is full of them and we will not always have the answers, but how we choose to respond will make all the difference for you and those around you.

2 Timothy 4:18
"The Lord will deliver me from every evil attack and will bring me safely into
His heavenly kingdom." NLT

"Lord, forgive them; forgive us for our wicked ways sometimes. Help us to entrust
our circumstances and our love unto You and please give us peace that sur-
passes all our understanding. To You be all the glory. Amen!"

Are you experiencing any hatred or animosity from others or deep within your own heart? Have you asked God for forgiveness or asked the Lord to guide you and give you a direction and a heart of prayer? He wants to protect you and give you and your potential enemy peace and joy everlasting. He is faithful to keep His promises. Now it's your turn to trust Him.

Week 34/ Day 34: On the Heels of Hatred

In a society where morals and values are in question with so many people, how do you react when something tragic happens or a heinous act is performed against you or others?

_____

_____

_____

_____

Have you ever felt offended, violated, or harassed by a stranger or somebody you know? How did you deal with the situation?

_____

_____

_____

_____

Do you feel our Nation has gone too far with "freedom of speech/political correctness"? Why or why not?

_____

_____

_____

_____

Are you or have you experienced hatred or animosity from others or deep within your own heart? Have you asked God for forgiveness or asked the Lord to guide you and give you a direction and a heart of prayer?

_____

_____

_____

_____

God tells us to love our enemies and pray for those who persecute us. What have you done to follow this expectation in your own life? How has it changed you or the individual?

_____

_____

_____

_____

_____

What life lesson have you learned through this story?

_____

_____

_____

_____

_____

_____

_____

_____

_____

_____

_____

_____

_____

_____

Dare...Laugh...Dream

"Mommy, what do you think of this title: Dare...Laugh...Dream? I am going to name my tumblr page with this title. I've decided to blog to share important things on my mind, words of encouragement, and lessons I've learned. Mommy, can you read my blog?" Immediately my heart filled with joy. I couldn't believe my ears. My daughter was inspired to blog similarly to what I've been doing for the past few years. Everything I have been teaching my daughter about encouraging others, living beyond herself, journaling and sharing her life lessons with others is already coming to fruition. "Absolutely Jacquelyn; I would love to read your blog."

Below is Jacquelyn's heart poured out on: www.darelaughdream.tumblr.com Check it out! Maybe this is a way you can begin telling the world your story, one chapter at a time.

Guess How Much I Love You?
By Jacquelyn Waltmire
Age 17

Do you remember reading this book? My mom would read this to me all the time growing up and I can probably recite it word for word. I loved this book. Little Nutbrown Hare expresses his love for Big Nutbrown Hare and is reassured Big Nutbrown Hare loves him back. He wants to show Big Nutbrown Hare how much he loves him-but love as big as his is very hard to measure! I loved this book because it shows the incredible love a parent has for his or her child. No matter how far or how wide Little Nutbrown Hare's love was, Big Nutbrown Hare's love was even greater. He loved the little one as far as *his* long arms could reach and as high as *his* strong legs could hop. The more I thought about this book, looking back on reading it when I was younger, I began to think of it from a different perspective. I imagined myself as Little Nutbrown Hare, once again, but Big Nutbrown Hare was not my mom or dad, but rather my heavenly Father. HIS love is immeasurable, and HIS love reaches right up to the moon and back, and even farther!

> *Ephesians 3:17-19*
> *v.17 "The Christ will make His home in your hearts as you trust in Him. Your roots will grow down into God's love and keep you strong. v.18 And may you have the power to understand, as all God's people should, how wide, how long, how high, and how deep His love is. V. 19 May you experience the love of Christ, though it is too great to understand fully. Then you will be made complete with all the fullness of life and power that comes from God." NLT*

It's mind-blowing to think about Christ's love. I heard this saying a while back and it fits perfectly with this story—Jesus asked me how much I loved him. I stretched out my arms as long as I possibly could and said, "This much!" I said, "Jesus, how much do YOU love me?" He answered, "I love you as far as the East is from the West" as He stretched out his arms and died. We are so undeserving of Christ's love, but he cares for each one of us so much that He gave up his life so that we may live.

Philippians 2:8
"He humbled Himself in obedience to God and died a criminal's death on the cross." NLT

His resurrection assures us of His great love and how victory is ours if we live through Him. Think back on the most self-less and humble act of love anyone could ever commit and let it consume you. You will never be the same once you encounter the love of Christ and I encourage everyone reading this post to remember how much He truly loves you.

Romans 8:38-39
"And I am convinced that nothing can ever separate us from God's love. Neither death nor life, neither angels nor demons, neither our fears for today nor our worries about tomorrow- not even the powers of hell can separate us from God's love.NLT

My Passions

What is passion? The Webster dictionary says that passion is an extreme or inordinate desire. The term **passion**, and its adverb passionately, often express a very strong predilection for any pursuit, or a kind of enthusiastic fondness of anything.

Lately, I've been thinking about what my passions are. I would say some of my greatest passions include singing, building a stronger faith with God, and working with children. Three different topics, but they all create a great part of me. Singing makes me feel like…me. I can express myself through singing and it has become a huge part of my life. In 8th grade, I had a surgery on my thyroid gland because there were two tumors in my neck. The doctors warned my family and me that they were going to take longer on the surgery because one tumor was too close to my vocal cord and one mistake could cause my voice to become raspy the rest of my life or could cause me to be unable to sing. This crushed me, but, by the grace of God, the surgery was successful, my tumors were benign, and my voice was not affected. This has been one of the motivating factors of my passion for singing. I love singing and cannot imagine life without it. I want to use my voice to bless others and to show what God can do. Passion must come from the heart. There is no passion if you do not mean it with everything inside of you. There is no inordinate desire in someone who does not mean anything from the heart. I hope that doesn't sound cliché, but when I say 'from the heart' I am talking of a sincere kind of love.

This easily connects to my second passion; my faith. People may think I sound ridiculous for talking about my faith or for putting this as my top priority, but it really is a sincere love of mine. I'm focusing on something I love. Each day I've been trying to become stronger in my faith. It's a challenge at times and not always easy, but, like singing, it comes from the heart and that is what pushes me each day. I know what I want. Not in a selfish way, but rather I know what I long for to make me happy. Happiness can be found in many things, whether love, family, friends, etc., but I feel as though a relationship with God truly fulfills one's happiness and I want to constantly have that happiness.

A third passion of mine is working with children. This has been one of my desires for as long as I can remember. Whether leading small groups at a kid's program at my old church, being a counselor at a kid's camp in New Hampshire every summer, babysitting, working in the nursery, or helping in my mom's classroom, kids have always held a special place in my heart. I love them. I love their innocence, their cute smiles, their laughs, the way they look up to you, the way they view the world. I love kids because they are still learning and have so much more to learn. I want to be an example to children. I want to be the one they can look up to and begin to love. There is nothing more special than a little child giving you a big, sincere hug. I love becoming their friend. I feel as though I am leaning towards Elementary/Special Education when I begin college in the fall of 2011. I've been struggling between several careers, but always go back to working with children. This is one of the reasons I know working with children is my passion. It is a fondness and attraction that I have had for many years. I feel as though this job will be the most rewarding job and I can see myself in this career easily. I also long to use my teaching experiences overseas for mission's trips. My heart aches for the little boys and girls in third world countries who just want to be loved. My family is sponsoring a little boy, Siblal from India. He is so precious. I only get to talk with him through letters every so often, but the letters I do receive make me cry each time. He has so little, yet feels like he has so much. He has someone in America who says she loves him and is supporting him. He draws me pictures and has learned to finally write in English which helps with the letters he sends. Thinking about him, thinking about many other children like him, and thinking about children in general just lightens my heart and I get so excited knowing that I can make a difference in a child's life.

Whatever plans God has for me, I am ready. I just know, that I know, that I know that God has placed these three passions specifically in my heart. I desire to sing for the rest of my life. I want to bless people singing. I want to bless children. I want to be remembered for my faith in God and my passions. I hope to show an extreme desire for His plans for my life. What are your passions? How are you going about fulfilling them?

> Psalms 37:4
> "Delight yourself in the Lord and he will give you the desires of your heart." NLT

Live for Today- By Jacquelyn

Imagine if life were a movie. I wish there was a remote that would *pause* and *replay* the special moments, *skip* over the difficult times, *rewind* back to the amazing memories, and *fast forward* to get a sneak peak at the future. I get so anxious sometimes, wanting to know where my life will be in the next few years, which will be in my life, and different experiences I will be able to encounter. Then, at the same time, I wish I could go back in the past and enjoy moments which I know I will never forget. I'd love to feel the emotions I had or see the smiles and excitement in others around me as they had during those times. What about those bad times? Sometimes I wish when life is difficult or I struggled with certain things, that I didn't have to deal with them. I could press a simple button and my worries would disappear. Life would be 'so easy' if nothing bad ever happened, right? Well, lately I've been realizing that everything that happens, whether good or bad, happens for a reason and makes me the person I am today. It is through these struggles that I become stronger and through the great times which help me appreciate the life I am living and who I am. I am truly blessed. Let's never forget yesterday, but always live for today. We shouldn't worry about what tomorrow may bring or what it will take away because today is what is most important and it affects the rest of our lives.

> Jeremiah 29:11
> "For I know the plans I have for you," Says the Lord. "They are plans for good
> and not for disaster, to give you a future and a hope."

Romans 5:3-5
"We can rejoice, too, when we run into problems and trials, for we know that they help us develop endurance. And endurance develops strength, character, and character strengthens our confident hope of salvation. And this hope will not lead to disappointment. For we know how dearly God loves us, because He has given us the Holy Spirit to fill our hearts with His love."

Jacquelyn is 21 now and it is obvious to me that another passion is her desire to write and writing is even more powerful than ever; what an amazing legacy already. I thank the Lord with all my heart for my daughter and the passions He revealed in her heart. Every life experience enables her to learn a lesson and now she wants to share her thoughts and words of encouragement with others. She is already creating a lasting impression on people's lives. Her writing is intentional and heart-felt. You see, age doesn't matter; it's a matter of the heart.

Nothing is holding my daughter back and nothing should hold you back either. Every day there is a lesson learned and another story to tell. We need to let God's Spirit and light shine through us and be an example to others. Every pain in your life will have a purpose, every decision in life will have a consequence, and every joy in your life will have a smile; so, share them. Journal your thoughts, write those letters, record your story and leave a lasting- legacy... Others will be glad you didJ

With Sincere Love,

Kim Waltmire

Jacquelyn's Mommy <3

Week 35/ Day 35: Dare...Laugh...Dream

Are you an encourager or discourager? Why?

_____

_____

_____

Think about a story you have read or someone shared that was an inspiration to you. How did this experience touch your heart?

_____

_____

_____

Have you learned a life lesson that you know others need to hear? Write your thoughts below.

_____

_____

_____

Have you considered sharing this lesson or experience with others? How would you encourage others, so they could be influenced by your experience?

_____

_____

_____

_____

We all desire to know we matter, but will our legacy last beyond our life-time? Life's fires, trials, joys and experiences will test the quality of our endurance, but if our choices are not eternal, our legacies won't outlast us. What an amazing legacy your life can be already. Every life experience enables you to learn a lesson and can become words of encouragement and inspiration to those around you. Think of ways you can share your life with others and show them that their 'life' truly matters and it is worth sharing yours.

Ideas: recording, journaling, Facebook, twitter, blogging, publishing, public speaking, and more importantly, building a personal relationship with others J

Share your lessons and stories.
Let God's Spirit and light shine through you.
Share them because you are the only one who can!

Epilogue

My goal was to complete my stories by the time my daughter, Jacquelyn, graduated from high school. I met my goal, but didn't have the money to self-publish at the time. Moreover, there were other goals that we committed to the Lord as well. We agreed in prayer that we would be disciplined and seek God for His guidance throughout our daughter's high school years and yes, we achieved these goals as well. The following is an account of my husband's journey through these years of writing this book. But, little did I know that there were more stories to share. God is faithful!

May 10, 2011

Dear Friends and Family,
It has been just over three years since my departure from full-time ministry to pursue my dream of leading a church as its head pastor. I can remember the time in 2004 when God placed this burden upon my heart and I began my pursuit of a Master's of Divinity in professional ministries. I looked at the 93-degree requirement and thought, "this is going to take a long time and a lot of money to complete" (3 years full-time or six years part-time). So, in prayer and with the support of my family, I set my goal and enrolled in seminary. It ended up taking me five years over a seven- year span to complete. As of May 2011, I completed my last few classes for seminary and I will receive my Masters of Divinity degree before the end of the month!

At the same time, I have fulfilled all my requirements for Ordination with the Assemblies of God. This process required me to complete a selection of reading materials, tests, and interviews. In March 2011, I was unanimously selected for Ordination. This was not an easy task, especially since my departure from full-time ministry and choosing to take on a full-time job outside the church.

Many have wondered why I chose not to continue full-time ministry at our home church. I realize my quick departure might have caused some confusion, but it was not a quick decision in my heart. The desire to prepare for leadership began in 2004. My home church provided me with many great experiences in ministry which I am forever thankful for, but I needed to step out of the boat and explore this calling. Over the past three years while Jacquelyn was finishing high school, I spent the first year filling in a few churches as the interim pastor. This gave me the opportunity to improve my preaching skills. After a year of helping churches, my family decided to settle and we began attending a new home church. I accepted a non-paid position as the adult ministries pastor. Many of my responsibilities were the same as my previous church, but I was involved in a lot of the strategic planning with the senior pastor and he let me preach more than once a month. Many senior pastors do not share their pulpit. Additionally, I grew in confidence as I began to see that my experiences could help other churches. Pastor Scott was supportive, encouraging, and provided many opportunities for me to grow, which I needed before becoming a lead pastor myself. Lastly, Pastor Scott's two eldest children became close friends of Jacquelyn during these years of transition. This helped as Jacquelyn missed many of her friends, especially the children that she taught in kid's church for many years. Pastor Scott and his wife Cathy, and the rest of the family have been a blessing to us during this time. Even though it was emotionally painful, looking back we can see the benefit of this decision.

As I mentioned earlier, Kim and Jacquelyn supported this decision knowing that it may not be easy. I can truly say I could not have done this seemingly insurmountable task without their support. Jacquelyn was busy in high school and understood when I had to go and hide in my office to study. Kim would bring me coffee late in the evening. They never once asked me to stop and when I thought of stopping they encouraged me to finish. Jacquelyn graduated in June of 2011and she has become a beautiful young lady respected by all her classmates and friends. She excelled with her singing at school and in church. She was the captain of her tennis team and graduated 25 out of 500 students. Jacquelyn made the high school honor roll every semester and is attending Liberty University in the fall, 2011. We are going to miss her very much. Kim has become my best friend throughout our marriage and this transition. While supporting me, spending time with Jacquelyn, teaching full-time, and being patient with my studies, Kim has written a woman's devotional of personal stories and plans to publish it soon. She continues to teach after 21 years, winning awards and accomplishing projects beyond the four walls. I love my wife and daughter!

I can say that our entire family has grown tremendously through this experience. We did not anticipate how difficult this transition would become when we left our church family of eighteen years, but we can see why it had to be done this way. We are forever grateful for our recent church family adopting us into their family so quickly, as well as miss our first home church family tremendously. We have been blessed with two church families. Looking back, I can see that this was the best decision for my family to pursue the goals God has placed in our lives. We lost some close friends who could not understand why we left. We made some new ones along the way and during our next ministry; we hope to rekindle the friendships lost and to grow with new friends in the future.

I have learned many life lessons through these experiences; drawing closer to God through circumstances brings security; having a loving family is essential, and having a dream beyond 'you' is a must. We want to make a difference in this world not only for our family, but for others as well. My relationship with God has grown immensely. My experiences forced me to rely more on God and that is the way it should always be, but sometimes it takes stepping out of the boat and taking our steps intently towards Jesus for us to really see it. Let me tell you, however, never step out of the boat unless Jesus is calling you. Remember, *the body must never lead the head; remember, God has put leaders in your life to guide you towards Christ and His purpose for you. Jesus Christ must be the center and purpose of everything we do in life. The journey is with Jesus, bringing us to the Father by the power of His Spirit and God does this through the church. My prayer is that this story helps you to keep in the center of your life, because when you do, He blesses you abundantly, even despite our own short comings. Christ has been faithful to me and my family and He keeps us and protects us from harm. When we left our home church, God showed me that He was having me step out of the boat and walk towards Him in faith, much like the Apostle Peter. Sometimes we get too focused upon our circumstances and begin to sink, but when we look to Him, we can walk. So, if you see or hear Jesus calling you to step*

out of your comfort zone, then obey and walk and begin to see what He will do through you. May God bless you abundantly and know that I am thinking of you.

Lovingly,
Hank
Jacquelyn's Daddy

Sometimes our plans are not our own...

September 25, 2011

Dear friends and family,
Kim and I miss all of you dearly and I hope this letter finds you well today. We are doing fine, but I would like to take a moment to inform you that I have resigned last Sunday from my position as Lead Pastor.

We do not understand the times or seasons of life, but Kim and I know that we were obedient to His call and now this season, although short, has come to an end. Let us reassure you, that I was not asked to leave and the district officials publicly recognized from the pulpit the great accomplishments achieved in such a short period and that my resignation had nothing to do with any spiritual or moral failure.

Through much prayer, it became clear that it was time for me and my family to leave. We wish the best for this church and we will continue to pray for the next leader to come and continue the blessing upon them as they forge ahead. I believe the church is positioned well to be successful with the next leader. In my short tenure, we built a worship team from scratch, implemented the first steps of the vision to reach the city with the Gospel, baptized new believers, launched small group ministry in the homes surrounding the church community, and reorganized the children and youth ministries for growth.

Additionally, God allowed me to expose some areas that needed immediate attention in the church which I felt required someone else to pastor; therefore, with much prayer, discussion with my wife and with the counsel of the district officials, we chose to resign. We are leaning upon God for guidance in our next steps. We are fine. We love God, our faith in His Word has not been weakened and we look forward to finding a healthy church to grow as we seek for direction in the next stages of life. We will be looking for new jobs and will be seeking opportunities immediately. We love you all and please understand that it might take time to get back to all your phone calls and emails. The magnitude of this decision is overwhelming. Kim and I believe this was God's will, despite the short season of this transition. Sometimes God moves us to point 'B' before leading us to His perfect plan of point 'C'. I am not sure what that is, but I know that as we seek Him each day, He will guide our steps. We have learned so much about ourselves, our faith and we are stronger for it. "There is a time and a season for everything." Ecclesiastes3:1

With love in Christ,
Hank and Kim

You Were Called Here; Not to Stay Here

I t is amazing to think in four months our lives can be turned up-side down and inside out all over again. Was this our will to pastor this church or God's will? Was this God's will for us to take this position, but man got in the way? Was this temptation or a selfish-desire? Our family prayed for months about this transition in our lives. We prayed God would open and close doors and guide us in His will. What happened?

> *"Lord, please shut every door if this job is not of you. Lord, we want nothing but to be in your will only. Please Father; you know how scary this decision is to leave our jobs and sell it all to follow you into full-time ministry. If we are not the ones for this job, please shut the door. Please Jesus!"*

God answered every private prayer along the way. Doors were opening and we were walking through each one by faith, even to the point of leaving Connecticut without selling our home during a struggling economy. We believed God would sell our house even though our home in its price range wasn't selling. What did the Lord do after we transitioned to Georgia? He sold our home in the middle of a hurricane that hit our hometown, sparing us the damage that so many others sustained. He also gave us a beautiful home to live in miles from our new church, all expenses paid except utilities. Imagine having to pay for two homes during this time; there was no way we could afford it, yet God provided. The chairman of the board was in close contact with us, reassuring my husband that he was the man for the job, our living arrangements would be taken care of if we needed; we were informed the church finances were fine, they were ready for radical change with the direction of the church, and the moral failure of the previous pastor was taken care of before our arrival. I remember the Christian Education Director calling and telling us that she told the board members that the next Pastor would preach from Acts 1:8 and that is exactly what Hank did the weekend he was elected the new lead pastor. I recall three friends calling me on our way down the coast within the same hour making sure I was safe. They each prayed that God's angels would surround us. It was incredible to me that neither one of them knew each other's concern, but prayed the same prayer within the same hour. The next thing I knew, I had a sense of urgency to have my husband pull over and check the trailer that he was pulling with Jacquelyn's car strapped behind. Hank immediately noticed that the straps on the car were unlatched and the car was just resting there in speeding traffic. Thank God we pulled over to check. Thank God He prompted three people to pray for us because I was the one driving behind Hank the entire way. I can tell you countless stories that prove God is good, He is alive, and He will never leave us. He proved it over and over through answered prayers and confirmation from others when we began this journey.

When we think back for a moment, it amazes me how we were about to leave our very lucrative positions in an unstable economy, sell our house, work out details with our realtor, get my mother care for a period of time, prepare for several graduation parties, complete personal paperwork, have a yard sale with help from our friends, and preach at our present church to 'say good bye' and 'thank you' to mentors and a few new friends. In the middle of that, surprisingly, our former church of eighteen years asked us back and Hank preached an incredible sermon. We were finally given an opportunity to be hugged and loved upon before we left Connecticut; an answer to a 3 -year long prayer. Still it continued to amaze me as we packed up a 4,000- square foot home, had to watch our daughter say good bye to all her friends and teachers, and get her on a plane for a mission's trip to Brazil for three weeks with no contact with family, while we orchestrated movers and said good-bye to immediate family members and friends. Hank even conducted board meetings through Skype with the new church as its' lead pastor during this time and everybody was jazzed and yes... God took care of it all in record time. We prayed for God's will and for Him to close the doors if this is not from Him. Yet, He allowed every door to remain open and God still took care of us as we stepped in faith to follow this call into full-time ministry.

As God allowed the doors to remain open, I was reminded in Mathew 14:27; of the words... "Take courage! It is I. Do not be afraid."

> Lord, you control the storms and I need to trust you; take heart; and engage my faith...

My husband and I both talked about Peter's response to Jesus... "Lord, if it's You, tell me to come to you on the water." Peter knew the Lord's voice and he asked to be called and yes, he responded and so did we. Hank and I wanted to walk with God into unknown places and take the necessary risks required because we knew He would be with us. Was this a call from God or were we tempted by our own will to leave Connecticut and pastor a church full-time? Did man just get in the way?

I feel like our lives have been equated to one little dash between two dates; May 10, 2011- September 25, 2011. What did we live for during this short time? Will it define our lives? What are our biggest regrets, mistakes, failures and successes? Will others judge us based on this little dash of time? How will this affect our walk with God? During this tenuous time, I have come to realize we don't have control over many things and life can just be difficult. No matter how many times we have played this scenario over in our minds, only God knows the 'why' and He knows the outcome. If Jesus says, "Come" then that word is going to accomplish its intended purpose. Whatever He starts... He completes. We may fail along the way, but in the end, God succeeds. The only thing we need to know is that He is God and our lives are in His hands, whether our circumstances are easy or hard. He gives us a free will to choose how we spend our precious time and we need to live with our decisions...

The moment we arrived in this lead pastor position, the real problems began to surface. We were informed that the air conditioning was not working, finances were very low and bills mysteriously may not be paid, hurt and pain was still present due to a major cover-up since the moral failure of the previous pastor, and some board members really didn't want change after all; which meant we were not hiring more staff to move the church forward. All programs that needed to be restructured and supplied with materials were stopped in their tracks until there was a firm handle on the finances, of which were controlled by a board member behind our back. Sadly, some district officials and current leadership were involved in various deceptions and although I can't disclose any more of the unbelievable lies, family-ties and circumstances, it was evident we were misled and several people are to be blamed; I only wish they took responsibility for their purposeful actions.

This reminds me of the life of Paul in the Bible. He struggled with discouragement just like we do. He was fatigued, he faced many set-backs, he was alone, and opposed by many. God came alongside Paul to see him through his struggles in many of the same ways He comes alongside us when we are discouraged. Paul needed to recuperate and God built him up in His way and in His timing. Our departure from full time ministry was difficult and these emotions were all too familiar. Both the departure and now this experience were the hardest, loneliest, and darkest times of our lives. When you step out of ministry like this, you are <u>not</u> to have contact with leadership or congregation members. Here we go again. Stepping out of leadership from our previous church left us lonely. Now we are faced with the same abandonment, but far from home, friends and family. You can only imagine the discouragement we felt when the district officials said, "This is a fight <u>we would not</u> even let our own son fight. Resign your position and let us come in and clean up this horrible mess. We will pay your expenses to get your family back home and put this behind us all. We are sorry about what happened and we are sorry we didn't tell you the truth about the previous pastor."

Unfortunately, to this day, the district officials never followed through with their promises and more. Two Board members tried to dismantle my husband's credibility while covering up many lies. So, we resigned our position and left gracefully. Sadly though, as far as the board or some congregation members were concerned, my husband just quit and gave up... not to mention the lies told about us behind our backs. We followed the directives given by the district which left many people confused and hurt. We have been totally abandoned by leadership again. We were left with no friends or family to physically support us. For the sake of the congregation, we were not to disclose the details of this unfortunate situation and nonetheless, had nobody to talk to for months. We became jobless in an area of the country we knew nothing about, using up our savings, awaiting my mother's arrival to live with us (who has dementia) and wondering how to conjure up moving expenses to bring us to our next destination. We lacked patience as hours turned into days that turned into months, mostly in disillusionment.

"Lord, how long will this take? We need you. Lord, please hear our heart's cry. You know the truth and the lies that were said, yet we were advised not to tell the truth. Hank turned the cheek Lord. Although we feel we were led here on false-pretenses by the church, you allowed us to come here and prayers were answered for us to follow this call. We are so confused and disenchanted with the church and leadership right now. Please forgive us for that. Where are you? We can't hear your voice Lord and we are scared? Will our lives ever be the same? Will we get jobs again? How can this be? You know we have a daughter in college and we are responsible for the care of my mother. So many lives are affected. What if family doesn't step up and care for my mother longer? Will others ever know the truth? Please take away our anger and frustration Lord. We need you more than ever... Forgive us for our failures or if man messed this up. Help us Lord; please! We can't make it without you!"

We know God should be the goal in our lives because He is the reason we exist; the Maker of every good thing that comes into our lives. Unfortunately, we lost sight of what 'good' has happened during this transition because of the whirl-wind of confusion and disappointment thrown our way. We soon became motivated by the immediate desire to be blessed with peace, clarity, and money, but when it didn't come, we found ourselves asking God where He was in this mess. When life doesn't go exactly as we plan, we tend to forget that God promises to be there in the midst, despite our circumstances. We couldn't believe we were not relying on God for His timing, as we have counseled so many others to do during their time of need. There were days of silence and times we felt God had abandoned us, while feeling guilty knowing these feelings were not of God…It was apparent we were not focusing on His promises for us. We were gripped by our necessity to get a job with financial security, assured we could provide for the family. We were in survival mode, second guessing ourselves and others, quickly getting things in order, making phone calls and contacts for prospective jobs, even sometimes without praying. Immediately we begged family to keep my mother longer, crying for help because we had no business putting my mother through all this stress and thankfully a family member heard our urgency and took my mother. We waited for phone calls and email responses day after day and week after week for our urgent need for a job. The stress of another expensive relocation, uprooting the family, and fear of not making the right decision prompted many sleepless nights. We became impatient and soon thereafter, we were forced to look inward and rediscover our true need for intimacy with a God who has loved us all along and cares for our every need.

When faced with life's challenges, we have a choice to make; either we will lean into Christ or we will choose to try and manage it on our own. I'll admit, after a painful experience like this and being misled on so many levels, we were done with church politics. We decided we would be happier volunteering and getting behind a Pastor's vision and supporting the Church from a whole new perspective. There were moments we cried. There were moments we felt paralyzed for fear that we were never called into ministry, or we wouldn't find a job, and we would run out of finances. How would we ever begin to explain this to Jacquelyn, friends and our family? We cried, yelled, and trembled at times, feeling inadequate and undeserving, confused and in a strange way feeling punished, yet released. Then anger and bitterness crept in like a vengeance. We were upset at all the people who were involved in the details of this hurtful situation and I even found myself frustrated with Hank because of all the stress. Before we knew it, a week passed without setting foot back into the church or having a daily devotion. Our words became more piercing at moments and more discouraging. Our prayer life wasn't as in-depth and we found ourselves taking more naps while our bodies became more and more fatigued. Finally, we stepped foot into a local church and we started to feel refreshed again. It was time to begin the healing process, one tiny step at a time. Thereafter, we could meet up with Jacquelyn and tell her the details, and to this very day we thank God for her relieving response;

"Daddy, you and mommy were called here, just not to stay here."

Jacquelyn's response was just what we needed to hear. She insisted we were going to make it and it will all work out. Suddenly, it was apparent that our transparency was what everybody needed to hear, including our daughter. We realized the details of this painful story allowed God to use our daughter as an encourager. As we became emotionally stronger, we began to call on more friends and family members so we could share our burdens. Every one of them poured out their love and concern for us. It allowed so many people to express God's love and moreover, make the choice to support us even during our darkest moments.

"Praise be to the God and Father of our Lord Jesus Christ, the Father of compassion and the God of all comfort, who comforts us in all our trouble, so that we can comfort those in any trouble with the comfort we ourselves have received from God." 2 Corinthians 1:3-4 NLT

As this season progressed, we were reminded to look for the small victories each day, but it wasn't easy. Sometimes we spent so much time getting resumes out and not enough time praying or reading the Bible. Other days we were right where we needed to be spiritually and then hours later right down in the valley.

"The Lord is my refuge and very present help in trouble." Psalms 9:9 NLT

We continued to look for the small victories and decided we had to enjoy the time we had together. During this season, we continued to be real with our conversations and prayers to God as He continued to bring us a message to carry us along our journey. It may have been a scripture, phone call, text message, a card, a song, a sermon, or even a blessing from a stranger. I couldn't believe it when a Christian hair stylist heard my story and knew funds were running out. She offered to do my hair and facial and insisted I receive this blessing for only $20.00. She said, *"Kim, God is trying to make a better you, not punish you."* I left the salon crying and humbled by a stranger's love. To this day, I know she is praying for me and my family.

You may be experiencing a painful time or a difficult decision. You may be frightened because change means going into uncharted territory and you must leave your comfort zone. No matter what your circumstance, He is your refuge and your strength. God wants all of you; your finances, relationships, and possessions. Have you given it all to Him? What is holding you back? God will make your path straight if you will seek Him with all your heart. It's tough to hear and see in the darkness, but remember God will not abandon us. He is in control of everything and will use friends, His Spirit, His music, our prayers and our service to move through the pain. Although we want the pain to go away now, we need to be patient. It's a process and He is in control!

Let me share an incredible letter we received from a dear friend...

> *Dear Hank,*
> *Many times, I've thought about the last moment I saw you. Sitting on the floor of your empty house wrapping pole lamps- [getting ready for the final move] wishing I could do more to help, but grateful for the opportunity to be able to help in some little way. Mostly though, I've thought about the things you shared with me that day... The sweat, the tears, the struggles, the fears... and the faith... All part of the transition process. It was almost as though I got to meet the REAL Hank all over again. To me, that was a moment in time that I will always remember and treasure- A moment which often serves as a reminder to pray for you, Kim and Jacquelyn.*
>
> *Knowing that you all sacrificed so much (in faith) to follow God, I can't begin to imagine the effect that this turn of events has had on you spiritually, emotionally, physically, and materially. That's why the thing that struck me as odd about your last voicemail Hank, was that you sounded almost upbeat. Based upon what you shared with me before you left, I must think that you aren't quite as upbeat as you would like us to believe. If I were in your shoes and was brave enough to put it all on the line, as you did, I think I'd be pretty much devastated. I'd be beating myself up and questioning my judgment a thousand times over.*
>
> *That said, I just want you to know that I admire you and Kim to the utmost, regardless of the outcome of this chapter of your lives. I admire you for your*

courage and faith, for your hard work and dedication as you seek to follow the Lord, and I admire you as people of principle. Though I can't see into the future, I don't believe for a moment that this was for naught. Some day all things will become clear, and the fruit of your labor and faithfulness will be rewarded. As for the here and now, please be assured that we love you, we care about you very much and we are always here for you all.

Love,
Paul

Thank God for friends...When we face discontentment, difficulty, or discouragement, often we put up a facade. It's time to tear down the façade. Be real, be transparent with God and others, be vulnerable; it's time reveal the naked truth. Admit you need support and encouragement, and be prepared to live with your decisions. Furthermore, remember those that are not discouraged must encourage and those who are discouraged need to be encouraged. Is there someone you know who can be encouraged today?

Only God knows the purpose for our leaving our home church and then leaving Connecticut for full-time ministry as the lead pastor of the church. He knows the final page of this chapter, but until then, I choose to lean into Christ for my next season and try to learn through these life lessons. He created the REAL me and I am not a mistake. Decisions have been made and I need to live with them, but I promise not to do it alone; and you should too! Share your story before someone else does and keep it real!

Hello, My Name is Claire

Finally, we arrived at the beach. We couldn't get out of the car quick enough. The car doors swung open and we rushed across the parking lot to the beach. Immediately, the walk through the soft sand squished between our toes. The pretty- bright blue sky appeared to melt into the horizon as the sun reflected off the smooth waves. The warm breeze was just perfect, sweeping across our bodies as the children's laughter enveloped us. Lana and I smiled as we watched Nathaniel happily run along the shore. I knew I needed this time with my new friend and her son and it made me feel very happy and peaceful to get away from some of the concerns that have been revealed about the church. I only wished I could tell Lana everything I learned, but this day was not about the church; it was about getting to know Lana and Nathaniel.

We stood along the shoreline talking and sharing stories when suddenly a ball flew right by us and towards Nathaniel. He picked up the ball and turned in the direction it came from. "Hello, my name is Claire," a voice remarked. We turned toward Claire and said hello. Thereafter, a young boy whizzed by us and right towards Nathaniel and before we knew it, they both were playing with the ball. Claire introduced herself and was not shy at all. She told us she was from outside the States and was away for the summer to spend time with her son and catch up on her studies before her Visa expired at the end of the summer. Lana and I thought it was strange that her husband was not with her, but everyone is different. By the end of our introductions, I told her what brought me to Georgia, as well as my God story and ended up inviting she and her son to church to hear my husband's message the following week. We exchanged numbers, Claire accepted the invitation and off we all went with our summer day.

The following week Claire arrived with her son. Hanks' message was a peaceful invitation to come to Christ, all those who are burdened, and receive His rest and comfort. After the prayer, I noticed Claire praying at the altar. I gently approached her and took her through the sinner's prayer as she accepted Christ that precious morning. My heart was filled and tears were flowing as we embraced with a new-found hope in her journey with God.

The following week, I visited Claire at her apartment and got to know her a little more. I was impressed with her independence and adventure. Apparently, she comes here every summer, but I couldn't help but wonder why her husband wasn't with them.

Claire came to church and got her son involved too. Everything seemed to be going well until we noticed she hadn't been at church for a few weeks. I contacted her several times, but to no avail, there wasn't a response. Both Lana and I were worried. We even drove to her apartment to locate her and still no response. What happened to Claire?

Then one day I got a phone call. It was Claire! I was so happy to hear from her, but what happened next would change everything, and I mean everything.

Claire was frantic on the phone, indicating she needed help to get out of a psychiatric ward located in the downtown area. I was shocked! "What? Where are you?" I asked. Claire proceeded to tell me the most outlandish story that I couldn't really contain, especially knowing she just gave her heart to God. How can this be? I thought to myself.

Claire said that she and her son were at the beach having a wonderful time together when suddenly an officer approached her. He asked for her name and the officer insisted she come with him to the station for questioning. On the way back to the car, the officer mentioned that he would be bringing the journal that was in the back seat of her car and that her son would be kept safe in the meantime. Claire struggled with the officer, trying to make sense of his reasoning to detain her and keep her journal, but more concerned about her son.

When they arrived at the station, Claire answered several questions about her journal entries and whereabouts over the past few days. She was also asked about her contact with a man in the area. According to the officer, they have sufficient evidence disclosed not only in her journal entries, but by the man he was referring to. The story wove its details in more circles than you can ever imagine; even to the point of no return and even that phrase has a whole new meaning.

Thereafter, Claire was taken to a local psychiatric ward on the account that she might be a threat to others and herself. Claire stated that the social workers were very rough to her, grabbing her by the arms and squeezing her arms tightly. It sounded like she was resisting because she also told me she had bruises around her waist too. Claire mentioned she was detained for several days. She didn't have a change of clothes, but rather, stayed in her suit with a cover-up the entire time, clenched to her Bible, of which she didn't mention until this part of the conversation. Claire proceeded to tell me that the social worker insisted that her journal entries were concerning, as some of the sentences stated that she wanted to walk straight into the ocean and not return. My head was spinning with questions and confusion. Claire needed help and I didn't have all the answers. All I knew was that I was a part of a story that I couldn't make -up and she needed our help.

Claire asked if we would come and pick her up and Hank and I agreed to transition her that same afternoon. Hank asked someone to preach that Wednesday night at our church and he and I set out that very afternoon to get Claire. When we arrived, she exited the door with the bible clutched in her hands. We signed release papers that seemingly declared her competency and immediately left the facility to go to the police station and pick up her journal and car keys. Next, we drove back to her apartment. We got into the apartment realizing her car keys, were missing along with her car and computer. We asked about her son and she said that her son was with her husband. Apparently, her husband flew to town to pick up her son, took the car, keys, her credit card and computer back to Canada. But it only caused room for more questions.

At this point we knew the church would be in good hands, so we took Claire to dinner for a nice, hot meal. We asked her how she managed to keep herself together and she mentioned that the Word of God was all she had. But that didn't explain why her husband wasn't here to help her and why her son is gone. Nothing made sense, but we knew we did our part for the moment. We finished our dinner and dropped Claire off at the apartment, agreeing to get together again and plan the next steps to getting her home.

Stress was certainly mounting for us. Not only were we involved in a concerning situation with Claire; we were being questioned at church as to our legitimacy not being there to preach on Wednesday night. It was one thing after another and chaos was prevailing everywhere we went. Not only was Claire's story about to take a twist, the church corruption was at an all-time high and Hank and I were about to be tested beyond imagination.

I visited Claire at her apartment and we talked for a while. She showed me the bruises and told me the anger she had when they detained her. She also mentioned that her husband has problems and she was concerned that he took her son. At this point, I'm even more troubled by her story.

We decided to talk about the best way to get her back home to be with family so she was safe and can get the help she really needs. We arranged to meet her the next day for breakfast. We talked about other friends and family members that we can contact for support. She then gave us her father's number, as well as discussed getting a one-way bus ticket or plane ticket home. Interestingly, it dawned on us both that she has a better chance of getting home if it was a plane ticket because she couldn't get off the plane and change her mind, as with a bus ticket, she could get off at any stop along the way. Claire seemed eager to get home, which was encouraging and at that point we agreed on a plane ticket. We decided the church would pay for the ticket and Claire was grateful.

That night we called her father to verify the story and get more information. He revealed that Claire has mental issues and she and her husband are at odds with many things, including her leaving months at a time. Additionally, he revealed that he wasn't fully convinced she will even go home once she gets off the plane. At that point, her father was so grateful that total strangers would take care of his daughter. He was hoping to donate money to our church in gratitude, but we thanked him and told him that it was unnecessary. We gave her father the flight information and felt good about the steps we took to get her back safely, but it became more evident that this story was even more involved than we realized.

We notified Claire about her departure and when to be ready for us to pick her up. She suddenly became despondent, stating that a friend can drive her and that she wouldn't be flying. It took a lot of convincing, but she finally agreed to meet us and take the flight after all. At that time, I remember telling Hank that I felt like we were being played and harboring a fugitive or something. He laughed and said he felt the same, but if we can get her home and share our love and kindness, then God will do the rest.

The next morning, we checked in with her father so he was prepared to receive her in Canada. Then we called Claire to be ready at 9:00am. She didn't pick up and I was convinced she was going to disappear. We arrived on time and unfortunately, Claire was not at the apartment. We waited along the sidewalk and twenty minutes later she walked around the corner. She apologized for being late, stating that she needed to drop off something at Fed-Ex. That struck me strange because she didn't have any money, but it didn't matter because we needed to get to the airport and get her home where she can get some help. We arrived at the airport and followed her all the way to the gate in hopes she would get on the plane and that was the last we saw Claire.

That very night we waited with anticipation for a call from her father. We called and left voice-mails, but no answer. We left a message with Claire, wishing her the best and letting her know that she would be in our prayers. There was nothing more we could do so we sat down and watched the news. No sooner did we sit down when suddenly; the newscaster requested any information about a local woman named Claire that is needed for questioning. If anyone had any information they should call the local police immediately. Our mouths dropped. You've got to be kidding. Seriously?

Hank called the local police chief and told him that he was the new local pastor and of our involvement with a woman named Claire. The police chief was relieved to know that she was the woman and out of the country. Apparently, she was stalking a local man who reported her deranged behavior to the police. She recently federally expressed a threatening letter to this man as well and they figured if they put something on the news and she was still in the area, it would scare her enough to leave. Although the man was not scared for his life, he was annoyed enough to tell the police to get her away from him. The police found a way to get her questioned, but just for a few days. Meanwhile the husband was contacted and took the son back home. The police chief thanked Hank for all he and the church did. Later that night we received a call from Claire's dad. She couldn't be found after the flight landed, but he was hopeful she would eventually come home and get the help she needs. The next day he called again and she was found. Praise the Lord.

Hello, My Name is Claire just sounded like an appropriate title. I never would have known her name if she hadn't introduced herself, but God did. He knows us all by name.

There is a time and a season for everything. And this chapter is the first account of a time that both Hank and I regretfully neglected to talk about. Why? We forgot about it because of our circumstances. We spent so much time focusing on our struggles that we completely forgot to focus on the amazing miracles that happened during our short tenure. If God purposed our transition to Georgia for such a time as this; meeting Claire, then wasn't this all worth it? If we were purposed to go to Georgia to only baptize new believers in Christ, shouldn't that be worth it all? If our purpose was only to preach for a few months and fill the altar with prayerful people seeking the Lord and giving their hearts to him, shouldn't that be enough? If we were purposed to go to Georgia to only set up a new worship team, a new mission and vision, new classrooms, new plans for a youth room, bible classes, reorganization, or donating our possessions to people who needed them, shouldn't that be worth it all?

> Lord,
> You know us all by name and you truly have a purpose in our transitions, even when they don't make sense. Forgive us Lord when we appear ungrateful or lost in our circumstances; forgetful of those around us or for the impact that may have been made. Forgive us Lord for not seeing the tiny miracles and only seeking after the bigger ones. Claire matters to you; then and now. I pray that she is well and leans upon you always. Thank you for reminding me to tell this story and look beyond my conditions.

There's a Time and a Season for Everything

T hings change in our lives, don't they? When things don't go our way, we feel pitiful, and when things go our way, we feel powerful. But what if we are in a season where things are not going well? What if we are in horrible circumstances? Well we can't have both… We can't act pitiful and feel powerful at the same time. It's a choice and how we respond to our situations makes all the difference. We must embrace change and seasons, one at a time. In my case I experienced multiple changes in one, short season. My family had so many changes; I felt like I was drowning. And when things were overwhelmingly hard or wrong, we asked why God allowed all these changes to happen <u>at once</u>?

He has a plan and a purpose for us and we need to remember our seasons can be a time of great blessing or tremendous pain and struggle. There are different types of changes. There is permanent change and temporary change, hard change and easy change. Hank and I learned a lot about ourselves when we wanted to change our conditions. Little did we know that our temporary change would ultimately change us. Perhaps if God revealed the reason we were leaving then we never would have left and we wouldn't have faced this painful season. Sometimes painful seasons are intended to change us; and all I know is that we didn't like our circumstances and we felt pitiful, but it was the power of Christ who saw us through and it took humility and our faith to persevere through these times of testing.

I always looked at change reluctantly. I never liked to accept change unless I understood it or controlled it. God allowed this season to happen and kept every door open and prayers answered so I would accept the change as He prepared us to leave. Even though it was a quick departure, every part of this journey included various decisions and answers. Was our departure perfect; no! We accepted the transition and obeyed, but little did we know that what we were about to go through would be so personal and difficult.

The good news about God is that you don't need to know the answer or understand. We are just called to obey and follow Him. That's what we thought we did, but we had so many interruptions during this season, we began to doubt ourselves. Was it possible that these interruptions were just great invitations; invitations for Kim and Hank to persevere and become stronger?

God invites us to have a vision inside our hearts and the timing seemed perfect. The path before us appeared clear and a vision was birthed. We wanted to transition by a certain time and it appeared to be happening, yet the amount of effort it took for us to prepare to leave and get things in order was unbelievable, but we did it! Unfortunately, the moment we left, all intensity prevailed; unending intensity from the moment we got in the moving- truck until we got back to Connecticut just 5 months later. I felt pitiful and not powerful in Christ in every aspect of my life.

We felt weak and useless at times when we were stranded in Georgia with no support, friends, family or jobs. It was the scariest moment of my life. We didn't transition with a huge savings and who knew that the leadership would lie about the monies they were paying us, let alone the money they were giving us to transition back to CT. We had to make creative financial decisions to get back home and our creative God helped us along the way. It is on this path we learned to persevere, depending on His strength to sustain us. And as we chose to live in His power and not in our pity more and more each day, we started to see and experience miracles on our way back to Connecticut and beyond.

Hank and I were working relentless hours to get as many interviews as possible. Day after day we were on the computer and phone. We were praying that God would give us a sign and give Hank an interview, perhaps a sign allowing the phone to ring from his former boss giving him an interview.

We couldn't believe our ears when the phone rang with his former boss on the other end offering Hank an interview for a position in North Carolina. Hank accepted the interview and we were immediately relieved and getting ready for the unknown. It took some pressure off us and we felt confident that Hank would do well and get the job, but that would mean another move with expenses. That would be the 4th move in three months. Where would the territory be? And can I live there? How will we transition my mother through all of this and who can take care of her during this extended season until we are settled? Hotel visits cost money and we didn't want to rush into another investment. Would I find a job in this territory? I thought we were going to pastor a church Lord? What has happened here? How could this be?

We put our dog in a kennel and drove to a remote part of North Carolina. I cried the entire time and Hank was so stressed getting ready for the interview of his life. I told him I couldn't imagine living in this barren area. I couldn't imagine caring for my mother and him traveling while I am by myself in an area surrounded with cornstalks. During these very hard discussions, his back went out and he needed me to drive everywhere. Every conversation was more and more painful, fearful, and debilitating.

> *"Kim, we have to do what we have to do to survive. I need to take care of this family and if we live in a part of North Carolina that you don't want, then I am sorry. We need to survive and I need to take care of my family. Go ahead Kim, blame me. Tell me this is my fault... Just do it! Tell me it is my entire fault."*

I cried my eyes out as Hank's back continued to worsen. The night before his interview, my brother called saying that he would be flying my mother to Georgia to live with us permanently and Hank agreed. I was livid!!! My brother can't do that. We don't have jobs and we can't have my mother with us full-time while we are struggling emotionally and financially. Somebody at home needs to care for her. We have done it for 16 years and we NEED HELP! I started shaking and dry heaving. Hank and I argued into a sleepless night of fear. He tried rocking me to sleep and praying for God's intervention. The next morning Hank had his interview and I stayed at the hotel contacting a family member to help us during this transition. She said she would help and called Hank later to express her love for my mother and willingness to help until after Thanksgiving so we can sort through all of this. Hank did not want to accept her offer because of his pride. He promised my father right before he died that <u>he</u> would see to it that my mom would be taken care of and this set-back shouldn't make it any different, placing the burden on others. Hank and I argued more. I couldn't look at him or speak to him rationally at this point. He got out of the car and could barely walk over to Starbucks as I sat in the car crying my eyes out. Moments later he came back and agreed to accept this gracious offer and a HUGE weight was immediately lifted. I can't begin to tell you the peace I received that very moment. We were given a gift of "time". We had a few more months to figure out our next move and location. The interview really went well except for Hank's back. We were encouraged as we drove back to Georgia knowing that North Carolina would be an option.

We waited seven weeks; the longest seven weeks of our lives, only to hear that they felt better giving the job to someone else. They strung us along for weeks! Really? We were heart-broken and angry. Hank looked at me desperately and said "Kim, I need you to call your old district and get your job back." I couldn't believe I was going to have to humble myself before my former principal. Due to some unique circumstances, I knew deep down inside she would never give me my job back. I called and although she and I both knew that I was only out of the class-room a few months and it would be easy to give me my job back, she took the opportunity to say, "Nothing personal Kim, but I can't. You understand, don't you? Our long-term substitute just signed a contract and it is out of my hands. Let me know if I can do anything." I said my good-bye, hung up the phone and slid it across the table in frustration. How dare her say this to me after all I have done for 20 years in that distract. I was even Teacher of the Year! Are you kidding me?

> "Lord, this can't be happening!!!This is not fair! She can get me my classroom back easily. After all I did for this town and all the children for 20 years. I think she found pleasure in telling me this. What are we going to do?"

Instantly the phone rang. I scrambled to pick it up and it was my dearest friend telling me that I need to get home as soon as possible because I have an interview with the best principal ever. No sooner did I hang -up, the phone rang again and it was the principal. He told me he was very impressed with my resume and wanted to meet with me. I gave him a date and Hank and I made plans to get to Connecticut, but where would we stay? What would it be like seeing my mother? Will she have to come back here? How can we do this and face our friends? Do they think we are failures? Our house sold at a loss and there is no place to go back to. We don't have jobs, and where would we live and how will it work with my mother? So many fears and unanswered questions flooded our minds.

I called a close friend and she opened her home for us to stay if we needed. She offered to act as our realtor in her neighborhood because several homes were up for sale and I wanted her to see if there was anyone willing to rent their home rather than sell. In the meantime, we packed the car and stayed at their house for 14 days to interview. It was surreal looking at some of the items in their home that happened to be ours from the tag sale before we left for Georgia. The quilts that covered us at night used to be ours; some extra pieces of furniture and a box of books stood in the corner of the garage as a constant reminder that we sold everything to move. As time elapsed, I cried frequently, shook incessantly, and had a very hard time dealing with my emotions and lack of sleep. Hank and I started to take sleeping pills to take the edge off sleepless nights. We were so grateful that our friend's son gave up his room as well. We tried not to interfere with their family routine too much. Hank and I tried to leave the house and look around for possible apartments, small homes to rent, and talk. It was painful because I had the responsibility of my mother. And who would rent to us with no proof of employment, let alone needing the perfect place for a mother with dementia? We had a few bags of clothes, but unfortunately sold a lot of our winter clothes due to our transition. I needed nylons and pants that fit so I would look professional for an interview. I couldn't believe we were living out of bags for 14 days. Is this really happening?

I interviewed with the Principal who called me and it was awesome. He would have hired me on the spot, but the position was not available until February. It was a long-term substitute position with no guarantee of a full-time position. I thanked him and he promised to call me in February. Next, I interviewed in our town for a second- grade position and it was in a HOT School (Higher Order Thinking) for the Arts which is my specialty area of teaching. I had this job hands down, I thought.... The principal I just interviewed with the week before created the HOT schools. If he would hire me, then surely, I could get this full-time position. It was the best interview, but unfortunately, I found out the principal was good friends with my former principal and she wouldn't hire me. Only one can assume "why" I wasn't hired, but I know that I interviewed with no flaws, especially having taught second grade for 20 years. I was saddened and my confidence weakened.

Hank had a scheduled interview after Christmas too. He was confident the job would be his, but still needed to research some more. In the meantime, Hank got a second interview with a company, but he hadn't a suit and needed dress shoes. Hank borrowed a suit from our friend and bought some shoes to wear to the interview. He knocked the interview out of the park, along with another interview set up with Bristol –Meyers. This interview was available to Hank due to our land lord in Georgia having a connection with this company. Who knew our very land lords, who agreed to break the lease and offer us financial support, would be used to help us in such a time of need. Their support was much more than even the Church offered and we were so grateful.

We continued our stay in CT with our loving friends, awaiting a visit from Jacquelyn for Thanksgiving break, while meeting with some other friends and family. One sunny Sunday morning though, Hank and I had just arrived back at our friend's house after a depressing trip to find an apartment. Not only did we realize that we could not show employment, but most of the apartments were multi-leveled, and not located in convenient areas for my mother to get senior care and be safe without falling. The pressure was mounting and my patience was lessening. We prayed for God to help and give us rest and to hear our prayers. Our friends were there for us through it all and they never gave up searching for a house to rent in the neighborhood. Thereafter, my sweet friend spoke to a neighbor and found out that not only were they willing to rent the house to us, but the owners were the parents of our previous neighbors before we left for Georgia.

> *"Rent to them Dad; they are good people and they will have jobs before you know it."*

This was the credibility we needed. We accepted the offer to rent their house. We felt the rent agreement would work and the creative financing helped us get back in a house near friends with more security, knowing full well that my mother would be joining us again; safe and protected.

Family needed to transition my mom back into our care, so we packed our car and invited my mother to drive back to Georgia to complete the packing. We had five days to repack and get everything in order again, with no support or financial help from the church. We managed to do what we needed and left, hoping to never look back.

As we drove up the coast, we received a call from the State of Connecticut. We were informed that my mother could receive Title 19 with Medicare, home care, and she was also eligible for weekly Senior Daycare hours. Additionally, I was called about an interview with another educational organization. The job sounded amazing and appeared to make sense why I left the state and moved back for such a time as this. Had I not moved, I never would have been looking for various job opportunities. What made this one so incredible is that they contacted me. What an amazing feeling!

We arrived back home and we moved into our beautiful rental just in time for Christmas and Jacquelyn's arrival. We wanted the house to look like we always lived there and fortunately, the transition was seamless. The house was orchestrated with the most amazing view of the city, and surprisingly, all our furniture fit. My mother had a sitting room, a bathroom, and her own bedroom as well. Everything was set up perfectly. We bought new curtains for the glass windows along the entire back of the house, helped the owners with their failing furnace and kept the house in great shape. Jacquelyn arrived and we had a seamlessly, special Christmas together.

We returned to our home church and people were very gracious. There were a few, however, who asked, "So how does it feel to fail?" We had to deal with a lot of emotions coming back to the church we transitioned out of. We were not on staff and still carrying minister credentials. The emotions were difficult... On Christmas Eve, I remember the church taking up an offering. This offering was for people in need; so, we put money in the bucket as it passed by and didn't think of it again until one night we were asked to dinner by one of the pastors of our home church. After dessert, we were asked to accept a manna jar as a gift from the church. We were taken back by this generous gift of money and shocked. We were asked to deliver the manna years ago when we were on staff and now we are the ones receiving. It was quite humbling and we were so grateful.

Meanwhile Hank's father had become ill while he was in Florida for several weeks. The family was quite concerned that he would not make it, and we prepared Jacquelyn for this possibility. Unfortunately, Hank's father died four hours before his final job interview. We knew that family in Florida would have to take care of the details. Sadly, there was nothing we could do and Hank was encouraged to stay in Connecticut and interview just a few hours later. Hank interviewed and was hired as the Director of Men's Health and Community Outreach at a local hospital. With mixed emotions and blessings, he accepted the job that afternoon. Unfortunately, it was not for the salary we know he deserved, but we were grateful he will have a job and can now concentrate on the family and lay his father to rest.

Before Christmas, I began the interviewing process for the most incredible job. I put together an outstanding portfolio and knew I could impress the interviewing committee. I got to the final interview which was postponed until after Christmas. All that was left was the presentation part and I knew I had the job hands-down because speaking is my gift. I completed the last stage of the interview and was complemented several times. I couldn't wait to get the offer, but they told me weeks later that I wasn't chosen. Thereafter, I was called in and asked to consider another opportunity that was better. At the same time, I was called by the previous Principal. "So, tell me who hired you Kim." I had to tell him that the interview fell through and I am in shock. He told me that he was extremely shocked as well, especially knowing my credentials, but would love to have me on his staff. I just needed to think about the long-term substitute position and call him by the following Tuesday. I called and he told me not to write a lesson, but to come in and just teach. In the meantime, after the previous interview for my dream job,

I was sent on a wild goose chase and they never responded to me again. I was devastated, as I have interviewed with this organization twice and they did the same thing to me both times. Lessons learned!

I interviewed for the first -grade position and was hired on the spot. It was amazing to think I was hired by the man who created HOT schools for the entire country and I couldn't even get hired in my hometown at a HOT school weeks earlier. God, what is happening here? Nothing makes sense. The next thing I find out is that this Principal made a call to human resources and told them to hire me at a salary-step so I wouldn't quit. I had no leverage when it came to my salary, now that I was officially unemployed. I was sent to human resources and found that I will be getting paid only $5,000 less than what I was getting paid before I left for Georgia. I was so grateful he made that call for me; truly a blessing from God. Sadly though, I was considered a non-tenured teacher and had to go through the observation process all over again to prove my competency. I was so upset, knowing I have taught over 20 years. It just wasn't fair, but I couldn't change it. I had to accept my circumstances and recognize the gifts God has given me with a grateful heart and begin my "new normal".

It's been two months since we got back to CT and I'm amazed by what God has done and accomplished through us. We are both employed, my mother is safe, Jacquelyn is back at school doing well, family is closer, friends are supportive, we have cars, food on the table and realizing the strength we must have to persevere and survive through dire situations. We have been humbled at times with decreased salaries knowing the resumes we carried, yet we have embraced the change and accepted our circumstances. We tried to continually thank God for everything because it could be far worse. Soon thereafter, Hank's brother-n-law had heart issues, my mother was hospitalized with an illness and Hank's father's funeral was scheduled. Tension and sadness left Hank upset, but all we could do is count our blessings and find forgiveness and understanding in our hearts.

A few more months passed and I am encouraged and very proud of myself. I didn't focus on my title as a substitute, but what I can do with my teaching strategies. The kids were great, the Principal was so happy and I am blessed. Finally, I am offered a job and now I am a full-time second grade teacher. I didn't have to teach a lesson; I was hired on the spot and valued by my Principal. Thank you, Lord!

Hank is doing well and using his skill sets with his new job. He is an incredible leader, learning more strategies and ways to communicate with key leaders and employees, especially when they don't tell the truth. He is being tested on all levels for sure.

In the meantime, we found a house for sale on the same street we were renting. We took incredible care of this rental home, but sadly the owners were upset and called us names after we legally gave them 60 days' notice. Unfortunately, it seemed to be the trend as our character has been slandered for all the wrong reasons. Nonetheless, we reminded the owners of what the lease stated with our lawyer's consent. We bought a smaller home down the street and in 7 months since our return to Connecticut, God orchestrated 2 jobs, gave us a rental and a home, took care of my mother, as well as provided a visiting nurse for 5 days a week. Jacquelyn completed a successful year of college and we were back on track.

This was the year of packing and unpacking. The summer we bought our new house, we packed Jacquelyn and she was off to Thailand on a mission's trip through her University. I received a call from my new school and learned that my classroom was painted which is unheard of in a public school. Soon after, I was gratefully getting my classroom ready with my sister-n-law's help, boxing and un-boxing, trying to find supplies and resources that I gave up or sold before we moved to Georgia. God provided me with all I needed and more, but at that point I didn't want to see another box again. I began reminiscing about the thousands of boxes I have packed and unpacked over the past year. I moved out of my home in Connecticut and into a temporary home in Georgia and moving some things to storage. We moved again into a townhouse from storage and the home we were living in at the time. We came back to Connecticut and moved the rest of our stuff back down to Georgia and then started moving things at the church to make new space. Then we packed to move back to Connecticut and unpacked to live in a rental and packed again to live in a new house and unpacked to put everything back in place. Now I'm at school boxing and un-boxing to reclaim my new space. You could say I don't want to see another box again, but God is good!

I had the most successful year with my new class and colleagues. Four months into teaching, a colleague nominated me for Teacher of the Year. I couldn't believe it!

Unfortunately, more challenges came Hank's way. He was hired by a Christian man, but his boss never acted like one. Hank was a Director and sadly had a horrible staff that had an alternative agenda to get him out of there, so they began to generate lies to get him to leave. It was messy and stressing. Just before Thanksgiving, as I was driving to pick Hank up from work. I was parked at an intersection waiting for the light to change and CRASH! A young girl was texting and struck my new car from behind, just as Hank was telling me on speaker phone that he no longer has a job and will be leaving. I am sitting there with $6,000.00 of damage waiting for Hank to find a ride and meet me in an intersection. He arrives with more boxes in his hands and all I could do is hug him and say, "God is good and those who are not must live with themselves."

For two more months, we struggled with the *"Why is this happening Lord?"* Another Christmas revolving around no job and having our character slandered. Why? It doesn't make sense! Hank put out several resumes and within two months was hired for a Medical Device company. Jacquelyn completed another fantastic semester and sadly my mother became ill again and ended up in the hospital and then in a long-term care center where she still resides. God provided us with a connection with the rehab center and because of that connection; my mother could transition seamlessly. We are so grateful for the support and safety for my mother. Even the Doctors said it was perfect timing. Hank rose the corporate ladder with such integrity and expertise that he was immediately named National Sales Manager for his company. Jacquelyn came back for the summer to work and we all enjoyed an incredible summer together on vacation in California; a much-awaited trip since the stress our family endured over the past several years.

When we got back from our trip, one of our close family friends informed us of their daughter's health. She had a tumor in her neck and unfortunately it was cancerous. Jacquelyn experienced this surgery years ago, and could be with their daughter through this experience. It was not an easy journey for this young girl, but we were honored to be there to support her and the family. What a reminder of how important it is to share our burdens with one another. Who knew God would use Jacquelyn's experience for such a time as this.

We began another school year, I with a new class and Jacquelyn with a start to another incredible junior year at Liberty University, and of course, Hank with his job. Sadly though, it didn't take long until we got an urgent text message in October from Jacquelyn telling us the concern about her neck. She sent us a picture of a growth in her neck and it was identical to the same situation she had back in eighth grade. Soon thereafter, we found out that Jacquelyn had two more tumors in her neck. We were in shock. We called a friend who is a surgeon and he decided immediately to set up surgery for our daughter. We notified our friends and family. Not only did Jacquelyn help a friend's daughter a few months ago, it would be her turn to support our daughter now. What is happening Lord? Jacquelyn's surgery was successful, having removed two benign cancerous tumors, but sadly, she lost her thyroid too. She recuperated for less than a week and left for a mission's trip to Jamaica before her next semester. Thank you Lord for all you have done.

Hank continues to excel at his job, but it is time for the next level. Right before Christmas, he put his resume out and finally landed the management job he was looking for. We are so happy for him, but more importantly, his former employer was so taken by his integrity and professionalism that he was told he could always return if he wanted to while even offering to pay him more money to stay. During this season, Hank is excelling, using his leadership skills as a manager, and still teaching at the church on Wednesday nights. I am so proud of his work ethic and all he is becoming. What a blessing!

This last semester Jacquelyn raised $6,000 to go on another mission's trip to live in Guatemala for two months. She ended her junior year with exceptional grades and all the money was raised. Jacquelyn's stories of Guatemala were incredible and heart-wrenching. We can't begin to understand poverty, starvation, pain and suffering until we witness it. All I know is that this trip for Jacquelyn and her team was life-changing and behind every pair of brown eyes, malnourished, or disabled child is a need for love.

Before I bring this chapter to a close, the following is only one of sixty journal entries Jacquelyn captured in Guatemala.

> July 2014
> *Don't get discouraged when refining times stir up your fears and flaws and show you your need for more of Jesus. When the enemy presses in hard to condemn us, we must remember that we have the authority to strike him down (Luke 10:19). When God makes us wait, He is making us ready. God has a protective, loving heart for us. Within each season, He measures out a boundary where we can thrive, flourish and grow. We have giants to face, battles to win, and victories to gain. These are all doable within the boundaries God has set for us. And the moment He knows we are ready, He will expand our territory in one way or another. Psalm 37:23 "As we delight in the Lord, He establishes us." 2 Corinthians 12:9-10 says, "My grace is sufficient for you, for my power is made perfect in weakness. Therefore, I will boast more gladly in my weaknesses, so that Christ's power can rest on me. That is why for Christ's sake I delight in weaknesses, in insults, in hardships, in persecutions, and in difficulties. For when I am weak, then I am strong." Jesus won't let us lose, but He must let us fight. He is always with us...Overwhelming victory is ours because of Him. 1 John 4:4 "Greater is He that is in you, than he that is in the world." Ephesians 3:20 tells us that God wants to do abundantly above and beyond all that we can ever ask or think, but it is "according to His work within us." To the extent that He's allowed to work in us, will be the extent that He does great things through us. Amen!*

Jacquelyn Face-timed us and shared her private thoughts and struggles one night. She was exhausted and wanted to come home for many reasons. No sooner did she ask God for a sign to encourage her and keep her focused, a note appeared on her bed...

My Beautiful Friend.... Good Night Beautiful

Hi Sweet Girl,
I'm praying for you and we all love you so much. Keep listening to His still small voice as He calls you closer to His heart and deeper into a relationship with Him. God whispers not because he is small or not powerful, but because he is close. You are so beautiful and I am very blessed to be on this trip with you. Love you... Bria

Towards the end of this incredible Guatemalan trip, Jacquelyn became real tired. She called us in tears and shared her heart more and more. Naturally, she focused on the heat exhaustion, her sickness the last week of her stay, saying good bye to her beautiful host family, and the needs she could not reach because there were so many. But what captured my attention were her journal entries. They were so transparent and revealed the 'Real Jacquelyn; the naked truth.' I read her entire journal and it warmed my heart as it gave me a glimpse into her experiences and feelings at a given moment. We are so blessed to see our daughter experience the world as she was made stronger in her weaknesses through Christ. Jacquelyn took her fear to the Lord and He gave her a fresh dose of confidence along with a heart of compassion for others, despite her circumstances. What more could a mother ask for?

It's the fall of 2014 and a year ago to the week, Columbus Day, Jacquelyn told us that she had another growth in her neck. I remember when we were taken back by the anxiety of the unknown again, but God reminded us that He has walked us through this journey before and He will be there again. He even used Jacquelyn's present scar to begin another conversation in Guatemala between our daughter and a young girl who would be having the same surgery months later. Our scars tell stories and we never know how God will use us or our scars. On November 25, 2014, we heard the good news. There is no growth and everything is fine. Thank you, Lord!

We are so blessed! Jacquelyn will be graduating in the spring with a teaching degree in Elementary Education and Special Education with a minor in Spanish. Hank has been promoted into an impressive role in a new company and I am still teaching. We have a beautiful home, debt is paid off, we are supported by a small family and friends and continue to try and bloom where we are planted. Let me say, blooming here is not easy for me at times and God is still working this out in me as I write this... I naturally find myself worrying about the next step out of the classroom as a Writing Coach and not feeling stuck in my career, committing to a ministry or small bible study group, making a difference, and more importantly being with my one and only daughter for this next transition after she graduates. I feel tired these days. I guess you can say my humanity combined with some of my painful experiences and now the possibility of not seeing Jacquelyn if she moves is just exposing my brokenness. The enemy of this world wants to continually remind me of my brokenness confirming my fear; that which has held me captive and he wants to make me think that I'm missing out on the abundant life due to my fears; now I'll never be able to move forward. But I need to remember that...

> *"My agreement with God's truths or the enemy's lies will have a significant impact on how my life unfolds."*
> Susie Larson

I need to trust in the Lord! I can't wait to move onto my next place of promise if I can just be patient and fully trust God with all my concerns and prayers.

Yet, my husband often says that when we tell our story, people tend to focus upon the blessings of God in our lives with jobs, health, home, and so much more, so Hank reminds everyone, many times in tears, that the real story is not the material blessings, but that God showered us in His love and grace despite ourselves. We felt abandoned. We were wrong; God was there all the time! The lesson is that God's grace is so big that we really cannot contain it. We believe that God chose to show us His love despite our circumstances and weakness, and He wants everyone to know that He loves us and He will let us fall and learn, but that He will also pick us up again if we let Him. Trust God and love Him with all your heart and your entire mind and all your soul because God is so good!

We are all doing fine and thank God for everything He has done and will continue to do in our lives. No matter what our circumstances, God has met us every step of the way. Will you let Him take you by the hand? He never promised us an easy life, but rather, He would walk us through it all if we would just ask him. Have you asked Him today? Really; have you?

It's time to ask God or even recommit your life to Him. It's time to pray and thank God for all He has done and will continue to do in your life. No matter what your conditions, God has met you and will meet you every step of the way... What is your prayer? Tell Him with all your heart. The Spirit of the Lord is here and the evidence of the Lord is all around. His love surrounds you... so tell Him!

Dear Daddy (My Father in Heaven):

_____

_____

_____

_____

_____

_____

_____

_____

_____

_____

_____

_____

The Pain of the Promise

"I need to trust in the Lord! I can't wait to move onto my next place of promise; if I can just be patient and fully trust God with all my concerns and prayers". Kim

My Journal Entry

Dear Lord,
Jacquelyn is about to graduate on my Birthday; 5/8/15, from Liberty University. Thank you for this incredible blessing. She is an amazing young woman. Lord, please take my worry away... I don't know the plans you have for her and our family, but you know my heart's desire is to be with her, near her, and to help be a part of Jacquelyn's family one day, whether in Charlotte or wherever you would take us. I am worrying too much and I need your peace Jesus! Help me wear your peace with royal dignity. Help me Lord and hear my heart's cry!!! Keep my heart and mind close to you.

Love,
Kim

Who do we invite to Jacquelyn's graduation? We need to get tickets because some may be driving quite a distance and even flying in for graduation weekend. Jacquelyn has interviews already and I need to take my vacation time and fly down to drive with her and spend some 'girl-time' together; talking about life, decisions, jobs and the future. What an exciting time to help plan for Jacquelyn's graduation and job hunting. I just can't believe this time is upon us already.

We had an amazing trip in April, just weeks prior to graduation, and I was so impressed with Jacquelyn's interviewing skills as well. I couldn't believe we were in North Carolina interviewing for a teaching position, the very place our family has talked about moving to for about six years. And wouldn't you know that she was given the job on the spot. Really? The school was a few miles from dear friends. It seemed perfect, but after talking it over, it was apparent that this school was not the place for Jacquelyn and we walked away, confidently believing there would be other opportunities. We decided to reach out to other friends in the Charlotte area and continued our visits with them in the pouring rain. We laughed and talked and cried along the way. We couldn't believe how beautiful Charlotte felt in the pouring rain. We drove back to Virginia and finished the trip together. What an amazing time. We said our good-bye's and hugged, knowing the next time we were together would be at graduation.

As graduation approached I became more anxious about meeting Jacquelyn's boyfriend's parents for the first time, as well as seeing that all the details were covered… Jacquelyn had other interviews in Virginia and Charlotte again; all of which were offered, but not accepted. So much was happening and North Carolina has been in the midst, but we all felt Jacquelyn made the right decision declining these positions.

A week before graduation, Hank was informed that his company was down-sizing and all positions, including Hank's was in jeopardy. How can this be Lord? Another job change? Really? In the meantime, Jacquelyn called to inform us that she had an interview at a wonderful school in Lynchburg and it is a school she would accept if given the opportunity. Oh my… The emotions were endless. Here we are in another transitional season with a potential job loss and school to pay off, graduation expenses, and the realization Jacquelyn wasn't returning to CT. My heart is aching and anxious beyond belief.

On May 5th Jacquelyn had her interview and it sounded like it went extremely well. On May 6th, we packed the car and her grandma Linda, Hank and I drove to Lynchburg. Jacquelyn spoke with us on the way there, letting us know that the Principal called and had some more questions. Along the way, we knew the stress was mounting again, as we were awaiting the call to learn whether Hank still had a job. As we journeyed along, the amount of conference calls was endlessly stressing to listen to, but we were finally informed that Hank miraculously kept his job. Now we didn't have to go through the graduation hiding our concerns about a job loss and finances again. Thank you, Lord!

When we arrived, Jacquelyn told us the Principal called to let her know that a Liberty graduate was hired for the position. Moments later she revealed that she was the graduate and she was a full-time k-5 special education teacher in the inner city. Let the graduation festivities begin! We screamed and were so excited.

Jacquelyn's graduation weekend went so well and we were very blessed. Family members made it and our interaction with her boyfriend's family went well too! Jacquelyn transitioned back home for the summer time. She had a few trips planned and soon thereafter, she broke it off with her boyfriend. Our hearts were broken and so many tears fell. I admire Jacquelyn trying all she could do to preserve his feelings and heart. Although a break-up is never easy, one of the things that impressed me the most was a comment that he made. He mentioned to Jacquelyn that he wasn't sure what God had planned for their relationship, but what was most important is that he preserve Jacquelyn's heart and their relationship with purity in case she is to be someone else's wife. I cried instantly! This was so precious to me and I can't thank him enough for saying that, for God answering my prayers of protection, and for Jacquelyn sharing her precious heart with her momma in tears that day.

> *"Apparently, Lord, you have a plan to keep Jacquelyn in Lynchburg this year. Wow! She has a job! She is happy and she is 10 hours away. Ugh! "*

Now that we know where Jacquelyn will be, our hearts feel more at rest, but still discontent at times. Why Lord? You have answered every prayer and in your timing. After a long talk with Jacquelyn, coupled with our own discontentment and realization that we really would love to make one more transition, Lord willing, to Charlotte; Hank noticed that one of his former companies had a position in Charlotte, NC. The position sounded incredible. Meanwhile, Jacquelyn shared her passion for teaching in the inner city, especially in a familiar area; but also, expressed her desire to stay south and not really return to CT, especially knowing we all discussed moving to Charlotte one day as a family. This decision was just the one we needed to help us finally transition and seek employment in North Carolina. Hank prepared for one of the most exciting interviews. Panic, worry and anxiousness flooded in immediately for fear that he would lose this opportunity. Could this be our chance to get to our destination? The timing seemed right. The job description was perfect. It was as if the job was created just for Hank. The recruiter called Hank stating he would never have called him if one of his biggest endorsers didn't reach out to him. As Hank prepared for the interview and obvious pressure was mounting, we kept reassuring ourselves that it was okay if he didn't get hired. Jacquelyn has a job and will be sharing an apartment with her dearest friend and we still have incredible jobs. Friendships are blossoming and family is growing closer, and who knows what can happen next with ministry in CT.

"God, it is in your hands. We give it all to you!"

Hank reached out to former colleagues and asked for character references. The letters made us cry. Hank's resume looked and sounded incredible too. Everything appeared to be going very well until the night before the interview. Hank received an email confirming flights and realized the name of the administrative recruiter was someone he knew. She was someone he happened to help during a previous interview when suddenly she was sick and began regurgitating right before he was called into the office. Hank left the waiting room to care for her, putting his interview aside, until she was better. He was very excited knowing he knew her and couldn't wait to acknowledge that they had a connection when immediately Jacquelyn came barging into the office stating that there was a huge discrepancy on his resume. Hank forgot to write the proper dates and it appeared he was unemployed for many years. How would he ever explain this error at an interview? Well, we encouraged Hank that this was God's timing now that he knows this administrative assistant; not to mention that she is working after hours. This is not by chance at all. Hank emailed her and she instantly remembered him and said she would do anything for Hank after all he did for her when she was sick. This woman let Hank send the new resume and letters of reference before the interview the next day.

We prayed together as a family and Jacquelyn was led to reference Romans 8:28...

"And we know that God causes everything to work together for the good of those who love God and are called according to his purpose". Romans 8:28 NLT

Hank flew into Dallas the next day as Jacquelyn, Linda and I shopped, awaiting the call. During the interview, Hank met a Christian man named Mark. He respected Hank from the start, knowing his resume shows many years of experience in the ministry. Not only was he impressed, he wanted to know Hank's story and followed it up with encouraging comments about how much he respects Pastors and their integrity. What a full circle it was! To think this man could see Hank's heart and the experience he could bring to this new position; It made us all cry. Hank was passed onto the next level in the hiring process. When he walked outside the office, he was greeted by the administrative recruiter. She was recounting the time by which Hank helped her and told others in the office that she would do anything for this man. As Hank begins to leave the office, she quoted her favorite bible verse from Romans- 8:28; the very same verse Jacquelyn quoted the day before. She smiled and told Hank he was getting the job. We were screaming and jumping for joy! Thank you, Jesus! Is this really happening? Can it be? It's been seven years Lord, since this desire has been placed in our hearts. Is this really happening?

I began my search that same afternoon. There was an email that kept coming my way. The school sounded so incredible, so I scripted a letter of intent. Off it went as I prayed that God would open the doors and hearts of those that received my letter.

> *"How am I going to get a job in July Lord? I live in CT? Nobody knows me! Lord, what will happen if Jacquelyn and Hank have jobs and I don't? Help me! I can't do this on my own Jesus."*

Within a few hours, I got a message back from an administrator who stated that she was extremely impressed with my resume and although the job I was referencing was not available, I was asked if I would be available to talk with her after the weekend. I told her I would love to talk. Our conversation the following Monday was three hours long. I had no idea I was being interviewed and before I knew it, I was offered a job over the phone. I accepted and our family was getting ready to move to Charlotte, North Carolina!!!

I couldn't believe what was happening. I was hired for the amount that we believed we needed to make the transition, financially. I would be teaching kids with learning differences like Jacquelyn is responsible for in her district. We would be three hours away from each other and not ten. My brother agreed to step up and see my mother as much as possible and my Aunt gave us their blessing after we cared for my mother for seventeen years. Grandma Linda gave us her blessing and so did our friends. The time has come and we had three weeks to accomplish this transition. Yikes!

Instantly, I called our friends in NC to refer us to a realtor. We flew to Charlotte in hopes we would find an apartment to rent until we could buy a home. Little did we know that it was impossible to rent and store what we would need. The price of a rental home would be just as easy if not better. We only had 4 days to do this and time was running out. Our realtor was incredible. She attended Elevation Church and took us under her wing right away. She and her husband were both in real estate and lead a bible study, as a part of Elevation Church. We hit it off right away and were invited to be in their small bible study group with our other friends when we finally get settled in NC. It made us feel welcome from the start. Then the next thing we found out was too incredible. Our realtor and now, new friend, mentioned that a friend of hers knows someone who is looking at renting a home and would rent it month to month, which is what we needed. We looked at the house and it was perfect! We immediately signed the lease and left a deposit.

The next day we visited Elevation Church. We couldn't wait to experience worship. We were beside ourselves. Is this really happening? As we entered the service of at least one thousand people, we noticed a woman seating us with a name that sounded familiar. We asked her if she knew our realtor and she said yes. We smiled, letting her know that we are the family renting her friend's home. She grabbed us and hugged us tightly; welcoming us to Elevation and the same small group we will be a part of when we come back to settle in Charlotte. Can this get any better? The worship experience touched our hearts deeply and Pastor Steven's message brought us to tears. Thank you, Lord! Thereafter, we exited the building and was greeted by a young, vibrant man named Sam. His personality was incredible. He was filled with life and our conversation continued for quite a while. His family is from Lynchburg and his father is a professor at Liberty University. Immediately there was a connection with the second person we met at Elevation. I stepped away quickly to get a drink in the Welcome Tent and was instantly greeted by a young woman named Britton. Her personality was contagious as well. She introduced herself and before I knew it, we learned that we were both adopted and her birth family was from CT, not far from where I grew up. Another gentleman expressed his interest in our conversation and stated he was headed back to CT and will be attending his home church; the very church we pastored at for ten years in CT. Just incredible…I exchanged numbers with Britton in hopes to connect for coffee when we get back. What a small world!

The last day of our trip was to visit my new school and connect with the Director. We had a tour and asked questions in hopes of making a connection. Interestingly, something didn't feel 100%, but I dismissed it. It's truly amazing to think I was hired over the phone and have a job teaching children with learning differences the second week in August. Thank you, Lord! We flew back to CT that day and then the fun began.

We spent every day organizing the house, packing, buying things for Jacquelyn's new apartment, clearing out my classroom and packing one hundred teaching boxes and loading them onto a U-Haul. We had to pack the first phase of things onto the U-Haul with all our things from the house. The house was officially up for sale and then the challenge was meeting deadlines for a very quick move, as well as seeing friends and family before we leave for NC.

Even one of our neighbors expressed an interest in renting our home, but she could not afford what we were asking, so we reassured her that if we can't sell it for the asking price then we would talk again. She was perfectly fine with that and mentioned that if it were to work in the future, she doesn't even have a deadline. We were certainly encouraged.

We spent as much time as we could, finding a balance between enjoying what little time we had left in CT, as well as completing the tasks needed to get us to Virginia on time. You see, one morning Jacquelyn woke up with a horrible swollen ankle and a possible infection that appeared to be spreading. Unfortunately, she couldn't walk and ended up on crutches. The doctor could not explain what happened, but put her on antibiotics for an infection. Where did this come from? We couldn't believe it. We had so much to do and really needed Jacquelyn's help. It was horrible. Then Jacquelyn received a call from her former apartment complex insisting we arrive to do a last walk though, as well as a removal of any items left a day earlier than we expected. This just couldn't be… We had the U-Haul for so many days and how can we possibly get the house and truck ready in time to drive to Virginia to meet an untimely deadline? If Jacquelyn wasn't healed in time, then how would we be able to drive her car? We pleaded with them and told them that this trip is breaking our backs, especially with Jacquelyn on crutches. They would not concede and reiterated that if we don't arrive by 1:00 a day earlier than planned, they would throw her stuff in the dumpster. Really Lord? How can we get all of this done on time?

> *Dear Lord,*
> *Our sweet Jacquelyn was stricken with something the doctors can't explain. Was it a spider bite Lord? Her ankle worsened by the day to the point of disabling her God. What happened? Help us Lord! Please heal Jacquelyn. Thank you, Jesus.*
>
> *Love,*
> *Kim*

We continued to do our very best and amazingly we could get everything done with family and friends helping and supporting us along the way. Sadly though, it was very difficult to carry things with Jacquelyn's inability to walk. That's when I decided to text some friends in NC and tell them what happened. Within a half hour of them praying, I received a call from Jacquelyn telling me was finally able to stand with little pressure on her foot and the pain lessened. Praise God! We were so grateful for this outcome!

> *Lord, it was hard to be still and know you are God while seeing Jacquelyn hurting and trying to meet deadlines. Forgive me for not always confessing that YOU are in control. I tend to take control and worry unnecessarily, but you never quit thinking about me and forgiving me. You meet our needs and you are our very present help in trouble. You answered our prayers and we are blessed. Thank you, Jesus!*

It was nearly impossible to say goodbye to everyone because we were running out of time with a new deadline, doctor appointments, shopping, and packing hour after hour, while putting the house on the market to sell. We prayed that God would bring us a buyer, and even though our neighbor offered to rent much lower than we anticipated, we reassured her again that if we didn't sell it that fall, we would let her know and talk some more. We knew we were moving in an act of faith without selling our home first, but what was also difficult was leaving my mom after all these years of caring for her. Now that she was in a long-term care facility for dementia, my brother and Aunt promised to be there for my mother and gave me their blessing to continue ahead. What a blessing to know after caring for my mother for seventeen years. We connected with a few friends, a special friend Dan, as well as Hank's sister, family, and his mother Linda, while exchanging hugs until we meet again. It was very emotional, but we knew we were supposed to continue this part of our journey to North Carolina. When we could leave, we realized there were a few others we were not able to say goodbye to. I only hoped and prayed they would understand.

We hit the road late evening with two cars and a truck packed to the brim. It took everything in us to stay the course. We slept in a parking lot and tried our very best to get to Virginia on time. When we arrived at to Jacquelyn's apartment the next day, we had ten minutes to spare, but we couldn't believe our eyes... someone's furniture and personal items were thrown into the parking lot. Immediately we assumed it was Jacquelyn's. Fortunately, it was not. We cleaned the apartment and a friend was kind enough to store the rest of Jacquelyn's things until she got back to transition into her new apartment. Hank dropped off the U-Haul trailer and car and drove the truck to NC while we stayed behind to finish closing the apartment. We left for NC thereafter, arriving to an amazing fan faire awaiting us at our new rental. Our realtors, now friends, gathered several people to meet us and unload the truck and welcome us to Charlotte. We gathered and prayed for our arrival and transition. God was clearly present and we were incredibly blessed and grateful for the support of our new friends. Our realtors invited us to stay the night and get some much-needed rest before we drove back to Virginia the next morning and move Jacquelyn into her new apartment. God was so faithful to us!

July 31, 2015

Dear Lord,
"Thank for bringing us here safely. You protected my family, orchestrated the details, and answered our prayers that began seven years ago, Thank you, Jesus!"

Kim

We arrived in Virginia with Hank not too far behind. Jacquelyn received her keys and we unloaded the car and waited for Hank's arrival with the truck, furniture, and more boxes. We arranged to have some friends help carry the furniture and as soon as Hank arrived we began the official transition, when suddenly we realized the 44 boxes on the truck were my teaching boxes stabilizing all of Jacquelyn's belongings. We couldn't believe our eyes. The truck needed to be returned that same evening or we would be charged, but what will we do with 44 boxes? Hank insisted he would drive back to NC and immediately turn around to get the truck back by the time the company opened the next morning. Off he drove back another 3.5 hours only to unload the boxes, take a quick nap and sadly sleep through his alarm. Hank only had 3.5 hours to get back to VA in time or we would be charged more money. This trip that was so perfectly orchestrated to the penny is now becoming another expensive adventure. In the meantime, Hank's new boss needed his biography and the deadline was at the same time while he was driving back to VA. We had to create it for him, read it on the phone so Hank could approve it, and send it to meet the deadline. We met the deadline for him and Hank arrived back in VA with the truck 30 minutes after the deadline. The U-Haul owner dismissed the extra charge and we were off to the DMV to register Jacquelyn's car. Hank was physically and mentally exhausted, but over time, Jacquelyn's apartment turned out to be amazing. We said goodbye to Jacquelyn with the notion we would see one another more often and off we drove to NC to begin our new lives.

Praise helps our perspective, doesn't it? We arrived in NC and I can't tell you how grateful we were when we stepped foot into our rental home. We praised God for a roof over our head, lots of space for all my teaching things, wonderful neighbors, new friends, new job opportunities, and a new church family. Our praises for God far out-weighed any negative perspective we had in our prior circumstances. In these moments, I felt as if God was bringing us right into a great land where we could be nourished and satisfied. We thanked Jesus for all of it. I guess you can say that is another reason why I am writing these stories- I am so grateful for all God has done through the pain of the promise.

"Delight yourself in the Lord and he will give you the desires of your heart." AMP

God impressed upon my heart to trust that He will make a way and that He would give us the desires of our hearts. It's only in these moments that we can graduate in gratitude and that starts with praise for all God has done.

> *Oh, the pain of the promise Lord. We have entered a new season, but in this season, I don't want to forget where I came from. God, you clearly have done countless things for me and my family. It was painful at times getting here, but now every week we are encouraged and filled while attending Elevation Church and volunteering, participating in an Egroup with new friends, reflecting on the weekend messages, along with starting our own group, volunteering in the community, housing church interns, succeeding at our jobs, as well as preparing for Jacquelyn's arrival in June as she makes a new life here in Charlotte, so it seems. This is an amazing answer to prayer; having our daughter living closer to us. I am so blessed! Thank you, Lord.*

We moved to NC in August 2015 and by November 2015, Hank and I received a heart-felt letter asking that we rent our home in CT and help them start all over again with a new beginning. Although this request was beautiful, we were instantly reminded that one of our neighbors asked to rent our home under the asking price, right before we left for NC. We decided to reach out to her and offer to rent the house, believing by faith that God will provide the rest of the rent if she couldn't afford the entire amount. How could we not when we are reminded of how another family did the same for us when we transitioned back to CT from GA. She accepted our offer to rent and to this day she and her family have been blessed, and so are we.

By December 2015 we bought our new home. Again, the blessings were amazing. The house needed over $40,000.00 worth of renovations and was the least expensive home in a prestigious neighborhood, of which we would never consider. Our realtors walked beside us in prayer and friendship as God opened doors to purchase this home. The owner agreed to all the renovations and in one year, the equity in this house has grown tremendously.

Two weeks after we moved into our new home, the church Intern Director asked us to consider a few boys for their program. The internship was scheduled for 15 weeks. They moved in with us on January 11, 2016. We were so encouraged and blessed by their commitment to God and desire to learn about the church. I remember meeting Jack's mom. Her tears of joy knowing that her son was with a family that loved God first, made her feel encouraged. The boys made me feel like an extended family. Our home and hearts are always full when we give back more and more to others beyond ourselves. And although my immediate family has not grown in abundance, I thank God for giving me a heart of love and compassion to invite others into our family too.

As the school year ended, Jacquelyn already began her search for a teaching job in Charlotte. Can this be happening Lord? Her interviews were incredibly positive and looked as if she would be moving to Charlotte this summer, 2016. Even her principal was encouraging; understanding her need to explore her teaching options, while moving closer to family. It was a dream come true.

Everything was going well as we prepared ourselves to go on our first Mission's trip to Guatemala as a family. We knew we would be blessed beyond measure and couldn't wait for all that God had in store for us. Just before we were getting ready for our trip, Jacquelyn met a young man named Josiah. He sounded wonderful, but the timing appeared difficult for me. Jacquelyn was getting ready to move to Charlotte. I remember thinking selfishly at first, wanting Jacquelyn to move here and if it was meant to be that Josiah is in her life, then he will pursue her heart and it will all work out, right? But as time went on and Jacquelyn told us how impressed she was with him, my heart turned toward God immediately. God's will be done!

Soon thereafter, we noticed that Jacquelyn was not getting the call-backs as promised after her interviews. It didn't make sense. She gave the apartment complex her 60- day notice and her roommate already found a new place to live for the following year. Everything appeared to be falling into place. This just doesn't make sense Lord; what is happening? Before we left for our trip to Guatemala, there was a moment that God prepared my heart to tell Jacquelyn that moving to Charlotte without a job would not be wise and we understand if she needs to continue teaching in Lynchburg for another season. Hank also contacted Jacquelyn to tell her the same thing, just as Jacquelyn received a call from her Principal asking how things are going with her decision for the next academic year. God's timing was incredible. We were all at peace. Not only were we at peace; her Principal was encouraging Jacquelyn all along, keeping her position available until the last minute in case things didn't work out in Charlotte. That's remarkable and of course, Jacquelyn agreed to stay in Lynchburg with peace in her heart. She got her same apartment and her roommate transitioned back in as well. To this day, Jacquelyn's job has allowed for new opportunities, while she and Josiah have gotten to know each other and date intentionally over the year. They were engaged February 11, 2017; to be married July 9, 2017, and we just adore him. God had a plan all along!

> *Dear God,*
> *You have answered our prayers! Since Jacquelyn was born, we have prayed for*
> *the man that you would raise-up to be our daughter's godly husband. It was*
> *Josiah all along. We prayed for his family; his parents, to raise this young man*

to love you first and honor our daughter as a princess of the King and you have provided. So many prayers answered... You are in the details Lord and we are forever; and I mean forever grateful. Thank you Jesus!

Even as I reflect on the teaching job God provided for me during this transition to North Carolina, I have decided to finish the year and resign my position. I felt trapped between my calling and character. It sounds ridiculous, but I couldn't align myself with corrupt leadership. There are many details I can't reveal. Therefore, during prayer and constant discussion with my husband, I've decided to move on and allow God to reveal a more integral opportunity. It's time for me to replace fear with faith. For years, I thought that all I can be is a public-school teacher and that I have reached my capacity. This has been a tremendous fear of mine for many years; taking a risk and trying something new. Today, in faith, I'm believing that God will provide the finances and reveal any dream He has placed within my heart. I can't believe I've been inspired to step away from the classroom and become an Educational Literacy Consultant. I hope to start my own business or academy, do something bigger than myself, and perhaps, be available to volunteer in the community regularly. Since I made this decision, not only have I been consulting and tutoring with no advertising; God has placed some amazing people in my path, speaking encouragement and words of wisdom into my life. God is meeting all our needs and I have felt a huge weight lifted and a sense of peace. Is it perfect? No! Are there moments when fear creeps in? Yes! But it's what I choose to do with these fears that truly matter.

So, off I go to accept the challenge. I needed to come to grips with my capacity. Pastor Steven Furtick once asked during a sermon, "How do you know what your capacity is without a challenge? Are you convinced of your level of capacity? What is your mental and verbal projection? Is it limited?" So many questions and yes, my heart began to pound. I knew it was time to stop surrounding myself with complacency because I will never be challenged; just comforted. It's time to be challenged out of my complacency and get beyond myself and my comfort zone because I will never know what is next if I am never challenged. We need to expect immeasurably more and we can, if we would just do it!! So, the challenge is to lift the lids that have become limitations in my life. I must believe that my comfort isn't my capacity because there is so much more left in me! How about you? Have you ever felt this way?

> *"It's time to show your situation your capacity; it's time to grow and challenge your capacity; it's time to move past your conditioning. But, we can't because we won't. And we could if we would!" Pastor Steven Furtick*

I need to see through the eyes of faith and not worry about my short-comings.

> *"Give your entire attention to what God is doing right now, and don't get worked up about what may or may not happen tomorrow. God will help you deal with whatever hard things come up when the time comes."*
> *Matthew 6:34; The Message*

We know that mistakes can turn to miracles and that which is aimed to destroy will develop us, but are you truly grateful for what God has done in your life? One of the lessons I have learned is that I can't live in fear! I don't want my fears to drive my faith-away, yet more importantly, my faith to drive my fears-away. Have you ever felt that way?

> *It's not to <u>have</u> the best of everything, but to <u>make</u> the best of everything.*
> *Pastor Steven Furtick*

And that is what I hope to do more. It's having an attitude of gratitude. Our heart forms habits in our lives, so I learned the importance of turning my blessings back into praise with less fear and more faith; thanking God <u>out loud</u> for my blessings. It's not that I deserved it or earned it, but more importantly, how much God deserves my attitude of gratitude, no matter if I must face my fears or move beyond my capacity. I learned the importance of thanking God for His provision even when I am down and out or even scared. This is what helps me to remember where I come from. Even though I walk through the valley of the shadow of dark times, fears, and struggles, His presence is with me through it ALL! My prayer is that I don't take His goodness for granted!

Dear Lord,
As I pen this last chapter, I can't help but remember the call Hank received about how his former company was sold; which meant that he would have lost his job back in CT after all. Oh, my Lord, how you have provided and protected us. Thank you, Jesus, for your faithfulness, even down to the tiniest details.

*Before Christmas, we said goodbye to one more intern who stayed with us beginning August 11, 2016. And yet to another Intern from Russia, months later. I am so grateful for the opportunity to open our hearts and home during this season of our lives. You know how much it means to me to be a mother, as well as care for, and show hospitality to our interns. I need my home filled with life, laughter, and love. You know how important family is to me and my desire to have Jacquelyn get married and live close to us so we can be a part of growing our families, as well as (in-laws) together with holidays and more. I can't wait! I will continue to pray every day for these opportunities. And now I thank you for inspiring Jacquelyn's grandmother Linda to move here. Be with her during this season Lord. She needs you. Even my birth mother lives nearby. These are exciting times and I can't wait to see what **you** will do next!*

*Lord, you lead me into a great land of plenty and I am believing I will be nourished and satisfied when I keep my eyes and heart upon you. Thank you, Jesus, for all of it. I want to be thankful always. My next level is just a praise away and I ask you Lord that you help me to not give up, even if I feel fear. Please help turn my fear into faith God. Forgive me Lord for giving fear access to your throne. Forgive me Lord for giving failure, anxiety, selfishness, rejection, regret, discontentment, frustration, worry, and abandonment access to your throne. It's time for me to look ahead, get above, and step aside because it is **you** on the throne. During this transition, I recognize that it was always **you** who got me through it all. Sometimes there is pain in the promise, but I am so grateful it is **you** Lord, whose promises I can and desire to stand upon and believe in. **You** know the vision and dreams I have, so Lord I give it ALL to **you**; believing **you** have my back; that **you** love and care for me, all the days of my life; no matter how naked I really am.*

Thank you, Jesus!
Love,

Kim

What Is Your Story?

"Etched in our children's minds and planted in their hearts is a permanent picture of who you are and how you've lived before them."

Dorothy Kelley Patterson

I have learned that my life and my time is not my own. My life belongs to the Lord and my life lessons and story belong to Him too. If I'm to leave a legacy, first, I need to remember that it's His name and His story that lasts forever. It's those God moments that can live on and leave a mark; but when I decide to live my life honestly and transparently, only then can I truly begin to influence others for Him. *Are you influenced yet?*

Before you write or share your story, think about a vulnerable moment when life really mattered. What did you look like before your trial, challenge, tragedy, or even before you met the Lord? Perhaps you were desperate to find healing, depleted, desolate, tried of everything, or even remained hidden and secretive so others didn't know the *'naked truth'.* Think about where you have been, what you have experienced and where life is taking you. What do you look like now that you have lived through these life lessons or gave your heart to the Lord? What defining moments can you share with others that will teach a lesson, leave a lasting impression, and a spiritual legacy for others to carry on? *Are you encouraged yet?*

Your personal life- lessons can serve, protect, and rescue others so don't hold back. It's time to reach deep inside your heart and reveal the *'real you'.* Your transparency can transform someone's life. If you could write and share your story from inception to completion, I guarantee, when you give it to the Lord, He will bring you healing, compassion, and touch you and others in so many ways. But you need to ask Him into your heart and let God help you share your story. *Are you inspired yet?*

You need to know your story matters and you matter to God. You are uniquely created and your life is significant to others and more importantly, God. I believe He is the Author and Finisher of our lives. He will determine when the last page of our story is written, but until then, it's up to you and me to live it and share it! It's time to live and give with an eternal legacy and perspective. *Are you ready to believe yet?*

I learned that if I share my struggles on this journey, I can ignite a purpose in others. So, I want to ask you; How are you? Are you tense right now? Are you hesitant to reveal the naked truth; the real you? Are you afraid that what you must say is a burden or won't be understood? I am tired of chasing perfection and making it appear that everything is perfectly fine. Why; because that's where the conversation ends. Perfect is where we keep it bottled inside. Purpose is making a real connection. Choose purpose over perfection dear friend. Will you purpose to reveal the naked truth? I promise God will see you through your joys and sorrows. You are your story, now bring it to life and give it away. It's time to reveal the real you!

You were created for a purpose and you matter-
Take a risk, be transparent, and reveal the naked truth. You will be glad you did!

Lovingly,

Kim Waltmire
Jacquelyn's Mommy <3

"Give thanks in all circumstances, for this is God's will for you in Christ Jesus." 1 Thessalonians 5:18 AMP